HUTTERIAN
BRETHREN

HUTTERIAN BRETHREN

*The Agricultural Economy and
Social Organization of a Communal People*

JOHN W. BENNETT

1967
Stanford University Press
Stanford, California

Stanford University Press
Stanford, California
© *1967 by the Board of Trustees of the*
Leland Stanford Junior University
Printed in the United States of America
L.C. 67-17299

For P. and J.

Preface

This study of six Hutterian colonies in Saskatchewan was made in 1964 and 1965. The research constitutes a major part of a study of ecology and socioeconomic development of the entire region in which the colonies are situated. Comparative data on Israeli collective agricultural communities were gathered in Israel in 1966.

I was a resident of one Hutterian colony during most of the two field seasons devoted to their study, and I visited the other colonies often. My resident study was participative, insofar as I engaged in the normal activities connected with farm and construction labor, shared the Brethren's regular meals, attended their church services, sat in on their policy discussions, and on one memorable occasion acted as boss of the women's house-painting crew. Extensive interviews were conducted with farming and ranching neighbors of the Brethren, and with townspeople with whom the Hutterites conducted business. I became an informal agricultural extension adviser to one colony, and helped to design an agricultural regime more suited to their specialized resources. I made many close friends among the Brethren in the colony where I resided, and became well acquainted with members of other colonies. Parts of the manuscript of this book were read by and discussed with members of several colonies, and numerous corrections were incorporated on the basis of their suggestions. However, final responsibility for the data and interpretations of them is my own. Heartfelt thanks are due to these Hutterian friends and collaborators. I have taken various precautions to disguise their personal identities and those of their colonies. The readers of this book are warned that we have altered and exchanged data in such a way as to make positive identification of people and places as difficult as possible. "Jasper town" and "the Jasper region" are fictitious designations.

After the Hutterite study was completed, I took advantage of an opportunity to spend a brief period in Israel. Background readings in the Israeli collective and cooperative farming communities had been done previously in an effort to understand the larger context of communal agriculture, and field observations on some of these communities seemed desirable. The comparative data and observations on the Israeli communities given here are the result of this study. Because the Israeli collective settlements resemble the Hutterian colonies very closely, yet differ greatly in origin and culture, this comparison is of special interest.

In preparing this book for publication I have enjoyed the professional assistance of the following persons: Seena Kohl, who assisted in the field with studies of Hutterian family life; Peter Rompler, who helped in the field with observations on education; Marvin Riley, who advised on compilation of the bibliography; and Myles Hopper, who assisted me during a visit to Israel, and who has contributed much to the comparisons between the Hutterites and the kibbutznikim. Professor Gan Sakakibara of Aoyama Gakuin, Tokyo, aided me by clarifying a number of historical points. John Hostetler of Temple University read the first draft and suggested important changes. Professor Erik Cohen of the Hebrew University, Jerusalem, offered me much information on the kibbutz, as did executives and members of Kibbutz Sha'ar Hagolan. Professor Joseph Kahl assisted me in preparing the final draft of Chapter 10.

Dorothy Altheimer assisted me as typist and general editor. Beverly Schneider worked on the statistical data and tables, and Harry Panagiatopolous prepared the original drafts of the diagrams.

The Social Science Institute of Washington University administered the National Science Foundation grant that was the major support of my research. Additional field work in Canada and Israel and certain data analyses were supported by grants from the Agricultural Development Council of New York, the Wenner-Gren Foundation for Anthropological Research, and the Graduate School of Washington University.

J. W. B.

1966
St. Louis
Tokyo

Contents

An eight-page picture section follows p. 160.

Tables and Diagrams

HUTTERIAN
BRETHREN

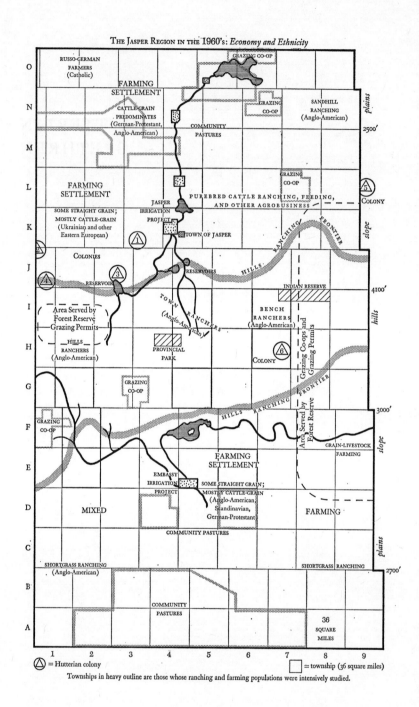

THE JASPER REGION IN THE 1960's: *Economy and Ethnicity*

Townships in heavy outline are those whose ranching and farming populations were intensively studied.

ONE

The Jasper Region

This book is a study of six colonies of Hutterian Brethren in the "Jasper" region of southwestern Saskatchewan—an area 4,700 miles square in the Great Plains section of western Canada.[1] In 1961 the total population of the Jasper region was about 7,300 persons, of whom 549 were Hutterites. During the period from 1962 to 1965 my assistants and I collected data pertaining to the region's social and economic development from the time of Indian occupancy to the present.[2] For this broad purpose we considered the "Jasper" region, as we have chosen to call it, to be typical of both the northern section of the Great Plains and the Plains in general.

The scientific objectives of this study may be described as ecological, inasmuch as we concerned ourselves mainly with the relationships between social and economic phenomena and the natural

[1] "Jasper town" and "the Jasper region" are fictitious designations.

[2] The overall study has been known as The Saskatchewan Cultural Ecology Research Program. Two books on the non-Hutterian population of the region are in preparation. For articles dealing with that part of the research, see the Bibliography for works by J. W. Bennett, Niels Braroe, and Seena Kohl. The best general description of the Cypress Hills region is found in Wallace Stegner's memoir *Wolf Willow* (1962), in which the "Jasper" region is seen from the town of Whitemud, a small community just beyond the eastern boundary of the region. This town was of lesser importance in the history and cultural traditions of the region. For a history of the Alberta-Saskatchewan-Montana region, see Sharp, *Whoop-up Country* (1955). Histories of settlement are found in MacEwan (1952), Mackintosh (1934), Hedges (1939), Dawson (1936), and Morton (1938).

environment. This portion of North America was settled largely
by peoples from more humid lands who were accustomed to a
type of small-scale agriculture unsuited to the semi-arid grasslands
and intermittent watercourses of their new surroundings. Walter
Webb, the foremost historian of this part of North America, summarized the problems of these settlers in his well-known book *The
Great Plains*.[3] Our own study was intended to be an examination
of Webb's key ideas in a particular microcosm. We selected the
Canadian West as our area of exploration because it was only recently settled and developed, and a wealth of statistical documentation and even some eyewitness testimony concerning this period of
its history is available. As in most regions of the Canadian West,
extensive resource development did not begin in the Jasper area
until after World War II. For this reason it was possible to observe
the process of adaptation in its earlier stages.

Our interest in the Hutterian Brethren was twofold. First, we
were concerned with their role as the newest and most important
immigrant group in Jasper, as well as with the reasons for their
relative economic success in this specialized region. Second, we
were interested in the colonies as examples of the world's most enduring form of cooperative-collective agriculture. Since the Brethren follow a way of life that differs greatly from that of the farming
and ranching population, it was necessary to study them more intensively than if they had been a group for which we possessed
many familiar points of reference. This book presents a specialized
inquiry into Hutterian life and places emphasis on the economy
and the formal or "instrumental" organization of the colony. Our

[3] John Wesley Powell forecast the basic problems in his *Report on the Arid
Region of the United States*, first issued as a Congressional document in 1878, then
republished and edited in 1962 by Wallace Stegner. For the Canadian section of the
northern Plains, comparable documents are Macoun (1882), Fleming (1877 *re*
Macoun), Palliser (1863), and Hind (1858). Walter Webb's *Great Plains* (1931)
was brought up to date by Carl Kraenzel's *Great Plains in Transition* (1955), but
there is no parallel volume for the Canadian side; however, the impressive group
of volumes titled *Canadian Frontiers of Settlement*, edited by W. A. Mackintosh
in the 1930's, covers much of the same ground. Other important items are Mac-
Ewan (1952), Howland (1957), Jones (1927–28), Gadja (1960), Alty (1939), and
Hedges (1939).

primary purpose is to show in all relevant detail how one group of typical colonies found their land and established their economy; how they managed their enterprises and worked out relations with local inhabitants. We have omitted much of the usual cultural, historic, and religious material, and have included only that which pertains to the socioeconomic and ecological aspects of the colony system and its changes. At this time several studies of Hutterian society are in preparation by other scholars; in all probability these surveys will give adequate attention to the details omitted here because of our specialized approach. In the meantime, the reader who desires a general description of the Brethren is referred to Paul Gross's unique book *The Hutterite Way,* an insider's view of Hutterian life written by the minister of a colony in the state of Washington; and to Victor Peters's account of the Manitoba colonies, *All Things Common: The Hutterian Way of Life.*

The Region

For the purposes of our study, we defined the Jasper region in terms of familiar criteria: historical factors of settlement, service centers and transportation routes, and persisting features of culture and economy. During the nineteenth century, the political distinction between Canada and the United States was vague; southwestern Saskatchewan, southeastern Alberta, and the neighboring Montana districts as a whole were called the "Whoop-up Country." The town of Jasper, founded in 1882 as a camp for workers on the Canadian Pacific Railway, remains tied to its pioneer past by geography and tradition.[4] Jasper was the first town settlement in the region, which up to that time had been an Indian frontier supervised by the Royal Canadian Northwest Mounted Police. It has remained the major railhead and service center in the area, even though the advent of the automobile has made it possible for local residents to do much of their business in other small cities of Alberta and Saskatchewan. All the major roads of the region, many

---

[4] For a detailed historical treatment of the "Whoop-up Country," see Sharp (1955).

of which are based on early trails, still funnel traffic into Jasper town.

Like all Western frontiers, the Jasper region was polyglot. The first pioneer settlement was begun by ranchers from the United States and the British Isles who established homestead ranches in the creek coulees and ran their cattle on the open ranges of the plains and the Cypress Hills. Then came the farmers, who poured in to the new frontier—the "Last Best West"—from about 1900 onward and were especially numerous during the years 1910–16, when the final increments of homestead land were opened by the Canadian Government. People from the British Isles, Ontario, the United States Midwest and Plains, Europe, and the Ukraine found their way to Jasper, often through special promotional arrangements between the Canadian Government and the Canadian Pacific Railway (CPR), which was still engaged in selling off its land grant in the region. A remnant band of Cree Indians, survivors of the days of the Mounted Police frontier and the Riel Rebellion, remained near Jasper, and their descendants live on a reservation in the Cypress Hills. A few Métis, French-Indian descendants of the men who served the Mounted Police as scouts, inhabit the coulees on the fringes of the hills.

By the 1960's the majority of the region's population was Anglo-American: that is, third- and fourth-generation citizens of North America or the British Isles who had lived in the Jasper area a decade or more. The direction of the cultural assimilation of agricultural settlers from loci other than Britain and North America was established by this Anglo-American group. The Great Plains area is the proverbial melting pot of nationalities; the use of European languages began to disappear during the second generation of the homestead farming settlement, and will be gone by the third, and distinctive costumes and food habits were gone by the end of the second.

Thus, in Jasper old-country customs died out among the majority of settlers during the second generation. Only the Cree Indians, the Métis, and the Hutterites offer a variant cultural profile. The Crees and the Métis, whose economy is largely non-agricultural, have long been outside the mainstream of the national economy and therefore have had no reason to change their customs. The Hutterites, on the other hand, have actively preserved their customs—the special beliefs and practices of a sectarian people—in spite of their important role in the local economy. The rapid assimilation of all other cultural groups has been the result of their being forced to adapt to the strenuous and specialized conditions of life on the northern plains. There can be few variations in ranching or farming methods in a region with highly variable natural resources and a rigorously imposed scheme of land tenure. Recurrent droughts and depressions over several decades have produced a continuing cycle of poverty and emigration.

Retention of old-country cultural patterns has been strongest in the districts where bloc settlement was the rule. In a few cases the old customs were clung to so strongly that the children's education was neglected, and as a result the second generation was largely illiterate. Shut off from full participation in the larger community around them, this generation grew up unaware of the changing requirements for adaptation and economic improvement. The Ukrainian settlement west of Jasper was an instance of this sort of isolation. There the peasant custom of dividing the land among the sons was strictly followed, and it resulted in the proliferation of a large number of substandard, unprofitable enterprises. Many of these holdings were bought up by the incoming Hutterites.

In contrast to the Ukrainian, the Hutterian way of life constitutes an almost ideal blueprint for success in this region. The purchase of large amounts of property, including both grassland and land suitable for crops, and the willingness to practice almost every available form of agriculture, have served to protect the Brethren against such hazards as economic fluctuation and drought. Operating costs have always been kept to a minimum by the colony's ability to concentrate a large labor force on essential tasks. The Brethren buy machinery in sufficient quantities to permit large savings, and keep it constantly in repair in their well-equipped shops. Many farm and home necessities are manufactured by the men of the colony, and most food items are produced, not bought. The practice of voluntary austerity in personal consumption is a basic means of effecting savings.

Among the Euro-American population of Jasper the distinction between ranch and farm is a more significant source of difference than is ethnicity. The ranchers, through their utilization of natural pasture lands, have made a more successful adaptation to the semi-arid and variable habitat than the farmers of any period have. The typical rancher-settler was of a different breed than the farmer was. Usually he was an adventurous wanderer, cowpuncher, or odd-jobs Western character who had come to the region before it was penetrated by either roads or railroad. The distinctive traditions and pastimes associated with frontier cattle culture have persisted in Jasper to the present day, and the far-flung nature of cattle-raising operations has served to perpetuate the rancher's cult of individuality and love for the open spaces.

Despite the differing cultural backgrounds of its individual members, the Jasper farming population displays a uniform conservative farming tradition and a social life of close interaction. Crop agriculture required a transformation, not a preservation, of the wilderness. The difficulties they encountered in marketing their grain crops caused the Canadian farmers of the nineteenth century to form cooperative groups with political objectives. The cooperative movement eventually took political shape at the Provincial level in the Cooperative Commonwealth Federation party (CCF). However, Jasper farmers, holding to a tradition of individualism borrowed from their ranching neighbors, were less active in this movement than were their counterparts in the more prosperous grain-growing districts of the Province.

The contemporary distribution of economy and ethnicity in the Jasper region is shown on the map facing page 1. Ranching operations, which once covered the entire region, are now confined to the hills and to the most arid corners of the plains. A greatly reduced remnant of the original homestead farming population inhabits the majority of the remaining land. At the peak of the homestead period, around 1915, the regional population was 9,828; this number increased slowly to 10,246 by 1930. During these years the considerable emigration was balanced by an influx of settlers. The lowest point of population, 6,813, was reached in 1950; by the 1960's the number had risen again, to 7,377. This fluctuation has taken place mainly within the farming and town-dwelling segments of the community, while the ranching population has remained quite stable throughout the entire history of the region. A recent upsurge in the general economy was mainly the result of increased resource utilization through such projects as the setting apart of community pasturage, the formation of grazing cooperatives, and the improvement of irrigation facilities.

These measures have permitted the farmers to supplement their failing crop agriculture with livestock production, and the small ranchers to raise more of their own feed, thus lessening the financial risk for both. The growth of the town population has been confined to Jasper and to one or two of the villages, where there has been an influx of retired people and an increase in the educational and service facilities offered by the few remaining town settlements. The many villages and hamlets established along the railroads between 1910 and 1920 have disappeared entirely or exist only as pickup points for agricultural products.

Both ranching and farming were at one time attempted in all parts of the region by enterprisers who paid little attention to resource differentials. The contemporary distribution of such operations represents a tendency toward realistic adaptation of modes of production to resources and transportation facilities. Thus the practice of specialized forms of agriculture like cattle-feeding and purebred-cattle-raising have developed near Jasper in an area of light soils suitable only for cultivated pasture. Grain-cropping is carried out only on the heavier soil areas in the farming settlements north and south of the hills, and ranching is restricted mainly to the hills themselves and to the slopes. Forage production on the Jasper irrigation project just west of town now makes possible the survival of a number of small ranchers and cattle-grain farmers in the vicinity.

The development of resource utilization is described in Table 1, where the alteration in types of tenure and land use in the Jasper

Table 1—Changes in tenure categories of agricultural land in the Jasper region

Tenure	1906–12		1960's	
	Number of acres (000's)	Per cent of total	Number of acres (000's)	Per cent of total
Deeded to individuals	1,351	52%	1,187	46%
Title held by government	1,248	48	1,412	54
Leased or in process of being leased to individuals for grazing (open range in 1900)	1,011	39%	935	36%
Open to individual use for grazing without lease or permit . .	237	9	none	18
Government acreage collectively used or managed:				
Community pastures	none		335	
Leased to grazing cooperatives	none		76	
Provincial Forest and Park, most under grazing permit . .	none[a]		52[b]	
Irrigation projects	none		14	
Total	2,599	100%	2,599	100%

Source: Municipal Secretaries; tenure and topographic maps; Saskatchewan Department of Agriculture Annual Reports; Prairie Farm Rehabilitation Administration reports.

Note: Our data for the years between the two periods shown on this table are incomplete, owing to omissions in the official records; however, it is relatively easy to reconstruct the events. (1) The 14,000 acres of irrigation land were almost entirely in private hands in the earlier period, and were acquired after their abandonment by former homesteaders. (2) Deserted land or land on which taxes were unpaid reverted to municipal tenure. In many cases such land was transferred to the Saskatchewan Land Utilization Board, and became part of the Community Pastures (about 150,000 acres). The balance had not been homesteaded but was used as open range. Some acreage had not yet been surveyed. (3) The Forest and Park land was open range in the earlier period, and the first step toward controlled collective use of the land was made when permits were required for grazing in these areas. (4) The 1960's figure for leased land is about 50,000 acres higher than that of 1930. This is because of the reappropriation by the government of tracts of land abandoned by farmers as unsuitable. (5) The community pastures, grazing leases, Provincial Forests and Parks, and irrigation projects came into existence between 1939 and 1941, with the exception of one community pasture that was established in the early 1950's.

[a] The grazing facilities granted by permit at this early period were not organized as cooperatives, and accurate records of acreage used are therefore not available.

[b] Organized as cooperatives after 1950.

area from 1900 to the present is shown.[5] The earlier figures on this table date from about 1906, when ranchers began taking out grazing leases in order to protect themselves against encroachment by homesteaders, and to divide up the remaining grazing land among themselves. There was only slightly less lease land available in the 1960's than there was in 1906, which indicates the stability of the ranching enclave; however, in the 1960's the figure was slightly larger than it might have been had not the drought conditions of the 1930's driven the farmers out of certain areas that consequently reverted to lease. The various cooperative and collective-use projects mentioned previously now constitute about 18 per cent of the total land area in the Jasper region. This is land out of individual tenure ownership and use, and it therefore represents the extent to which land tenure and utilization patterns in the region have moved away from purely private ownership and exploitation.

The position of the Hutterian colonies with respect to land area and tenure in the region is shown in Table 2. This table breaks down the land area into rural municipalities (similar to counties in the United States, but usually smaller) so that the differential impact of the colonies can be clearly seen. More will be said of this impact in Chapter 3; for the present, it is enough to note that the colonies' land holdings are extensive in some municipalities and nonexistent in others. It is also important to observe that all Hutterian land, though cooperatively and collectively managed, is "deeded": that is, it is owned in private freehold tenure. By administrative ruling of the Saskatchewan Department of Agriculture, the colonies are not entitled to grazing leases or grazing facilities in the community pastures and grazing cooperatives. This decision

---

[5] A word about land purchase and tenure arrangements. "Deeded" land is the local term for land privately held with clear titles or bought and sold by individuals. "Lease" land refers to tracts of pasture land held by the Government and leased under fairly stringent regulations. Tenure is mixed, however, since it can be transmitted to heirs by testament. It can also be "sold" in the following manner: the lessee can charge for the "improvements" on the lease, but the price must be no greater than 20 per cent of the valuation as assessed by the Provincial Land Bureau. Even so, the lease does not automatically transfer to the buyer; the buyer must be approved by the Bureau as a prospective lessee, in accordance with the criteria established for suitable candidates.

Table 2—Land in private tenure in the Jasper region, 1960-64
(*Acres*)

Land tenure arrangement	Rural Municipalities						Total for the six rural municipalities	Per cent of total land	Per cent of land in private tenure
	Jasper	Sunrise	Embassy	Big Bear	LID* No. 1	LID* No. 2			
Total land area	201,658	197,558	202,773	206,183	1,218,286	587,119	2,613,577	100%	100%
Land in private tenure . .	167,702	136,529	139,040	183,983	315,116	244,520	1,186,890	45	100%
Agricultural, Gentile . . .	157,783	136,529	139,035	178,846	308,764	213,000	1,133,957	43	96
Commercial, Gentile . . .	93	0	5	17	112	0	227	0.009	0.01
Hutterian	9,826	0	0	5,120	6,240	31,520	52,706	2	4

Sources: Municipal Secretaries; tenure and topographic maps; Saskatchewan Department of Agriculture Annual Reports; Prairie Farm Rehabilitation Administration reports.

* LID: Local Improvement District. This designates an area too sparsely populated to afford an adequate municipal tax base. Such an area is managed directly and partly financed by the Provincial Government.

is based on the philosophy and the regulations of lease assignment: leases are to be given only to single-family enterprises that lack the capital required to purchase sufficient grazing land; the Hutterites, on the other hand, have the reputation of being able to pay large sums for extensive tracts of land. Moreover, the colonies are not single-family enterprises, but corporate entities. This justification of the government's policy seems straightforward enough, but there exists also a diffuse feeling, at least on the part of the local non-Hutterites or "Gentiles" that the Hutterites can "take care of themselves," and do not need government help as the other farmers do.

The percentages of land held in collective operation in the Jasper region from 1960 to 1964 were as follows: land held by the Hutterites, 52,706 acres, or 11.3 per cent of the total land area; land held in government tenure as community pastures, 335,239 acres, or 77 per cent; land held by grazing cooperatives, 76,176 acres, or 15.7 per cent of the whole. In Table 2 it can be seen that Hutterian land consists of 4 per cent of all land held in private tenure. The ultimate tenure rights to all other land in the area under cooperative-collective operation are vested in the government.

The Hutterian colonies are the largest individual landholders in the region operating diversified farming enterprises. The only comparable holdings are the medium-sized and larger ranches. At the time of our study only about twelve of these had land areas of 6,000 acres or more, most of which was held by grazing leases, not by private tenure. The average holdings of the Gentile farmers practicing diversified production comprise parcels of about 1,500 acres each. As owners of large private agricultural enterprises operated as collectives, the Hutterites occupy a unique and important place in the regional economy.

The Environment

From the standpoint of its key habitat gradients, the Jasper region is typical of the northern Great Plains. As J. W. Powell pointed out in his 1878 *Report on the Arid Region*,[6] the semi-arid West is

---

[6] Quoted in Stegner, p. 16.

divided into three major geographical zones: the level plains or "prairie" lands, where there are treeless, semi-arid stretches; the lightly wooded watershed slopes, with their fairly heavy rainfall and occasional watercourses; and the plateaus, characterized by trees, more abundant rainfall, and short growing seasons. In the basic pattern of Western development, the highest elevations have provided timber, game, and grazing facilities, the slopes have been used as watersheds for irrigation purposes and as a setting for ranching, and the level plains have been used for grain production and mixed-crop farming. The topography and economic development of the Jasper region have followed these general patterns.

The characteristics of the resource parameters of the three zones of the Jasper region may be described briefly. On the plains, the altitude averages 2,500 feet (north of the Cypress Hills, i.e., at the northern edge of the ranching frontier), and the north-facing slope of the Hills is quite steep. The slope on the southern side is a more gradual one, and the farming area just south of the Hills is situated at 3,000 feet. The extreme southern boundary of the Jasper region has an altitude of 2,700 feet. All parts of the plains were at one time shortgrass country, and have an average annual precipitation of between 9 and 13 inches. Growing seasons average 120 days long, and are slightly longer north of the Hills because of the lower altitude and heavier rainfall there. Wind speeds are high, as they are everywhere on the Great Plains: gusts up to 50 m.p.h. are not uncommon.

The altitude and rainfall characteristic of the whole area make for a habitat marginal for agriculture but adequate for drought-tolerant crops like rye, barley, and forage crops (though somewhat less satisfactory for wheat). However, problems of crop production are caused not only by the marginal nature of the habitat parameters, but also by the extremes in weather. Rainfall may vary from 5 inches to 17 inches annually, and both early and late frosts are frequent. Heavy spring rains are sometimes followed by hot, dry, extremely windy summers that destroy the benefits of the early moisture. Snowfall may be abundant one year and scanty the next, thus limiting irrigation and forcing forage crop reductions.

Torrential rains and hail may hit at any time, completely destroying a crop in minutes.

Soils in the plains area vary greatly, owing to the extensive glaciation of this region, which is situated on the margins of the final melt-off of the Keewatin sheet. Districts with fortunate moisture patterns sometimes have extremely light soils, whereas heavier soils are often located at higher elevations where growing seasons are extremely short. The watershed slopes vary in altitude from 2,500 feet at the plains level to 4,200 feet at the crest of the Hills. Precipitation, which rises proportionately with the altitude, ranges from 9 to 17 inches annually. There are between 75 and 125 frost-free days a year, depending on the district and the wind pattern. The stream coulees, heavily overgrown with brush and small trees, afford excellent cover for cattle. The grass is a mixture of shortgrass species, with fescue associations at the higher elevations. In general, the slopes are very well suited to ranching, and the flood-irrigated meadows easily sustain forage crops.

The upper edges of the slope are riven by deep coulees caused by drainage from the crestal plateau. These coulees contain a heavy growth of lodgepole pine, spruce, aspen, and other sub-montane plants. Shelter from the wind and cold provides an opportunity for the growth of forbs and grasses generally found only in locations farther south.

The highest part of the Jasper region, the crestal plateau, is situated at about 4,000 feet, with elevations of 4,200 feet in some places. This plateau, which is covered with excellent fescue prairie, is an irregularly shaped peneplain where few trees grow, save in the coulees and other rugged areas. The frost-free season averages around 46 days, which is insufficient for wheat but possibly long enough for artificially fertilized forage crops. Winds are strong here and the precipitation averages 15 to 17 inches annually, which compensates somewhat for the temperature limitations.

Some slope and plateau areas were homesteaded in fairly recent times, after the plains had been occupied. However, these settlements had nearly all disappeared by the 1960's, and the land was once again being used for grazing. A deeply dissected and hence wooded part of the plateau has been made into a Provincial Park, and the remainder is held as deeded and leased pasture by ranchers with headquarters farther down the slope. In the 1960's a small handful of bachelor ranchers were the only ones who lived permanently on the plateau.

Socioeconomic Adaptation

The direction of resource development in the region has had a direct influence on the social continuity of the farming family. The establishment of livestock-raising facilities such as community pastures and grazing cooperatives by the Provincial and Federal governments has aided the marginal farm enterprise by offering the opportunity for a more balanced income. Because of this the farming population, after decades of influx and outgo, is becoming more stable, and the culture of the Jasper farming community is, in varying degrees, beginning to resemble that of the ranchers.

Ranchers' sons, most of whom can look forward to inheriting relatively prosperous enterprises, are much more inclined to stay at home than are the farmers' children. This has a stabilizing effect not only on the ranching community's economy but also on its family structure. Some farmers are willing to admit the drawbacks of farming and to actively encourage their sons to leave home and educate themselves, and for this reason the farm family may be more outward-looking and urbanized than the ranching family. Moreover, farmers continually deal with the unpredictable world of markets and prices, whereas the rancher nearly always does his selling at the ranch, directly to the buyer, in an atmosphere of relative price stability.

The Hutterian colonies represent the most stable social units in the region. They diversify their economy in order to distribute their risk, they maintain an economy of scale to provide enough capital to cover failures, and they participate in a unique socio-religious system that provides a basic continuity for the family and the kin group. Retirement is built into the system, and there is no need for the son to shoulder his father's debts. Increasing population is taken care of by the formation of new colonies; and until the new colony becomes self-sufficient, it can expect support from its "parent" colony. The economic and social stability of the Hutterian colonies is the prime cause of the resentment with which they are viewed by their neighbors, the Gentile farmers. The farmers find it hard to accept the fact that they, the "true" pioneers and builders of the Jasper region, have a less secure place in it than the "upstart" sectarians do.

A major feature of social and economic change in the region is the shift toward organized cooperative forms of enterprise among the Gentile population.[7] These people, like most North American farmers, have traditionally adhered to a rigorous and individualistic mode of life mitigated only by the practices of neighborliness and voluntary mutual aid common to all farming societies. As farming has become increasingly more mechanized, these latter customs have tended to wither. However, since small-scale individual enterprise has been, on the whole, unsuited to this region of variable resources, it has been necessary to devise new expedients to put such endeavors on a more stable footing. These projects have had in common some aspect of cooperation. The community pastures and the irrigation projects of Jasper are essentially collective-use institutions in which there exist varying degrees of cooperation among the users. The grazing cooperatives and the Forest Reserve grazing-permit groups come closer to exemplifying true producer cooperation, insofar as the members must govern themselves and their assigned land. All the farmers of the region have been members of the marketing cooperatives for grain and cattle for one or more decades. During the 1950's, the number of consumer cooperatives and credit unions increased rapidly.

The various forms of cooperative endeavor among the farmer producers superficially resemble the basically cooperative nature of

[7] For studies of the cooperative movements of Saskatchewan and the Canadian West in general, see the following: Moorhouse (1918), Nesbitt (1962), Wright (1956), Yates (1947), and Boyd (1938). The classic analysis of the political consequences of the cooperative movement and agrarian protest in Sasketchewan is S. M. Lipset's *Agrarian Socialism* (1950). See also Oliver (1961), Patton (1928), Sharp (1948), Tyre (1962), Zakuta (1964), and McHenry (1950).

the Hutterian colony; but ironically enough, the colonies are barred from participation in these local systems, by administrative regulation as well as by their own cultural autonomy. The colonies contribute to the general quotient of cooperation and collectivism that is a major adaptive trend in the region, but they comprise a separate segment of this trend. They do, of course, participate in the pooled-grain marketing system, which is open to all producers, regardless of ethnic identity.

The Hutterian colonies can be considered a progressive element in the farming community, for they are generally more receptive to agricultural innovation than their neighbors are. This ability of the Hutterites to experiment and thus to prosper is another mark against them with the Gentiles. Decades of drought, deprivation, and family instability have produced in many of the older members of the homestead farming society a reaction pattern of conservative management and cautious investment. The first generation of farmers, the "building" generation, showed much courage and daring in establishing their enterprises under harsh conditions. Their sons, the "sustaining" generation, suffered frustration and privation in the course of their attempts to expand the family endeavors, and as a consequence worked out adequate but conservative methods of coping with the market. However, the third and fourth, or "improving" generations, who were taking over the enterprises in the 1960's, are much more inclined to accept government aid and to use a scientific approach to agriculture than their fathers were. They are less conservative and independent, more daring and flexible. However, at the time of our study, the farms of the Jasper region were just coming under the stewardship of the improving generation, and therefore the Hutterian colonies still represented the large-scale and innovative element in local agriculture.

In spite of the hostility felt by the Gentiles toward the Hutterites, there were few acts of discrimination or vandalism. We believe this to be a result of the strong tendency of the local culture to suppress overt manifestations of aggression and hostility—a phenomenon found in most rural regions. In the judgment of our field workers and associates in Saskatchewan, the Jasper residents exhibited this trait to an unusual degree. Open quarrels and arguments between neighbors were unusual, and personal criticism was delivered privately. A man was measured not by his personal habits but by his performance as a conservative, unostentatious agricultural operator or businessman. A woman was judged by her pleasant disposition and her "nicety"—a term chosen by the researchers to convey the tone of locally approved female behavior. The reasons for the exceptional passivity of interpersonal behavior in Jasper are probably to be found in the hardships of the recent pioneer period and the drought and depression years, when economic difficulties led to conservative operation. Other factors are to be found in the severe competitiveness necessary if one is to establish an enterprise in this variable region. Without some behavioral check, such competitiveness would have torn the community to pieces. Still another cause may be found in the Canadian emphasis on middle-class virtues. For these reasons, the Jasperites must tolerate, even if they cannot love, their Hutterian neighbors. To do otherwise would be to endanger the serenity of the Jasper social system.

Ecology as a Frame of Reference

As mentioned previously, our study of the Hutterites was informed principally by the perspectives and interests of social and ecological anthropology. The term "cultural ecology" has been used in recent years to refer to these interests,[8] but in some respects an alternative, "social ecology," would seem to describe more clearly the approach we adopted. In any case, the methods of cultural ecology have been worked out mainly with reference to peasant and tribal peoples; and the Hutterian Brethren, while possessing some qualities of both, are really neither. Therefore a key question underlying this research was to what extent the ideas associated with the

---

[8] The following writings in the general field of sociocultural ecology have particular importance for this study: Firey (1959), Freilich (1963), Fried (1952), McHale (1962), Murphy and Steward (1956), Steward (1955), Odum (1953), Park (1962), Sauer (1963), Birdsell (1953, 1958), Lévi-Strauss (1963), Geertz (1963), and Sahlins (1962).

cultural ecology approach in anthropology could be found applicable to a North American agrarian economy.

The classical anthropogeographic approach to ecology was usually concerned with a single descriptive task: the demonstration of the degree of fitness of the culture and its subsistence technology to the natural environment. At given levels of subsistence, this fit is often exceedingly good in tribal peoples, owing to the long period of adaptive change that generally precedes the time of observation. However, ecological studies of peasant economies and fully developed market agrarian economies must proceed in a different fashion. The peasant or farming society must adapt not merely to a chosen set of natural resources but also to constantly changing external social and economic forces such as landlords, bureaus, taxes, and markets.[9] The response to the natural environment is thus only one facet of a larger problem of adaptation. The concept of adaptation can be used as a master interpretive idea, but it must include more than the idea of fit between culture and environment.

Adaptation was the key concept used in the Jasper study, and we conceived of it as a dynamic, not a static, concept. We viewed adaptation as a series of processes, not as a state already achieved, for the adaptive strategies used to manage both natural resources and the external agencies and forces that affect the conduct of economy are always changing. Since the societies studied in the Jasper project were of relatively recent origin, and since we possessed historical data describing their experiences with the environment, we were able to trace the development of adaptive processes in detail.

It was important to approach the Hutterian Brethren in this manner because of the significant differences between their adaptive background and that of the Gentile farmers. The Hutterites brought with them to Western Canada customs and institutions well suited to the region and to most of the forces and agencies governing access to financial and natural resources. Unlike the Gentile

---

[9] The need to recognize the influence of external institutions that help mold the microcosm constitutes the most important single change in sociocultural anthropology in the post-World War II period. This change and the reasons for it are illustrated in Wolf (1956), Steward (1950), and Ray (1959).

farmer-settlers, the Brethren did not pass through the harrowing experience of discovering that their farming traditions and social customs were almost totally unsuited to their new environment. The Hutterites did encounter some difficulties with climate and habitat, but they soon recognized the need for change, and began to experiment. Adaptive response has always been a characteristic of Hutterian culture. This fact gave the Brethren yet another advantage over the heirs of the Gentile farmer pioneers.

Whether or not a modern agricultural society is adapting successfully to its environment can be judged in general terms by standards of economic survival and population continuity. These factors, however, must be carefully defined. The size and continuity of a population are always relative to the level of the society's technology, system of land tenure, and economic practices. In the case of the Gentile farmers of Jasper, the success of their adaptive measures can be seen in a reduced and stable population and in contemporary economic arrangements (such as individual farming and land tenure) that require larger farms and fewer farmers. However, the Gentile population is still in the process of changing, and its numbers may continue to fluctuate as prices and costs fluctuate.

The case of the Hutterites is different: the large scale of their operations and the economic diversification of their colonies provide adequate margins against most financial vicissitudes. For this reason, the Hutterian adaptation is characterized by large colony population per land area. Characteristically, a colony's population continues to increase until it reaches optimum size, as defined by the colony economic and social system, whereupon it divides, and half its members leave the region to set up a new colony. This system of fission protects the Hutterian colony from the necessity of increasing its economic means to keep up with its expanding population.

Though survival and continuity may be used to measure long-term adaptation, productivity is the short-run measure. Other things being equal, a man who has attained the skills needed to practice farming in this region of specialized and variable resources will be able to increase or stabilize the productivity of his enterprise. But productivity cannot be guaranteed in this area, owing to its extremely variable resource parameters. Droughts and depressions may bring out errors in the land operator's approach to variability and uncertainty, and he may be forced to migrate. Over time, the only generally successful approach to these conditions has been the accumulation of land. The man who has added to his property holdings has had the greater guarantees of productivity than the man who has failed to do so. In general, the Gentile farmers learned this lesson painfully, whereas the Hutterites had long understood the value of land accumulation as a means of ensuring survival.

All measures of adaptive success are affected by the standards people hold with regard to life values. In a society based on a market economy, where the key socioeconomic unit is the farm enterprise, the appropriate values can be defined in such terms as "level of economic satisfaction," "aspirations" (for consumption goods, for children's education, and so on), "social prestige," and the like. Since some people are willing to settle for fewer satisfactions, mere survival at a very low economic level is possible. There were a few of these people in the Jasper region, but other forces besides their own low standards were at work against their survival. Owing to the competition for land, these extremely poor families were being bought out rapidly and forced to emigrate. The Hutterites were among the enterprisers with higher satisfaction levels who were doing the buying. This process might be called an example of *ecological competition* or *replacement*.

We also found it necessary to inquire into the various processes of *adaptive selection* at work in the combined cultural, economic, and environmental systems of the Jasper region. The basic questions in such an inquiry are those of who stays, who goes, and why. The gross measure of adaptive selection is arrived at by studying the population dynamics with reference to particular micro-regions and districts and reinforcing this knowledge with detailed genealogical studies of family continuity and migration. At different times the factors pushing people out of the region or keeping them in varied. Sometimes the most adaptive person was he who exhibited extreme caution, conservatism, and postponement of gratifications. At other times, the most adaptive was the more daring operator, who was willing to go into debt to get what he wanted or to give his family a better break. Generally speaking, Hutterites possess all or most of the characteristics or strategies that make for favorable adaptive selection.

Another important ecological process is *adaptive assortation*, or *adaptive specialization,* aspects of which we described in earlier sections of this chapter. This is a process by which modes of economic production move toward or develop within geographical zones with suitable natural and socioeconomic resources. Such movement has been important in the economic development of the Jasper region, where the original settlement was based on a uniform grid survey that did not allow for resource variation. For example, in the Jasper region wheat has disappeared as a crop from nearly all of the dryer and light-soil districts, cattle production has been restored to certain areas where cropping was attempted and failed, and cattle-feeding and other agricultural enterprises possible on small holdings with poor soil have accumulated in a belt of poorly drained land near the town of Jasper, where they are in a position to benefit from the proximity of various transportation services.

In general, the ecological point of view is one that emphasizes economy and natural resources as conditioning or determining factors for particular cultural forms. This does not mean that cultural forms themselves do not have an influence on adaptation. Once established, a given mode of adaptation can persist by virtue of its associations with particular social relationships, prestige criteria, and other cultural factors. Moreover, the ecological point of view is obviously not equally relevant to all human societies. In general, it is most relevant to agricultural societies, and especially to those who must contend with specialized and limited environments. So far as the Jasper region is concerned, we do not see how any approach other than the ecological could make sense out of its history and development.

It is important to remember that the ecological approach is basically a point of view and not necessarily a disciplined theory. It is a point of view that emphasizes resources and the means of managing them as interpretive principles of social analysis. The particular concepts associated with this analysis will vary, since the role played by environment and by various sociocultural features varies from society to society. For that reason, we found it necessary to examine the literature of economic development, agricultural economics, and farm management as vital adjuncts to the materials of anthropological ecology.[10]

There are, however, certain generalizations one might make. Clearly the relationship of environment to society for all market economies differs consistently from the patterns in tribal and peasant economies—although farmers and peasants are probably much closer to each other than either is to the tribal mode. The market agrarian society is more dependent upon its environment than the tribal is, in the sense that it generally must use its natural resources to the hilt in order to survive. Any change in the availability of these resources can lead to social and economic disaster. The tribe characteristically has more latitude than the agrarian society, although here the degree of specialization of the environment is an independent variable, and tribal peoples in extreme habitats are as vulnerable to fluctuations in resources as modern agriculturalists are. The experiences of prehistoric Pueblo peoples in the Southwest during drought periods constitute a case in point: adaptation to drought conditions resulted in massive population movements and extensive and rapid cultural changes among these peoples. On the other hand, though the modern agrarian society in a resource-deficient area must depend on its available resources for survival, it receives help from outside agents in the form of capital and development programs. These inputs facilitate adaptation; in this sense one may say that the modern agrarian society is less dependent on its natural environment than the tribal society is.

---

[10] See, for example, Gee (1954), Johnson and Barlowe (1954), Parsons *et al.* (1963), Schwartz (1954), Bozeman Conference (1953), Thorne (1963), Meij (1960), Knight (1921), Rogers (1962), Lionberger (1960), and Robertson (1958).

TWO

Hutterian History and Beliefs

The current scientific concern with the Hutterian Brethren is one phase of a revival of interest in the various sectarian groups associated with the Anabaptists of the sixteenth century, who were the founders of a religious and social movement called by George Williams, its latest historian, the "Radical Reformation" (Williams, 1962).[1] This second Reformation, different in many ways from that led by Luther and Calvin, has largely been ignored or slighted by both Protestant and Catholic historians. During the sixteenth and seventeenth centuries the orthodox churches let loose a flood of polemic literature supposedly containing the truth about Anabaptism. The general acceptance of this misinformation did much to prevent historians from forming a true estimate of the spiritual and historical meaning of the movement.[2]

---

[1] The brief account of Hutterian history and beliefs in this chapter is based on, but is not necessarily in agreement with, the following sources: Horsch (1931); Clark (1924); Eaton (1952); Deets (1939); Hofer (1955); Arnold (1940); Friedmann (1961); Williams (1962); Gross (1965); Klassen (1962); and Peters (1965). A careful reading and partial translation of certain portions of the *Älteste Chronik* (Ziegschmidt 1947) and the *Klein Geschichtsbuch* (Ziegschmidt 1947) were made by the writer. The principal difficulty in reconstructing Hutterian history from available primary and secondary sources is that these sources are so exclusively concerned with the Brethren that they ignore the larger context; for example, many overlook the fact that during the Russian episode the Hutterites were part of the entire Ukrainian and Volga German minority picture. There is also some inconsistency of detail.

[2] Only recently have historians of the Reformation begun to acknowledge the revolutionary role of the Anabaptists. Ronald Bainton's one-volume history *The*

Three contemporary groups in North America have Anabaptist origins: the Mennonites, the Amish, and the Hutterites. The Mennonites, who have abandoned communal living and have largely accepted the world and its institutions, often consider themselves members of the general Protestant communion. The Amish and the Hutterites stand aloof, rejecting both Protestant and Catholic kinship, in accordance with their tradition of exclusionism and cultural distinctness. These three groups differ from one another in the degree of their exclusion and in their practice of communal life: the Amish, who reject nearly all that the modern world has to offer, including advances in agricultural technology, have abandoned communalism, but cooperate on economic matters, while the Hutterites, who accept technology, live a strict communal life. The Mennonites, the Amish, and the Hutterites all recognize their common ties with the Anabaptist tradition, but have no official or traditional patterns of interrelationship, and are generally silent on the issue of formal membership in the larger Protestant body.

In any case, the specifically doctrinal issues that separate Hutterites from orthodox Protestants are no longer of great significance, since the major problem of infant versus adult baptism was dissolved when the Baptists became a part of the Protestant body. It would seem that Hutterian religious beliefs and observances place

---

Reformation of the Sixteenth Century, published in 1962, was probably the first to make a sympathetic estimate of this role.

However, the older, less sympathetic approach to the Anabaptists is by no means dead. In a recent history of the Reformation, G. R. Elton (1963) states: "The true nature of Anabaptism ... always embodied a conviction of sole salvation for the particular group of believers, and often also the chiliastic dreams of salvation realized in the destruction of the wicked with the establishment of Christ's kingdom on earth. ... It was in its essence markedly more intolerant than the institutional Church. Its victory, where it occurred, led to terror." This is an overgeneralized and biased conclusion, and does not follow from some of Elton's own materials. The vast majority of Anabaptists were retreatist pacifists, and their program was one of specific religious tolerance: all persons who did not follow Anabaptist teachings were asked to leave the Anabaptist ranks and practice their religion elsewhere. The "victory" and the "terror" associated with Anabaptism occurred only once, in the famous Münster incident, and all reliable accounts of that episode indicate that the Anabaptists involved had been exploited and seduced by an unprincipled group of adventurers. Elton, like so many others, seems to confuse rejection of the world with animosity against it.

the sect close to the Fundamentalist tradition. The Hutterites' celebration of Pentecost, their constant use of the Bible as a source of guidance in private and social matters, their literal acceptance of the Creation myth and the Jesus legend, their strict moral and sexual code, and their use of a traditionalized body of sermons and religious literature are shared in common with the Pentecostal sects; but they refuse identification as Fundamentalists, on the grounds that their practice of communal living and consumption austerity sets them apart. There are a few signs, however, that they are changing their position of general opposition to any identification with existing church bodies. As their willingness to take a more intimate part in the social life of the Gentile community grows, the Hutterites show some tendency to play down their self-concept as the Elect and to relate to Protestant groups in a spirit of friendliness and cooperation.

History

The Protestant Reformation is conventionally presented as a spiritual revolt against domination of the individual conscience by the hierarchical Catholic Church. It did embody such a revolt, but it was also a product of the general social unrest in Europe during the sixteenth century. Economic development had altered the medieval social pattern, and growing urbanism demanded the establishment of new forms of government. Resentment over high rents, taxes, and tithes kept the peasantry in a state of turmoil. The spread of literacy and the translation of the Scriptures into the vernacular exposed the common people to new ideas and suggested possible solutions of their economic and spiritual problems. The orthodox Protestantism of Luther and Calvin was viewed by many people, in particular the peasants and small tradesmen, as simply a continuation of the old, oppressive institutions.

Unrest among the German peasantry finally erupted in the brief but bloody Peasants' War of 1524–25. The emergence of Anabaptism as a recognized movement coincided with this revolt. On January 21, 1525, George Blaurock, a former Catholic priest, was re-baptized by Conrad Grebel at the home of Felix Mantz in Zurich. The followers of these three men came to be known as the Swiss Brethren, and they are generally regarded as the first true Anabaptists. Blaurock and Grebel had both been followers of Zwingli, and in the first two years of the sect's existence, the Brethren conducted public disputations with Zwingli on the issue of infant baptism. Zwingli first tolerated, then openly opposed, the Brethren. Finally, he joined those who encouraged the authorities to arrest and persecute them.

During the period from 1530 to 1536, other Fundamentalist groups with beliefs similar to those of the Swiss Brethren emerged all over Europe. The common bond between them was their literal interpretation of the Bible and their hope for a revival of the Apostolic Church of Jerusalem. The Brethren's insistence on adult baptism was one of the issues that set them apart from the rest of Christianity and led to their persecution by both orthodox Protestants and Catholics. Although the majority of Anabaptists were peaceful protestors in the Waldensian tradition, they were thought of by the civil government as flouters of constituted authority because they refused to participate in military service, rejected established political forms, and refused to accept public office. Their advocacy of rural "innocence" over urban bourgeois and aristocratic conceptions of social order reached an unfortunate climax in the capture of the city of Münster in 1532 by a fanatic faction with Anabaptist affiliations. This naïve group, led astray by clever malcontents, established an increasingly tyrannical and bloody rule over the city and imposed their tenets, including the practice of polygamy, on the populace. In 1535 Münster was liberated by the forces of Francis of Waldeck, the deposed Bishop, and the leaders of the Münster rebellion were tortured and executed. This episode blackened the reputation of the Anabaptists for many generations to come and contributed heavily to the already prevalent ill-feeling against them.

By the early 1530's, persecution of the various Anabaptist groups had led to their flight or expulsion from most of central Europe. The behavior of the Anabaptists in western Europe and England attracted less ill-will, and so the Dutch Mennonites and English

Baptists were spared the searing experiences and hopeless wanderings of the central European groups. The Hutterites, however, underwent the full impact of persecution and prejudice, and their troubled history represents the Anabaptist experience in its classic form.

In 1528, a number of Anabaptist groups in the Austrian Tyrol and in Moravia decided to unite. This federation was unharmonious from the start, and its later years were marked by a vigorous and confused factionalism within and considerable persecution from religious and secular authorities. During a period of persecution in the Tyrol, a congregation of Anabaptists under Jacob Widemann and Hans Hut moved to Austerlitz, in Moravia, at the invitation of the Lords Kaunitz. During the journey to Moravia, the migrants spread a cloak upon the ground and cast all their personal possessions onto it; this symbolic act is thought of by modern Hutterites as the conclusive beginning of their practice of owning all property in common. The Münster disaster in 1535 led King Ferdinand of Austria to demand that Moravian officials persecute the Brethren, and for the next decade the congregations suffered acutely; but in 1547 tolerance was restored and the patronage of the Moravian lords resumed.

In 1533, an Anabaptist minister from the Tyrol named Jacob Hutter joined the Brethren. He persuaded three groups to accept full communalism, and thereby established the first three communities of *Hutterische Brüdern,* or Hutterian Brethren. Hutter was executed at Innsbruck in 1536, and his successor was Peter Rideman, author of the *Rechenschaft (Confession of Faith)*, the basic Hutterian catechism. Other Anabaptist leaders denounced Hutter's principles as incorrect or extreme, but the groups stayed together.

Moravian landlords had offered the Brethren their protection largely because of the efficiency of these peaceful people as craftsmen and managers. After 1547, the Hutterian population continued to prosper and increase. An estimated 20,000 Brethren lived in some 90 community villages or *Bruderhöfe.* Some of these villages had as many as 1,000 members. There were numerous converts to the Hutterian way, including a number of educated professional people as well as peasants and artisans. During the peaceful phase of the Moravian period, the diversified craft manu-facturing industry, managerial activities, and agricultural produc-tion of the Hutterians permitted a population ratio per colony larger than at any subsequent time in their history (in North America, for example, the population per colony has rarely ex-ceeded 150).

The year 1622 marked the end of this so-called "Golden Age" of Hutterian development; not until recent times in North America were the Brethren to enjoy an equal measure of prosperity and peace. In 1622, the Moravian nobles who had befriended the Hut-terites were persuaded once again by Church and government offi-cials to drive them from their estates. They did this reluctantly, for the Hutterites had proven their worth as talented and efficient stewards. The Brethren were ordered to forfeit their homes and possessions without compensation and to leave Moravia immedi-ately. They scattered eastward into Slovakia and Transylvania, where they managed to survive despite persecution and privation.

By the end of the seventeenth century many Hutterian com-munities had dissolved, and great numbers of Brethren had been persuaded or forced to swear allegiance to the Catholic or the Protestant faith. During intervals of relative peace, the remaining Brethren continued to welcome converts, including Mennonites from Holland and, according to legend, some survivors of Jewish *shtetl* communities. While they managed to retain their identity and even to increase in number, the Brethren ceased to adhere to the traditional communal principles, and by the first part of the eighteenth century the idea of a Community of Goods was largely a memory. Harassment by the military is usually given as the cause of this falling-away; evidently it became impossible for the colonies to remain self-sufficient when their food and other supplies were subject to confiscation by the foreign troops stationed in Hungary. Throughout the rest of the eighteenth century the Brethren con-tinued to observe their traditional rules regarding costume and worship, but the practice of communal living and property owner-ship declined.

From 1761 to 1767 the persecution of the Brethren in Hungary was intensified, with government sanction, under the Jesuit Delpini. A decree was finally issued ordering that all Hutterian children be taken from their parents and raised in orphanages. This intolerable edict was obviously an attempt to stamp out the sect in Hungary once and for all by forcing the Hutterites to leave the country en masse. The Brethren and their families fled to Rumania, where the Russo-Turkish war was raging. In 1770 the Brethren requested the protection of the Russian General Sametin against marauding soldiers. This officer brought their plight to the attention of Empress Catherine, who invited the Brethren to settle in the Ukraine, where Mennonites and other German-speaking colonists were already involved in a pioneer attempt at resettlement and the improvement of local agricultural conditions.

The sojourn in Russia was a peaceful period for the Hutterites for the government lived up to its promises of protection and toleration. Former Hutterian groups scattered over central and southeastern Europe were invited to join them, and the Brethren increased in numbers. The Community of Goods was reinstated, and for a time the colonies functioned in the traditional way. However, by the nineteenth century the Hutterites were being plagued by dissension, the communal principle had been virtually abandoned, and some land was divided among the separate nuclear families. Mennonite help, both spiritual and financial, was probably responsible for the survival of the Hutterites and their traditions.

Some Hutterites prospered as individual farmers, and this prosperity contributed to the decline of the communal system. In any case, by 1850 communalism was largely dead. A few communities were re-established as collectives, but the majority of Hutterites remained as private landholders, and were essentially lost to the sect. Many of these people joined the Mennonites, and formed a special unit called the Krimmer Church, whose members today consider themselves "kinship Hutterites" (in the United States, these people are called *Prairieleut*). The Krimmer Church people migrated to North America in the 1870's with other Ukrainian Germans, including the communal Hutterites. This suggests that the present-day communal Hutterian Brethren are the descendants of a hard-core revivalist group that transferred itself to North America and increased in numbers and wealth.

In 1870 the Czarist Government withdrew its protection from the Hutterites because they and other German colonists had refused to intermarry with Russians and kept themselves aloof from the mainstream of Russian society. This forced the Brethren to migrate once more. They came to North America, the only part of the world where large amounts of land were available to them, and where freedom of worship was a reality. In the 1870's the North American Great Plains were in the throes of settlement and colonization, and Europe was full of land and railroad agents looking for desirable settlers. The Ukrainian Germans were visited by these men, and the Hutterites were among the many who signed up for the move to the new continent. In this way the Brethren became a part of the great wave of German-speaking Russian minority group members that washed up onto the North American shore during the latter half of the nineteenth century.

The Russian government attempted to stem at least a part of this mass migration by offering to excuse the Hutterites from active military service. But most of the Brethren were determined to leave; only the wealthiest decided to remain behind (those who stayed behind, and their descendants, were virtually annihilated during the Russian Revolution and World War II).

After a brief sojourn in Nebraska, the Hutterites, along with some Mennonites, chose as their new home the southeastern corner of South Dakota, where the farming conditions resemble those of the Ukraine. In the generation preceding the North American migration, certain Hutterites had decided to re-establish the communal way of life and property ownership. It was these three groups or *Leute* whose members identified themselves as "Hutterites" after their arrival in South Dakota. Two of the Leute, the Darius and the Schmieden, had been living in colony groups in Russia, and they simply continued this practice in the United States. The third Leut, the Lehrer, was the last to arrive in North America. This group had not lived a communal life in Russia, but a few years after their arrival in 1877, they decided to establish communal colonies. The members of the Lehrer Leut are quite conscious of the fact of their late entry into full Hutterian status, and so are understandably more orthodox than the Schmieden and the Darius. *Lehrer* means "teacher"; the Leut's founder, Jacob Wipf, was an exceptionally well-educated man, and the Lehrer have always emphasized scholarship and a high level of skill and accomplishment somewhat more consistently than the Darius and Schmieden Leute. ("Darius" was the first name of that Leut's founder; *schmiede* means "smith," the trade of the Schmieden Leut's first leader.)

Today many Hutterites regret their early division into three branches; and informal discussions concerning reunification are carried on at intervals. A "United Hutterian Brethren Church" with a printed constitution exists;[3] this organization was created at the urging of the Canadian government, which found it easier to deal with the Hutterites on some issues as one group. Each Leut sends Elder delegates to an annual meeting of this church's administrative body, which confines its actions to issues concerning Hutterian relations with the government. Each of the three Leute, as we shall note in Chapter 5, has its own councils of Elders; each has an *Älteste* (a chief Elder); each is an endogamous marriage group; and each differs from the others in minor customs and rituals. The Lehrer comprise a kind of cultural-conservative wing, although they are very progressive economically and technologically: the Schmieden, especially those in the Canadian colonies, are the most liberal in terms of permissiveness toward customs and attitudes from the "outside"; the Darius fall between these two extremes. The dress of the women is one of the simpler means of identifying members of the three Leute: for example, Lehrer women are allowed to wear brighter colors than their Darius and Schmieden counterparts. From an outsider's viewpoint, the differences between the Leute are negligible; and indeed all three adhere to the same religious beliefs and way of life.

[3] See Fletcher, n.d. Since this writing, a transcription has been published by Victor Peters (1965, pp. 193ff).

The colonies prospered in the James River Valley of South Dakota until World War I, when they became the target of local anti-German prejudice, and also fell afoul of the draft laws: since conscientious objection was not legal in 1918, the United States government jailed many Hutterian youths as draft evaders; two of these young men died as a result of brutal treatment by prison guards, thus joining the long list of Hutterian "martyrs."[4] The accumulated social pressures forced the Brethren to think of migrating once again. At this juncture they were invited by the Canadian government to settle in Alberta and Manitoba. Both the government and the Canadian Pacific Railway were anxious to bring hard-working settlers to the parts of Alberta and Manitoba that had hitherto remained empty because of lack of resources or unfavorable climate. Assured that their pacifistic principles would be respected, the Brethren accepted the invitation. The Schmieden colonies went to Manitoba, and the Darius and Lehrer to Alberta. In the late 1920's, the Schmieden sent branch colonies back to buy up the old South Dakota colony sites that had been taken in trust by the state government. The other two Leute have sent branch colonies to the state of Washington, to Montana, and to North Dakota, and have recently settled in Saskatchewan. The six colonies in the Jasper region constituted the first Saskatchewan contingent; other groups have followed, and are located elsewhere in the Province.

The Brethren's first major encounter with official harassment in Canada occurred in 1942, when the Alberta legislature passed the Communal Property Act, a law expressly forbidding Hutterian colonies to locate closer than 40 miles from one another. There is evidence that the passage of this law was encouraged by Mormons in southern Alberta who feared the continued expansion of the colonies and resented the refusal of the Hutterites to accept the Mormon faith. On the other hand, some highly placed Mormons, including men in the Alberta government, opposed the legislation

---

[4] The *Martyrs' Mirror,* a Dutch Mennonite compilation of the lives of early Anabaptist martyrs, first published in the late sixteenth century, has recently been republished by the Mennonite Church.

and later sought its revision. Such a discriminatory statute is clearly unconstitutional both in the United States and in Canada, and the law has recently been modified to permit the government to approve any land purchase by the Hutterites regardless of proximity factors and provided the local people approve. This provision has resulted in some situations in which the local community has at first approved, then later rejected, the Brethren's entry. Hutterian principles include an injunction against litigation, but recently one colony caught in such a dilemma decided, against the advice of the Leut council of ministers, to resort to legal defense.[5]

Hutterian expansion has some problematic aspects. In at least one county of southern Alberta, the Brethren constitute the majority of the population. Yet their customs prevent them from assuming any political responsibility. The problem of local overpopulation by the Brethren has been handled in a variety of ways. For example, the Schmieden Leut has worked out an agreement with the Manitoba government not to establish more than two colonies in any one Rural Municipality. When colonies began branching into Saskatchewan, the provincial government obtained from the Darius and Lehrer Leute their agreement to consult with a special committee in Regina, the capital, before attempting to buy land. The committee is set up to help them find land in a district where local reaction will be favorable, and where Hutterian colonies are not already numerous. The Saskatchewan plan has worked well, and some of the colonies are beginning to settle in the north and to develop this frontier area.

In 1965, there were approximately 17,800 Hutterites in North America: 12,500 in Canada and 5,300 in the U.S. This entire population, comprising 164 colonies, is descended from the original

[5] During the fall of 1964, one Montana and one Alberta colony tried the expedient of purchasing their land through the individual male members, with each member taking title to a separate portion. These cases were still in litigation at the time of this writing. Another Alberta colony received the permission of the local municipal council, began purchasing land, and then was stopped by a spontaneous protest movement of farmers in the district. At the time of this writing, however, the colony was holding fast to its original agreement, and had a cadre of workers on the new site. For more details on the difficulties of the Brethren with state and Provincial governments, see Peters (1965, Chapter 2).

three groups of 800 Brethren who moved to the United States in the nineteenth century. While this group represented a hard-core conservative element, they were nevertheless lineal descendants of the sixteenth-century Brethren, and therefore their sons may be considered the present-day representatives of the old tradition.

There exist three quasi-Hutterian colonies or movements. The best-known and most important is the Society of Brothers, or "Bruderhof" group, founded by Eberhard Arnold, a German intellectual and refugee from Hitler's regime who established a "Hutterian" colony and publishing house in the Cotswolds in the 1930's as a utopian settlement.[6] This group moved to Paraguay, and was eventually disowned by the orthodox Hutterites after some of its members joined and subsequently disrupted the Forest River Colony in North Dakota (a colony now operated as a separate group by various outsiders and former Hutterites). Branches of the Bruderhof society are now found in Pennsylvania, New York, England, Paraguay, Uruguay, and Germany. The Pennsylvania colony operates a tourist hotel. The Bruderhof is a serious scholarly movement, and has published English translations of the basic Hutterian texts used by the orthodox colonies. Another group, the Community Farm of the Brethren, was founded in the early 1960's by a former Hungarian immigrant, Julius Kubassek. It is located in Bright, Ontario, and includes several families from Alberta Hutterian colonies. This convert group is not generally accepted by orthodox Hutterites as legitimate.

Beliefs

The Swiss sectarian groups that made up the nucleus of the Anabaptist movement founded their doctrines on the teachings of Erasmus. The central concepts—adult baptism, self-help, and avoidance of worldly affairs—were shared by many sects in Europe which, in their own ways, were attempting to re-create the church of the Apostles. Thus the doctrines of all Anabaptist groups are remark-

[6] See Eberhard Arnold (1964a, 1964b) for histories of the Bruderhof movement. A brief account of this group and others like it is found in Peters (1965, Chapter 12).

ably similar, despite the fact that the Radical Reformation had no single founder or even a central group of major theologians such as those participating in the Protestant Reformation.

As noted earlier, the relationship of the Anabaptist sects to Protestantism is complex and subtle. Although a sense of separation is maintained, all the important surviving groups—the Mennonites, the Amish, and the Hutterites, for example—still use the Protestant Bible and share certain basic doctrines with Protestantism. On the other hand, the Mennonites, save for the members of some purely agrarian communities, participate freely in "the world"; the Amish (who are really ultra-conservative Mennonites) eschew modern agricultural technology; and the Hutterites, who accept the benefits of technology, refuse to become involved in society. The Baptist faith practices adult baptism, but is thought of as a part of Protestantism, rather than as an Anabaptist sect. The Baptist movement began in England, and was comparable in many ways to Anabaptism, but its members lacked the revolutionary zeal of the Anabaptists, and so were more easily able to identify with Protestantism.

The relationship between Anabaptism and early Protestantism was equally complex. Though the Anabaptists and the Protestants were mutually hostile, the Anabaptists used the Luther translation of the Bible. Emphasis on faith rather than works, rejection of ritual and ecclesiastical paraphernalia, hostility toward monasticism, hatred of greed and hedonism, and the cultivation of such virtues as modesty, thrift, and self-abnegation were as characteristic of the Anabaptists as of any of the better-known Protestant sects.

The principal doctrinal difference that set Anabaptists apart from both Protestants and Catholics was their rejection of infant baptism on the grounds that the infant has neither the will nor the ability to accept God in a conscious manner. More important than this point of dogma was the fact that the Anabaptists and the Protestants had different aims: on the one hand, social change; on the other, religious reform. The Anabaptists were activists and millenarists who believed that the perfect society could be established here and now. Luther taught submission to the State and Calvin accepted capitalism as a positive good; the Anabaptists rejected both positions. Their rejection of existing institutions alienated both Luther and Erasmus. The Anabaptists foresaw in a general way the consequence of Protestant beliefs, that individualism and covetousness would eventually triumph, and they believed that the Christian virtues they hoped to practice and encourage would be compromised unless the teachings of the primitive Church were quite literally observed; hence their attempts to emulate as closely as possible the life of the first Christians of Jerusalem as related in the Acts of the Apostles. In the light of their puristic objectives, they had no alternative but to withdraw from society and from participation in the aims of the orthodox Reformation.

Is Anabaptism—and therefore Hutterian belief—a part of the Protestant movement? This question cannot be answered simply, and Anabaptists themselves differ on the point. Mennonites are inclined to identify with Protestantism because they have joined the majority society and follow the same basic institutional patterns. The Amish and the Hutterites, on the other hand, reject the Protestant Church as vigorously, or almost as vigorously, as they do the Catholic, and they refuse to forget the persecutions they suffered at the hands of both. Thus, the further an Anabaptist group may be removed from the institutional system of "the outside," the less inclined it is to consider itself part of the Protestant movement. This pattern of identification emphasizes the fact that the Anabaptist religion, in its communal version, is really a fusion of religious beliefs with a way of life. In this sense it is closer to Judaism than to Christianity, and bears a general resemblance to Buddhism and other Oriental religious systems. Communal Anabaptism is a continuation of the ancient principle of ascetic or withdrawn communalism practiced by such diverse groups as the Essenes of the Qmran community, the early Christian communes, and the medieval communal sects.[7]

[7] The resemblances between Hutterian communities and the Qmran community can be grasped by reading any description of the latter, for example, Jean Danielou's brief book *The Dead Sea Scrolls and Primitive Christianity*. There are detailed resemblances among all the sects that have modeled themselves on the Apostolic church community of Jerusalem. For example, the Zoar Separatists of the American nineteenth-century frontier duplicated many Hutterian practices, such as separation

While the Hutterites conceive of their way of life as a replication of the early Christian church, the question of the nature of early Christian life is a complex and ambiguous one. We have noted that the Anabaptists, like other millennial communalists, based their way of life on certain passages in the Book of Acts (2:43 and 4:32 in the Revised Standard Version). These passages can be interpreted as presenting a case for relinquishing all private property and sharing equally in the group's pooled possessions. However, a careful reading reveals ambiguous elements: there is an insistence on the distribution of goods to "any that have need," which suggests charity, not necessarily equal division or communal property. And there is the famous case of Ananias (Acts 5:1–11), who was castigated not so much for having failed to share all his property as for having lied to Peter about the amount. In the light of the thinness of evidence that true communalism prevailed in the church of the first and second centuries, it is difficult to make a sound historical case for early Christian communalism, although some form of voluntary sharing and charity to the poor were probably practiced.

Another mark against the communalist theory is the conflict between the nature of a true communal social order and the messianism and proselytizing of Jesus and his disciples. The Dead Sea Scrolls and modern historical analysis indicate that Jesus and his family existed in an atmosphere of Galilean sectarianism, with its several and conflicting aims, and its hostility toward Judean Judaism. There is historical evidence that Jesus' brother Jacob (or James) was an Essene-type sectarian who abstained from animal food and alcohol, possessed the gift of healing, and used Essenic terminology (e.g., the "Just One"). On the other hand, there is Biblical evidence that Jesus was opposed to the holier-than-thou, retreatist aspect of sectarianism. The Essenic pathway was withdrawal from

---

of the sexes in the dining hall, election of officers by the whole society, separate education of the young by the community, consumption austerity, and so on (Nordhoff 1875). The Amana community, an American religious communal society, still flourishing in northern Iowa, also resembles the Hutterites, and several *Prairieleut* Hutterian families intermarried with Amana people in the late nineteenth century. The Zoar and Amana people, like other German-derived communalists of the nineteenth century, trace their origins to seventeenth-century German Pietism, which has distant Anabaptist affiliations.

the world, as we know from the evidence found in the Qmran community, and from other historical sources.[8] In Matthew 11:12, Jesus is made to say, "From the days of John the Baptist until now the Kingdom of Heaven suffereth violence, and the violent take it by force." This passage is often interpreted to refer to the withdrawal sects with their "forced" approach to holiness through rigorous communal living, and their doctrine of the elect. A messianic leader like Jesus would have been opposed to this: his ministry was to all the people, and while he approved of the charity and sharing element in sectarian doctrine, he could hardly have approved the attitude of rejection of the world and mankind. Schonfield suggests that this may have been "a cause of friction with his family," as hinted at in Mark 6: "A prophet is not without honor, except in his own country, and among his own kin, and in his own house." Throughout the Gospels Jesus is shown associating with all kinds of people, drinking wine and eating freely, and in general comporting himself in a manner that must have offended the sectarians.

The spirit of the earliest movement, therefore, does not justify the strict interpretation of communalism made by the later communal sects—although there are some resemblances to the ascetic itinerants of the medieval millennial movement, such as the Beghards, who usually did not live in true communal groupings. During the first century, the small, beleaguered communities of Nazarene Christians might have lived communally out of fear and need for protection, as a functional adjustment to their social position; but the messianic element in Christianity seems antithetical to this as a permanent pattern, and in any case it did not prevail as a majority expression of the faith.

There is evidence, therefore, that the spirit or basis of Hutterian communalism is sectarian, not Christian. The Hutterian commune more closely resembles descriptions of the Zadokite-Essenic communal sects than it does any existing description of Christian groups, including that described in Acts. Hutterites themselves early perceived these similarities.[9]

---

[8] E.g., Josephus, Clement of Rome, and others. See Schonfield, Part 2, Chapters 1 and 2.

[9] See "True Surrender and Christian Community of Goods," by Peter Walpot (1577) as translated by Kathleen Hasenberg. The passage occurs at the end of the

However, there is no direct historical connection between the later communal sects and the pre-Christian Jewish sectarian groups they so closely resemble. Their ancestry is ideological: a mingling of sectarian, early Christian, and even classical elements, implemented and fused by feelings of social deprivation. In the most basic sense, the communal tradition is part of what Norman Cohn (1947) calls the "egalitarian state of nature." The origin of this doctrine is to be found in the Greek and Roman myths of the Golden Age, the time when all men held all things in common and lived together in perfect peace and equality. The early Church fathers such as Clement of Alexandria often quoted these myths, but gave them a distinctly Christian orientation by defining "equality" as God's grace—His creation of all things for the equal enjoyment of all men. Cohn notes that by the third century, Christian writers had "assimilated from the extraordinarily influential philosophy of Stoicism the notion of an egalitarian State of Nature which was irrecoverably lost" (Cohn, 1947, p. 201). The irrecoverability of the ideal condition functioned as a rationale for the prevailing social inequalities that were either furthered or tolerated by the Church. The *Pseudo-Isidore,* a work produced about A.D. 850 by a French monk, took the final step in the conversion of the "State of Nature" concept into a Christian doctrine. The author of the *Pseudo-Isidore* extolled the Apostolic Church of Jerusalem as the ideal egalitarian communal society. By the late medieval period, Christian scholars had accepted as a fact the teaching that the early Christians had rejected private property, and that this rejection was commendable because it brought man closer to God.

The Anabaptists chose to follow this trend of thought. Their advocacy of communal ownership of property and egalitarianism was enunciated in the form of a revolt against the established churches. The Anabaptists did not merely sigh for a vanished Golden Age, but they proposed to restore it and, by so doing, to revive "true Christianity." This proposal came as a profound shock to orthodox

---

selection, in section 147, and refers to the accounts by Eusebius, in turn borrowed from Philo, of the *Theraputae,* an Essenic Jewish sect living in Alexandria. All the elements are present: communal life and property, withdrawal from the world, and the "fervent, fiery faith."

church authorities and scholars, implying as it did that they were hypocrites who knew the nature of the true path, but who continued to follow and teach others the way of corruption.

During the Middle Ages, the sects following egalitarian and millennial ideals displayed varying degrees of adherence to revolutionary or militant doctrines, depending upon the extent to which the ideals of purity and withdrawal were influential in their culture. Those who took the militant course became itinerants, or established semipermanent communities that may or may not have had communal customs. Those who set out on the communal pathway followed an implicit blueprint, or what Lévi-Strauss would consider *imagines mundi*—a particular pattern of thinking about social life that inevitably produces like consequences regardless of time period or culture: i.e., withdrawal means departure from the urban community; self-sufficiency means agriculture; communal property means discipline and suppression of factionalism and individualism.

While the Hutterian Brethren did not participate in the more extreme revolutionary and eschatological versions of the millennial movement, their descendants do possess the generalized ideological mind-set that millennial beliefs produce. The millennial ideal is uniquely Western, for it embodies a goal that most Oriental religions view as a delusion—the establishment of a perfect society. In the Judeo-Christian tradition the millennial ideal has played an important role as a revolutionary force and as an impetus for renewal and reform. It has led some men toward a utopian vision, and others toward the active reform of contemporary institutions. It has functioned as a corrective to individual rapacity and excesses of achievement by emphasizing brotherly love and the right of all men to share the fruits of the earth equally.[10]

[10] Yonina Talmon has summarized the relevance of millennial religious movements for social change in a useful paper, "Pursuit of the Millennium: The Relation between Religious and Social Change," *Archives Européens de Sociologie,* 3, 125–48 (1962). Talmon's paper also raises by implication another important issue: the question of classification of these millennial societies. Talmon follows an old tradition in sociology which uses the utopian or millennial spirit as the independent factor; in this book, the implicit classifier is communal-type social organization. The two methods of classification yield an overlapping, but not identical, array of

If there is a single basic belief common to all Anabaptist sects, it is simply that all Christians must be united in a bond of love for Christ and for each other. Any important manifestation of individual self-seeking destroys this bond and thus injures the social fabric and separates the individual from Christ. In order to maintain the bond of love and self-effacement, the Anabaptists—and most particularly, the Hutterites—seek to organize their society and economy according to egalitarian principles. This effectively separates them from the "Gentile" world. The chief spiritual concept in the Hutterian version of Anabaptism is *Gelassenheit*—literally, "giving-upness"—which most authorities refuse to translate into English, since there is no accurate or euphonious equivalent. The term implies a submission of one's whole nature to God's will, and a voluntary surrender of everything that might come between oneself and God. The colony becomes the living expression of this submission: "He who is accepted into our communal life has to show obedience in his whole life" (see Friedmann, 1960). Worldly goods are hindrances to the pursuit of spirituality, but one must live in the world and contend with its forces. One of the paradoxes of Anabaptism is that its members must avoid contamination by the world, yet be able to deal with society successfully so as to further the mission of Christ.

The basic Hutterian beliefs (*Die Glauben,* as they are called by the Brethren) are based on a collection of Biblical passages. These passages are used as justification for particular rules of daily living and social organization.[11] The most important Hutterian document is Peter Rideman's *Confession of Faith,* written in the years 1540–44, an explication of the rules of conduct formulated from these passages (Rideman–Hasenberg 1950). The entire second portion

---

societies and sectarian groups; e.g., millennialism includes all of the medieval groups, while communalism leaves some of them out. Moreover, there is a change in the classificatory position of any given society relative to its historical development. Thus, the Hutterites were most certainly millennialists in the sixteenth century, but in the current North American phase much of their millennial spirit has faded, and it is probably more meaningful to consider them at present as examples of communal social organization and economics.

[11] Perhaps the most penetrating study of Hutterian beliefs is provided by Robert Friedmann in various articles (1961).

of the *Confession* is an exposition of the distinctive Hutterian doctrine of election: that the true Christian way is the communal way and no other, and that only those who follow this way can properly call themselves true Christians.

The world, or "World System" as it appears in certain Hutterian and Anabaptist writings, is carnal, corrupt, and idolatrous, concerned with pleasure and therefore removed from God. The world consists of the works of men, which are to be avoided (as Jesus told Pilate in John 18:36). At the same time, the Brethren exist in this world, and must contend with it in order to live. Thus it is all the more important that they "behave wisely [and] unobtrusively, and, unoffending, keep their lights burning ... so that the light shines through, convincing the world that they have something better than unbelievers" (Hofer 1955, p. 35). Man is imperfect, and while the Brethren seek to come as close to God and to Jesus' way as humanly possible, the road is hard: "The communal way of life is not an invention or social system devised by the Hutterites, nor is it to their liking to live this life" (Hofer 1955, p. 7).

The avoidance of worldly things is expressed by the Brethren in their refusal to hold political office, to bear arms, to take oaths, or to pay taxes if the tax money is to be used for military purposes, as well as by their practice of austerity with regard to personal possessions and pleasures. "Love not the world, neither the things that are in the world. If any man love the world, the love of the Father is not in him" (John 2:15-17). The Hutterian attitude toward government is a complex one. Though the Brethren cannot hold office, since they regard governments as corrupt, they agree to cooperate with rulers, since rulers are unconscious agents of God who by government punish men for their transgressions and their falling away from God. Thus, Hutterites withdraw from, but must deal with, the outer world.

Nevertheless, one must make money in order to live, and therefore one must meet the Gentiles to some extent on their own ground. The Hutterites are permitted to make money by selling the fruits of their production. They are specifically enjoined from buying goods and selling the same goods at a profit, but they may sell for a profit those things produced by their own hands. This does not include manufactured goods, since on the whole these seem to the Hutterites to be "commercial" articles; their manufacture and sale would bring the Brethren too close to the practices of the world. However, craft manufactures were sold by the colonies during the sixteenth century; there is no specific traditional taboo against manufacturing itself.

"Then they that gladly received his word were baptized. . . . And they continued steadfastly in the Apostles' doctrine and fellowship, and the breaking of bread, and in prayers. . . . And all that believed were together and had all things in common; and they sold their possessions and goods and parted them to all men, as every man had need" (Acts 2:41–47). The principle of communal ownership of property, or "the Community of Goods," is the basis of the Hutterian economic organization, and it is also the feature that distinguishes the Hutterites from the other Anabaptists, who gave up or never completely accepted communalism. Without their communal practices, the Hutterites would be indistinguishable from those Mennonite groups that use technology. The Brethren are well aware of this; they know that the entire Hutterian system stands or falls on communalism. So long as the Hutterites share goods, especially land, in common, and reduce their personal possessions to a minimum, the colony can exist as a colony and Hutterian life can maintain its continuity; hence the Brethren's relative freedom in adopting anything that strengthens the colony as a communal system. At the same time, the colony framework permits much greater control over austerity than does a "church" system in which individual families live separately and are merely exhorted to refrain from consumption. Thus the Brethren have not experienced the tendency to schism that has characterized the Mennonite and Amish groups, whose various sects differ in the kinds and amounts of modern equipment they may adopt and use. The Hutterian system is a truly functional social system: their religious beliefs establish a social frame, and the social frame makes it possible to observe the beliefs. Conversely, the Hutterian social system is a static one, for its functionalism makes radical change almost impossible.

The Brethren's basic rules of conduct were laid down during their years in Moravia, and were followed, often with great difficulty, throughout their many years of migration and persecution in various parts of Europe. On several occasions the Brethren departed from their principles of community and austerity, and the sect was in danger of extinction more than once. The expectation of martyrdom at the hands of religious or secular authorities is an important part of the Hutterian attitude toward the world; they are always prepared for persecution, and are proud of their 1,700 martyrs.[12]

The Jasper colonies have not departed significantly from the observance of these principles. Their wholly agrarian economy makes it relatively easy for them to maintain a controlled engagement with the world. The efficiency of their large-scale economic operations is appropriate to communal-cooperative agriculture carried on by a growing population, since this form of agriculture provides the savings needed for financing the establishment of new colonies. In the Jasper colonies, some features of the original commands are less emphasized today than in the past: the Brethren are more willing to enter into the world than a reading of the commentaries would lead one to believe—but they continue to avoid voting and public office, and firmly refuse to bear arms. They continue to educate their children in their own "German School," although they will accept a minimal 8th-grade public education if the schoolteacher comes to the colony. They continue to make their own clothes, both to save money and to preserve their external distinctiveness.[13]

At the time of our study, there were differences of attitude toward the basic Hutterian principles on the part of the older and younger generations of Jasper colony men. The older men often gave the visitor the impression that they were wise, conservative mentors who dealt with the world only in order to maintain the

---

[12] See Rideman-Hasenberg (1950); also Friedmann (1961, Section III).
[13] This was the original reason for the costume, as enunciated in Rideman-Hasenberg (1950, pp. 133–34). See also Gross (1965).

continuity of true Christian existence. The younger men tended to put the emphasis on Hutterian life as the best form of an agricultural society and the most efficient system for supporting a large and growing population under modern economic conditions, especially in the Great Plains. In short, they resembled practical, cooperative ideologues, not religious philosophers. It is doubtful that this represents a growing change, for there is evidence that such a difference has characterized the Hutterian generations from early times. The young men are engaged in the business of running the practical side of an intricate social system, the colony. The older men, though they are responsible for guarding the colony finances, have the leisure, since many of them are retired, to read over and ponder the sect's history. Thus the contrasting attitudes of the old and young men reflect the remarkable Hutterian functional synthesis of the philosophical and the practical.[14]

It is instructive to view the Hutterian ideology in the context of its relationship to the instrumental and social values of the Jasper Gentile community. It is apparent that the Hutterites share the Gentile orientation toward money as a medium of exchange and a measure of general economic worth. The Hutterites are proud of their savings, their credit ratings, and their efficiency in management. Production for the most favorable cash sale is as much a fundamental economic principle for the Hutterites as it is for the rest of the agricultural operators in the area.

The Brethren do not, however, subscribe to the idea of money as a measure of all things. They reject the "consumer culture" around them and they especially resist spending money on luxuries, for they consider this "idolatry." Since their economic goals do not go beyond the secure financial establishment of the colony, the Breth-

---

[14] Children are exposed to Hutterian beliefs as a matter of course, and each one is expected to study the traditional books on his own. A few do, and become philosophically oriented in their 20's and 30's. All tend to become more conservative—that is, devoted to the Hutterian way—as they get older and assume responsibility. In any case, the Brethren do not like to emphasize the sectarian character of their religion, since they prefer to see themselves simply as Christians who live as Christians should. They are communal because they are Christians, not because they are a separate sect of Christianity.

ren only partially accept the doctrine of continuous economic progress. They lack any concept of an expanding standard of living; of the aim in life of coveting and spending money in order to live more easily and enjoyably. Though individual Hutterites may envy their neighbors and secretly desire more possessions, to show such feelings openly is taboo. If envy becomes a serious problem, the colony has formal ways of dealing with it.[15]

Unlike the Gentiles, the Hutterites are not forced to cope with a dual value system in which help of one's neighbor is esteemed, but a man's worth in the world is determined by his success in competing with others. The cooperative-communal frame of Hutterian life is the alternative to both competition and individual altruism. Within it, human effort is regarded as innately cooperative; hence it is felt that the individual exists only to serve the welfare of the entire group, not to feather his own nest or to help another from private motives, although at the same time, Hutterites recognize that men—including Hutterites—have strong tendencies in these directions.

The Hutterites do extend aid to other colonies, in fulfillment of their obligation to maintain desirable social and economic relations, and they sometimes engage in "neighboring" practices with their Gentile neighbors for the same reason. But the Brethren do not enter organized cooperatives, mutual aid rings, or work exchanges with the Gentiles, nor do they seek to compete directly with Gentile enterprisers. They need not make a shibboleth of cooperativeness, since their very way of life is cooperation incarnate.

These instrumental and social values of Hutterian life, which all the Jasper Brethren follow, are based on the colony organization, but at the same time they are also the functional expression of the religious framework underlying it. So long as the Brethren adhere

[15] The Hutterian refusal to regard money as an end in life, or as the measure of other things, had its analogue in the actions of the first generation of Gentile settlers in the Jasper region, who placed financial accumulation low in the hierarchy of goals, and who did not spend money on luxuries. However, they also refused to spend it on capital improvements; in this sense the approach of the Brethren has always differed from conservative entrepreneurship in Gentile agriculture. The Hutterian values concerning money appear to combine Anglo-Saxon or Scottish frugality with contemporary ideas about the value of credit and the measure of monetary values in investment.

to communal principles, they cannot share fully in the values of the Gentile community; and their failure to share in these values reinforces their dependence on communal ways. Since the Brethren are manifestly successful commercial agricultural enterprisers, they demonstrate the possibility of carrying on such an enterprise with a value system other than that of individualism or covetousness. Their success as a type of cooperative organization stands in contrast to the difficulties of some of the Gentile cooperative farmers in Saskatchewan, whose irrepressibly individualistic or covetous motives have led to the decline and breakup of the cooperative farms.[16] Hutterian communalism is not a universal blueprint for successful agricultural or community development, but it does indicate what can be accomplished within the communal framework. It remains the most enduring form of collective agriculture yet devised.[17]

The Meaning of Hutterian History

The Hutterites are proud of their nearly 500 years as a harassed religious minority, and they never tire of pointing out that they are living proof of the doctrine that persecution simply strengthens

---

[16] See Cooperstock (1961). Most cooperative farms in Saskatchewan were established after World War II by veterans who wished to enter agriculture but were unable to find farms. The cooperative enterprises were transferred to them by the Provincial Government by means of grazing leases. Most of the original farms had disappeared by the 1960's; those that were left had converted themselves into limited co-ops: for example, machinery cooperatives in which only the machines were owned collectively. For an optimistic study of the Saskatchewan cooperative farms in their early stages, see L. E. Drayton, in Infield (1950).

[17] The Israeli *kibbutz* is a new and, thus far, a successful form of agricultural collectivism. As we shall note in a later chapter, the organization of the kibbutz resembles that of the Hutterian colony very closely. The ideologies of these two outstanding types of the agrarian collective community provide interesting contrasts and similarities. The kibbutz is based on the Marxist principle of "to each according to his need," which implies a degree of difference based on function in the distribution of goods. However, the *kibbutznikim* also believe in the Marxist egalitarian distribution of profits, and hence much property and all money are communally held, and consumption and individual differences in property ownership are controlled. The Hutterian practices are more consistent: there is no recognition of "need" differences in property, and the entire emphasis is placed on communal ownership and equal sharing. The Brethren's insistence on austerity and equality of ownership results in a consistently lower level of living than is found in the kibbutz, and also greater control over demands for a higher level.

the persecuted. There is truth in this claim, but it must be remembered that on two occasions, in Hungary and in the Ukraine, the Brethren abandoned their central principles and communal way of life; and that perhaps a majority of the members of the European communities eventually were reconverted to the orthodox Christian faiths. The Hutterian sect survives today because a few deeply committed groups managed to flee in time from persecution and establish themselves in new locations.

In any case, today's Hutterite has no "crisis of identity." He knows exactly who he is and where he came from. The Brethren have written their own history, and possess a voluminous literature of chronicles, epistles (mostly written in prison), catechisms, songs, and other documents, all preserved by the useful custom of hand-copying manuscripts. The Brethren's sense of identity is reinforced by the fact that in all historical periods they have confronted the world in the same way. In a sense, history does not exist for them, since they have always been outside the mainstream of society. They have repeatedly migrated, established themselves anew, and worked out adaptations that permitted them to keep their distance and yet survive. In the recent North American phase, they have had to move and establish themselves twice—first in South Dakota, then in Canada—and their current troubles with the Alberta government represent still another episode of a type familiar to the Brethren. In connection with their struggle to represent Christ in a corrupt world, a world essentially hostile to Christian ideals, one modern Hutterian writer remarks, "It is the same today." The modern world offers them the same hostility or grudging acceptance, and shows the same self-seeking departure from Christ and the Word of God as it ever did; the same opportunities await enterprising colonies, and the same temptations beset those Brethren who fall away from the "true path." This historical continuity reinforces the Hutterite's traditional view of himself and his position in the world.

Still another factor that helps the Hutterite maintain his identity is his acceptance of a rural existence. Agriculture has not always been the Brethren's mainstay, but it has been so for most of their history, and even in the "Golden Age" on the Moravian estates, they were essentially rural communalists. They have always avoided the city because it is apparent that no way can be found there to maintain a colony mode of existence based on communal landholding. Agriculture, with its relative isolation and its earthy tasks, shields the Brethren from contamination by worldly life and minimizes the necessity of wage labor (although in poor colonies today, as in the past, the men frequently take temporary jobs on the "outside"). The traditional rural setting of Hutterian culture lends it a "peasant" quality that contrasts with its basic economic rationality and tradition of respect for education and craftsmanship.

The rationality of Hutterian culture stems from the period of its founding, when converts from every trade and nearly every profession known in sixteenth-century Europe joined the faith. A complete listing of these occupations is to be found in Hutterian historical documents. According to Klassen's recent compilation and description of Anabaptist economy (1962), the converts included professionals, intellectuals, artisans, and merchants. Klassen includes as professionals and intellectuals physicians, tutors in classical languages, humanist-scholars, theologians, professors, translators of religious literature, clergymen, former monks, magistrates, mayors and other civic officials, members of the nobility, lawyers, bookkeepers, and stewards. Artisans included weavers, tailors, printers, teachers, booksellers, furriers, millers, bakers, hatters, cartwrights, goldsmiths, farriers, blacksmiths, locksmiths, watchmakers, tanners, saddlers, cobblers, carpenters and cabinetmakers, coopers, cutlers, vinedressers, gardeners, butchers, masons, bookbinders, potters, wagoners, glaziers, and painters. A substantial number of merchants dealing in almost every commodity of the time are also listed in the Hutterian chronicles and in the records of heresy trials. However, all these people probably constituted only a fourth of the total sixteenth-century Hutterian membership, for the majority of the Brethren were peasants. It is possible, however, that the professionals listed by Klassen comprised the most progressive element of the group at that time.

Since the movement was largely rural, the majority of the early

Brethren came from farms; but there seems to have been no discernible tendency to favor the members of certain occupations over others. Everyone was welcome to join and to practice his trade as part of the colony life and economy. The economic strength of the Moravian colonies owed as much to the diverse skills of their members as to their faith and steadfastness, and it was because of this wide range of skills that the Moravian lords extended their protection to the Brethren and allowed them to work as stewards or in technical and agricultural cadres on their estates. A better bargain could hardly have been struck, since the Brethren sought no profits for themselves, and asked only peace and protection in return for their services.

The experience of service on the estates of the Moravian lords influenced the form of the Brethren's instrumental organization (see Chapter 6). The chief executive of the colony was and is the Minister, who governs the spiritual life of the community, but the economy and finances are under the direction of the Householder, or, as he was known in the sixteenth and seventeenth centuries, the *Wirt, Diener Notdurft,* or *Rentmeister.* This officer not only played a necessary role in colony affairs, but also acted as general director of the economic activities of the lord's estate. The Hutterian estate steward was a supremely rational man: a man of practical affairs whose task it was to conduct the economic affairs of his employer in the most efficient possible manner. The manager of the craft and agricultural enterprises on an estate was often the Householder of the Hutterian community as well.

The organization of the colony system is not a simple projection of basic beliefs, but the result of a particular episode in early Hutterian history. No other Anabaptist group experienced this particular form of patronage, and none of them display the intricate organizational rationality that characterizes Hutterian life. The Amish have retreated into horse-and-buggy traditionalism; the Mennonites accept individual enterprise, though they often practice cooperation as well. Only the Hutterites have persisted in practicing the rationally organized communal collectivism developed during their service in Moravia. But these are perhaps chicken-and-egg questions. It is difficult to see how a colony could be operated successfully, even at bare survival level, without a highly rational form of decision-making and direction. The colony system is inherently "rational" insofar as it requires highly efficient production for the support of a relatively large population on resources that are always relatively limited. We know this is the case under the present conditions of Hutterian life in the Northern Plains, but the basic dimensions of the situation must have characterized Hutterian life at all periods.

The colony system seems to function most successfully where resources and returns are just adequate or slightly deficient— either absolutely, in terms of survival, or relatively, in terms of felt deprivation. The Hutterites are aware of this; they fear excessive prosperity because it removes the necessity for the many intricate regulations of conduct and economic activity on which their daily life depends. The relatively wealthy colonies of the modern period must exercise vigilance lest their young people begin to demand personal possessions or even excessive communal purchases. The Hutterian colony is able to control demands; the Israeli kibbutz, with its ideological tolerance of individual differences in needs, is less successful.

The dynamic of Hutterian history in periods of relative security has been one of constant proliferation of daughter colonies. In the North American phase, daughter colonies have generally split off when the population of the parent colony has reached about 150 persons—although in recent years the split has been occurring even earlier, at about 130. These new colonies are regarded as independent communities, although their members intermarry and lend each other money. There is no central purchasing agency, cooperative, or bank to which all colonies in a given area can resort.

Hutterites conceive of themselves simply as "Christians," or "Christian Brethren." Though they use the adjective *Hutterische,* they recognize it as an informal term applied to them by the Gentiles. Their own world is circumscribed, but they interact with each other much as people in the outside world do. Colonies criticize each other freely, and even develop feuds that become public knowledge (however, because of the prevailing emphasis on brotherly love, interaction that is less than benevolent tends to be soft-pedaled or concealed). Repeated persecution has led most Hutterites to feel that they should present a united front to the world. In spite of their unity, however, they elude easy classification. They are an ethnic group, a culture, an economy, a sect, a branch of Christianity, and a kind of "nation." They are, in a way, peasants, but they are also highly rational entrepreneurs. They are, in short, a unique people; a people from whom there is much to be learned, especially on two important subjects: the nature of the control of social tensions, and the key aspects of successful cooperative agricultural management.

THREE

The Hutterian Settlement

The coming of the Hutterian Brethren represents the most recent large-scale migration into the Jasper region. The members of the first colony arrived in 1952, and over the next decade five other colonies were established. Additional colonies were established elsewhere in the Province at the rate of about one a year during the 1960's. The Saskatchewan colonies were all offshoots of parent groups in Alberta that had reached the maximum population allowed by Hutterian custom. (By the late 1960's the Saskatchewan colonies themselves would begin their process of fission.) The original move to Saskatchewan was prompted by Alberta laws that restricted the location of new colonies and imposed obstacles to the purchase of land.

Hutterian settlement differs from colonization by individual pioneers in that it is virtually self-contained. Much of the equipment necessary for the initial establishment of residence and an economy are provided; and if shortages exist they are tolerated, in accordance with the Hutterian practice of austerity. The self-containment of the Hutterian colonization resembles that of the Mormons, who, in a similar migration, settled portions of southern Alberta in the nineteenth century.[1] The Mennonites too came into southern Saskatchewan very early.[2] The feature of self-contain-

---

[1] See Lowry Nelson (1952, Chapters 10 to 14).
[2] See A. S. Morton (1938, pp. 54–55).

ment gives all these sectarians a considerable advantage over the individual pioneer: a frontier, in the sense of penniless pioneers contending against a wilderness, does not exist for sectarians, and while there is a growth pattern, it is not as marked as the extreme privation-to-prosperity cycle that has typified the societies of individual farmer pioneers. Moreover, the Hutterian colony is a world unto itself; it is peripheral to the regional networks of social relations and shared experiences that characterize all former western frontiers. The Brethren's inability to participate fully in regional tradition is a barrier to their participation in contemporary regional society, and in some Northern Plains districts this arouses feelings of hostility toward them.

The Hutterian colonies represent a unique adaptive response to the Jasper habitat and economy. In Chapter 1 we defined the problem of maldistribution of natural resources in the Northern Plains, and showed how relatively small-scale private land tenure tends to reduce the chances of each settler obtaining an adequate share of these resources. Hutterian practices of large-scale land ownership and resource development counteract this tendency. Consumption austerity and self-help enable the Hutterites to amass capital and purchase land, and thus increase their overall financial returns. Their nucleated communal mode of living and working permits them to obtain maximum labor efficiency, and their broad diversification of agricultural enterprise makes it possible to distribute risk.

The strategy of our research on the Jasper colonies was as follows. The southwestern portion of the Province contains a total of seven colonies. These colonies are distributed in two groups: four colonies are located from 15 to 25 miles west of the town of Jasper, and three colonies are located from 25 to 30 miles east of the town. The western colonies are adjacent, with much of their land touching. The three eastern colonies are widely separated from each other: one is on the north slope of the hills, one (not shown) is on the south slope just outside the Jasper region proper, and the third is near the crestal plateau. The four western colonies and two of the eastern group were included in our study because they used Jasper town as their mailing address, service center, grain delivery terminus, and livestock sales and shipping point most of the time. Since Hutterites "shop around" for services, the south slope colony used the town from time to time also, and hence we included it in some aspects of the research; however, we studied the six other colonies much more intensively, and selected one of them for a prolonged residential study. Brief comparative studies were made of some of the Alberta colonies from which the Saskatchewan groups originally split off. This approach provided us with both intensive and survey data on the Hutterian settlement.

We noted that the typical Hutterian colony divides when it reaches a critical mass of about 150 persons. A colony of this size becomes difficult to manage by means of the intimate forms of social control used by the Hutterites, and difficult to support on the amount of land usually available. The colonies split vertically through the generations, and therefore the new colony possesses a population pyramid approximately resembling that of its parent. This means that the new colony is in effect an extension of the old; and its relationship to the parent colony remains exceptionally close for a decade or so, while it is achieving economic maturity. During this formative period, the two colonies are to some extent operated as a single enterprise, and exchange various forms of assistance, financial and other. This makes spatial location particularly important. The Brethren have long considered a distance of about 30 miles between parent and daughter colonies as ideal, since this is far enough to avoid Gentile accusations that Hutterites dominate the district, but close enough to permit ready contact. However, with the increased use of automobiles and trucks, the colonies now think of 100 to 200 miles as close enough for desired relations. The colonies in the Jasper region are about 200 miles from their parent colonies in Alberta.

The initial land purchases in Saskatchewan were made in a district west of Jasper town whose previous settlers were ready to sell their land. Owing to the availability of this land, eventually four colonies came to be located within one to twenty miles of one another. Since population in this district was sparse and the resources uninviting, there seems to have been relatively little criticism of or hostility toward the Brethren. Three more colonies, arriving at a later date, were able to find widely separated tracts of land east of Jasper without difficulty.

The Hutterites seek to balance distance and proximity. Much distance between colonies would make it hard to maintain relations between related or unrelated colonies, and to exchange information and labor. Too great proximity of colonies would invite Gentile criticism, and would lead to competition between colonies in local sales of garden and farm produce. By Hutterian standards, the colonies west of Jasper are too close for comfort; the spacing of the eastern colonies is ideal.[3] Regardless of distances, however, the seven colonies in southwestern Saskatchewan constituted a social region of their own. Though contacts between them were governed to some extent by distance, all seven considered themselves "neighbors," and interacted accordingly. The six colonies selected for study were those that interacted most frequently.

[3] *Kibbutz* settlement patterns and their consequences both resemble and differ from those of the colonies. Resemblances are found in the difficulties which emerge between *kibbutzim* when they are too close together. In the Jordan Valley, as in other places in Israel, kibbutzim land borders adjoin to form a continuous strip of kibbutz-settled land. Many of these communities are engaged in constant small running battles over land adjustments, land-use planning, and the like. Competition for local markets, however, which was prevalent in earlier years, no longer exists, because the produce of all kibbutzim is now sold on a national market. Differences between kibbutz and colony settlement patterns also emerge in the degree of rational assignment of land areas by the Israeli government. All land used for agricultural purposes is considered the property of the state; a kibbutz must receive its land on assignment, and is not in the free market. Thus the placement of kibbutzim for a number of years—at least since 1950—has been governed by rational considerations outside the wishes or needs of the new kibbutz members. Another difference in settlement loci resulted from the need, during the early years of Palestinian settlement, to locate kibbutzim on the frontiers for defensive purposes. Kibbutzim sometimes share farm equipment and exchange information, as do the colonies, but the writer received the impression that there is less and less of this, because of the extensive involvements of the communities in national systems, and because the several kibbutz federations have set up their own organization. A recent trend in the federations is the establishment of regional "service centers" serving the repair and processing needs of local kibbutzim belonging to the particular federation. Hutterites, of course, have nothing comparable to this, nor do they have the numerous cooperative stores and services that have developed within the federations and between them.

The Ecological Significance of the Hutterian Settlement

In 1964 the four western colonies and two eastern colonies studied had a total population of 549 persons, or 7 per cent of the regional total of 7,300. Of these, 176 lived in the two eastern colonies, and 373 lived in the western (see Table 3).[4] Since Hutterian colonies reach a maximum of around 150 persons before dividing, the projected maximum population of the colonies is 900, but it will always be less, because of the increasing trend toward early fission. The rate of growth of the regional non-Hutterian population is about half that of the Hutterian, owing to the high rate of emigration and the relatively small size of families among the Gentiles. Therefore, as the colonies reach their maximum projected size they will

Table 3—Population of colonies on arrival in 1964

Colony	Year of arrival	Population	1964 population	Mean increase per year (persons)	Per cent of increase since year of arrival — Period (years)	Per cent of increase since year of arrival — Per cent
Western Group						
1	1952	45	72	2.2	12	60%
2	1956	79	100	2.6	8	27
3	1958	68	105	6.2	6	54
4	1960	79	96	4.2	4	22
Subtotal . .		271	373	15.2		
Eastern Group						
5	1954	72	106	3.4	10	47
6	1959	50	70	4.0	5	40
Subtotal . .		122	176	7.4		
Total . .		393	549	3.8		Average: 42%

[4] According to Eaton and Mayer (1954), p. 44, the population doubles every 16 years (see Table 3 above, for data on the Jasper colonies). There is no reason to foresee any slackening of this growth rate, although younger Brethren sometimes show concern over Hutterian fertility and the need for a population policy in the future. This may be the beginning of a change, but it would take a generation or more before this could become official or effective. Some form of control is probably inevitable, because colony sites will eventually become unavailable. See also Cook (1954).

constitute a somewhat larger proportion of the regional population than they now do—perhaps as large as 10 per cent.

The Hutterian emigration to Jasper spanned the twelve years preceding 1964. The first Hutterites to enter the region purchased land in the western area about ten miles from the town of Jasper. Other colonies followed at a rate of about one every two years, and the last one came in 1960. The successful entry of the first colony encouraged others to locate in the same area. By 1964, all immediately available land had been purchased, and the few remaining Gentile farms in the area were wholly or partially surrounded by colony property. We have noted that in contrast to this nucleation of the western settlement, the eastern colonies were widely separated and each was completely surrounded by Gentile farms and ranches. These differences in the settlement patterns of the two groups of colonies suggest the existence of particular ecological and economic factors affecting colony location.

We have emphasized the fact that it is the Hutterites' practice to buy up very large tracts of land. This practice increases their chances of acquiring adequate resources. However, problems arise when the differences in the availability or quantity of resources require modifications in the standard traditional Hutterian agricultural regime. This regime is perhaps the most complete form of diversified agriculture to be found in single, large enterprises anywhere in North America.

In the Jasper area there are farms without a single good well, ranches without a permanent creek, and land with nothing but sandy soil. No colony, however, is without an adequate water supply, and all colonies have some heavy, water-retaining soil. On the other hand, some colonies have better groundwater than others; one colony lacks a creek, and one has heavy soil but is located in a hail zone. Such differences result in a need to redefine the pattern of diversification in order to adapt to the particular resource picture in each location. In the most general sense, this means shifting the emphasis either to field crops or to livestock, and it may also mean changes in living habits. Underlying this pattern of adaptation is the issue of management flexibility: the diversification regime has deep roots in the Hutterian economic philosophy, is linked to the emphasis on self-help in their religious dogma, and serves the major practical end of supplying a relatively large number of responsible jobs to colony men, thus providing rewards for the self-discipline of close communal life.

Table 4 shows land productivity as measured by wheat yield, and gives altitude and growing season data also. One can see that the two eastern colonies (5, 6) differ greatly from the rest: Colony 6 is at a high altitude and has a high percentage of poor yield (Class 1) land, but the largest percentage of good (Class 3) land is owned by Colony 5. The other four colonies do not differ significantly. At the time of our study, the colony at 3,700 feet was experiencing critical resource problems based on its short growing season; its members were responding by introducing intensive fertilization to give crops a fast start, by clearing the brush in coulee areas where the only heavy soil is located, by planning to build a greenhouse for starting garden crops, and by emphasizing livestock over crops. These innovative responses are a matter of some importance, insofar as all these things diverge from the traditional Hutterian extensive

Table 4—Wheat productivity of colony lands

Colony	(as % of total acreages)				Altitude (feet)	Growing season (days)	
	Class 1 (poorest)	Class 2	Class 3	Class 4 (best)		20-Year average	Minimum on record
1[a]	65	30	5	0	2,600	123	85
2[b]	50	40	10	0	2,700	120	81
3[b]	50	40	10	0	2,600	123	85
4[b]	50	40	10	0	2,700	120	81
5[c]	35	25	25	0	2,700	120	81
6[d]	75	25	0	0	3,700	50	8

Sources: Land data: Map, "Productivity of Land by Wheat Production, Saskatchewan," issued by Department of Agriculture, University of Saskatchewan. Altitude data: project measurements and topographic maps. Growing season data sources: Canadian Government climatological surveys, and local observers.

[a] Poorest productivity pattern of low-altitude colonies, compensated for by large acreage and abundant pasture for livestock.

[b] No significant differences; percentages smoothed.

[c] Best soil pattern; good growing season.

[d] Poor productivity of soil and short growing season require livestock specialization.

agricultural routine, which is based on Northern Plains conditions at the 2,500-foot level.

Colony 5, which has relatively abundant high-productivity land, is located low on the north slope of the Hills in a high-frequency hail belt, and has been "hailed out" twice during its decade of residence in the region. The colony is almost completely surrounded by government-leased grazing land, to which the Hutterites are denied access by Provincial administrative regulations. This means that the colony is limited in its ability to raise livestock, and thus deprived of an effective cushion against crop failures resulting from hail. As can be seen in Table 4, its response has been to emphasize cash-crop production in an effort to build up financial reserves.

A western colony, Colony 1, has the second largest proportion of Class 1 land (after Colony 6). For about ten years this colony made attempts to cultivate much of its low-productivity sandy soil. After repeated difficulties with soil blowing during fallowing operations, the decision was made to sell part of this land and to re-grass much of the remainder, thereby making it possible to incease the livestock population. A decade was the amount of time required for this colony to shift its cropping emphasis from that developed in the Alberta colonies in a relatively abundant rainfall zone, with heavier soils. In a sense, all the Jasper colonies were being required to make some such adjustment, because the moisture and soil resources of the new settlements were inferior to those of the parent colony locations. However, the extent of crop shift differed: Colony 6 made the most radical changeover; Colony 1 the next. All colonies were in the decision-making phase during the period of study.

We made no precise measurements of available water supplies, since such measurement is difficult in a region of extreme moisture variability and unpredictability. Because of its high-altitude location on the crestal plateau, Colony 6 had the most abundant and predictable precipitation. The other colonies did not differ from each other significantly in this respect: all were in the prairie-plains moisture regime, where marginal precipitation and high variability are the rule. Groundwater supplies were adequate for all the colonies except Colony 1, which developed a shortage of well water on some portions of its grazing land during the period of study. Colonies 1 and 5 did not have a continuously flowing stream on their lands, although both had developed check dams in strategic locations to impound runoff waters. Colony 3 was situated on the shores of a partially artificial lake used as one of the reservoirs for the Jasper Irrigation Project, and thus was assured of ample garden irrigation. We may conclude that in all colonies but Colony 1, ground- and flowing-water supplies were adequate. Where water shortages existed, the colonies were taking appropriate remedial steps.

The adaptive situation of Colony 6 may be compared with that of the former individual farmers and ranchers of the same district. This district once had a homestead farming settlement that failed completely, owing to the short growing season, the small scale of land ownership, and the discontent of the settlers over the geographical isolation and difficult winters. Colony 6, located in the same district, had several adaptive advantages over these individual operators: it had more land, and a larger labor force to perform the many special tasks, like brush clearing, needed to obtain soil resources in the more favorable locations. The colony's ability to obtain loans from other colonies permitted it to purchase a snowmobile, a two-way radio for communications (telephone lines do not exist in this remote district), and a variety of other special equipment that rendered its isolation more bearable. The colony was under strong compulsion to adapt and succeed, since its population and the extensive investment involved made leaving extremely difficult. Individual farmers and ranchers, who were more mobile, had less incentive to persevere or adapt.

The large land area of all of the colonies provided them with a more abundant supply of resources than was available to the individual farms and the smaller ranches. While resources did differ among the colonies, they did not differ as radically as among farms in comparable districts. This is illustrated by the case of the farm discussed in Chapter 9. This farm comprised nearly 2,000 acres, which were concentrated in an area of severe water shortages; if the farm had owned 100 additional acres on any one of three sides of its perimeter, adequate wells or streams would have been available. It is apparent that the sheer size of the colonies helps to reduce the risks of farming to a great degree. Still, hail, seasonal changes, light soils, and water inequalities create some problems necessitating adaptive change.

We noted earlier that the colonies had bought up the land of individual farmers in their several locations, and subsequently had more or less successfully farmed these submarginal tracts. We may now analyze this process as a case of ecological competition, because the conditions that made possible the economic act of land acquirement were rooted in the local resource situation and in the maladaptation of the previous economic modes, as well as in the superior adaptive position of the Hutterian system of life and production.

In the western district, before the coming of the Brethren, the population consisted mainly of Ukrainians and others of eastern European origin who had come to the area toward the end of the homesteading period, about 1912. These farmers were heirs to a small-farm tradition, and it was the custom among them to use their savings to purchase small tracts of land for their many sons, in order to establish these young men on their own farms. Cooperative father-son enterprise management was even rarer among these people than among the Anglo-Americans. By the second generation, the district was occupied by a relatively large number of farms ranging from half a section to a section and a half in size.[5] Those few farms larger than a section and a half were the most viable. The remaining individual farmers adjoining Hutterian land either possessed these larger acreages, or were members of a grazing cooperative, or both.

About half the small farms sold to the Brethren were owned by aging farmers whose sons had left the area, or by their surviving relatives. Some of the remaining farms were occupied by younger men attempting to make a living on the small tracts left to them by

[5] One section contains 640 acres, or one square mile.

their fathers. The remaining farms were sold to the Hutterites by farmers in early middle age, who used the cash to finance the expansion of other holdings.

It is interesting to note the details of ownership of the properties purchased by one colony during its development. Of a total of 10 farms purchased (about 15,000 acres), three belonged to aging first-generation farmers with no successors, who sold out in order to retire; two of the farmers went to Jasper, the third to an Alberta town. One farm had been operated as a part-time occupation by the son of a deceased farmer; the son now works in an Alberta town. The fifth farm had been operated on a rental basis by an absentee farmer; it had originally been rented from the aging widow of the former owner. The sixth farm had been operated by an aging farmer; he died shortly after the sale, and his wife retired to an Alberta town. The seventh had been bought by a farmer father for his son; the son now lives in Jasper and farms an additional tract (in local jargon, he is a "sidewalk farmer"). The eighth farm had been operated by a man in his forties, who used the purchase money to buy two new farms and to finance his livestock production; after the sale, he remained in the Jasper region. The ninth farm had been operated by a bachelor; after the sale of his land, he retired to Jasper. The tenth farm had been operated by an aging farmer and his wife; they too retired to Jasper town. The population subsisting on these ten farms at the times of purchase totaled 17; the colony's population was between 65 and 73. Thus the entrance of the colony into the region meant that about four times as many people were to be supported on the same amount of land. The Gentile occupation averaged about one person per 1,150 acres; the Hutterian, about one per 200 acres.

Table 5 summarizes the property value and ownership data available for the colonies we studied. A relatively small number of farms were displaced by the coming of the eastern colonies, owing to the smaller acreage of one colony, and also to the fact that the farms on the Bench and east of Jasper, in the Big Bear district, were larger; these latter farms were owned by Anglo-Americans from eastern Canada and from the British Isles who did not fragment

Table 5—Value and ownership of property bought by colonies

Colony	Number of farm units	Average price per acre	Total acreage	Total price	Owner stayed in region		Owner left region		Expansion stage of colony
					Owners	Other family members[a]	Owners	Other family members[a]	
1	10	$21[b]	14,800	$ 310,800	6	2	3	2	Complete
2	12	27	10,700	288,900	9	3	3	2	Small amount expected
3	10	23	9,440	224,930	9	3	1	0	Nearly complete
4	12	35	9,220	336,100	5	1	5	2	Small amount expected
5	6	22	10,400	109,760	2	1	2	1	Nearly complete
6	5	13	6,080[c]	79,040	2	1	2	0	Large amount expected
Total	55	$23.50	60,640	$1,349,530	33[d] + 11		16[d] + 7		
					44		23		

[a] Approximate.
[b] Two periods of purchase: 1951 and the early 1960's.
[c] Bought in 1956 by the first group to colonize. The present group came 1959, after the first group had failed.
[d] Total does not equal 55 for various reasons: some property is rented, owned by the railroad, vacant, or part of existing farms.

their properties to afford their sons a start, as did the European families in the western district. We attempted to determine the number of farms that changed hands as a result of cash being made available to former farmers who had sold out to the Brethren. Six may have changed hands for this reason in the western district; we were unable to find that any did in the eastern area. There would have been no such cases in the Bench district, the location of Colony 6, since this area was depopulated, and the land either was in the hands of absentee owners or was held in trust estates. The majority of operators of purchased farms retired to Jasper, and some of their younger family members left the region; a total of 44 remained in the area. Thus, only about 23 persons left the region as a result of the Hutterites' purchases. This per-enterprise loss of population was low because the majority of units were held by aging persons without families.

A total of 55 farms were sold as a result of the Hutterian entry. Between the census years 1946 and 1961, a reported 685 individual enterprises were dropped from census totals; about 7 per cent of this number had been purchased by the Brethren. The local impact of these purchases was considerable. The western colonies bought 44 farms in an area approximately 162 miles square—the northern third of L.I.D. No. II, in which most of the land owned by the colonies was to be found.[6] (Colony holdings accounted for 6.48 per cent of all the land, and 14 per cent of all the private-tenure land, in this L.I.D.) The 44 farms comprised over a third of all farms in this major settled farming district of the L.I.D. Colony purchases were not completed at the time of the study, and all but one colony anticipated further land acquisition.

We noted in Chapter 1 that toward the end of their expansion in 1963 the Hutterian colonies controlled about 4 per cent of all private-tenure agricultural land in the Jasper region (see Table 2). Since Hutterian land is communally or collectively managed, it constitutes a significant addition to the amount of regional land

[6] L.I.D.: Local Improvement District. These entities exist in very thinly populated districts in Saskatchewan where the tax revenues are insufficient to permit regular Rural Municipality government. The L.I.D.'s are financed in part and supervised by appointed Provincial officials.

not under individual management or subject to relatively small-scale individual farming. Seen in this light, the Hutterian presence in the region appears as part of the prevailing trend toward alteration of humid-lands styles of land tenure and management.

While we have shown why the colonies were able to find sites in particular areas, we have not explained why they did not attempt to purchase land elsewhere. The simplest answer to the question is that the particular conditions they desired were not available anywhere else. North of the western colonies the soil was largely sandy and the land was useful only for pasturage; north of Jasper the farming community on the 2,500-foot prairie-plains level was economically viable because of increases in the size of individual holdings, and because of the presence of community pastures. South of the Western colonies there remained some individual farmers, but most of them had access to grazing cooperatives, and hence were better established than their neighbors and relatives who sold out to the Brethren. Farming conditions in the municipality just south of the Cypress Hills were good, due largely to the presence of irrigation facilities and community pastures. However, a number of farms on the 3,000-foot level of the south slope immediately south of eastern Colony 6 were experiencing difficulty, and further Hutterian expansion could be expected there. Colony 5 could not expand in any direction, owing to the large amount of leased land, and also because farming conditions in this district were very good and the existing units large and profitable. The plateau increases in elevation toward the west, and this district supports an established ranching economy. Thus, in all districts except the one south of Colony 6, individual agricultural economy was well established, succession rates were high, and the possibility of large bloc sales virtually nil.[7]

[7] Another Alberta colony has recently purchased land in an area about ten miles north of the northern boundary of the Jasper region. This district resembles the area west of Jasper town insofar as it consists of submarginal Class 1 soils, is very dry, and is populated by a diminishing mixed-farming community. The district has its own small-town service center, which means that the new colony will not be closely tied to Jasper town. The author has also learned recently that another colony has indeed been considering a tract in the area south of Colony 6 as a likely spot for further expansion.

What disposition might have been made of the colony lands if they had not been sold to the Brethren? In the case of the western district, the land would probably have gone to a group of farmers near Jasper town who, in the five years preceding the study, had embarked on a program of purchasing failing enterprises and isolated single tracts in order to increase their holdings and advantages. A prime cause of resentment against the Hutterites during the 1950's was their ability to outbid these farmers on particular parcels and thus remove a considerable number of available properties from the market.

With regard to the eastern district, the possible alternative to Hutterian colonization can be inferred from the past pattern of development. In the cases of the failed homestead settlement and similar settlements eastward in the Hills, the departure of some homestead farmers might have meant that the few who remained could acquire more land. In fact, most of this land was purchased by members of the Bench ranching community, whose headquarters and home grazing lands lay on the slopes both north and south of the crestal plateau. The lands purchased on the plateau were given over to grazing and hay production. In the early 1950's these ranching families were unprepared to invest large amounts of cash in expansion, and the relatively small scale of their cattle operations did not provide them with much surplus cash or credit even during the high livestock price period of the late 1950's and early 1960's. Moreover, since the available lands were deeded properties, the cattlemen would have shown a considerable reluctance to invest relatively large amounts of money in grazing land when leased pasturage was so much cheaper. Despite these inhibiting factors, it is highly probable that if the Hutterites had not come, the eastern district would eventually have been split up into individually managed and deeded ranching properties, and the lands in the western district would have been used for diversified, individually managed farming. The conversion of these lands to communal diversified agriculture under the Brethren was made possible by the economic conditions of the time, and by the prevailing lack of incentive to expand on the part of the individual farmers and ranchers. At the same time, the land was available because the relatively small-scale individually owned farms were not remunerative enough in that habitat, nor were the climate and location sufficiently congenial to permit a viable individual enterprise system.

The Hutterian Pattern of Land Acquisition

When a colony in the process of fission selects a new location, its first step is to negotiate for available land. Most colonies employ the services of a land agent from some distant community, since resistance to Hutterian entry invariably develops and local real estate operators are unwilling to represent them. The agent visits farmers in the area and sounds them out. This is done as quickly as possible, since the more prolonged the negotiations, the higher the price is likely to go: farmers meet together and agree to "stick the Hutterites," as the local phrase has it. The Brethren are well aware of this situation and accept the necessity of paying prices considerably above the prevailing level. However, since they pay cash they can sometimes make quick deals, and thus acquire land at lowered prices.

The first colonies to enter an area have an advantage over late-comers in that they can generally obtain land for lower prices. The later entrants resent the inflationary influence of their predecessors; suppressed tension between the colonies on this score is often apparent. Hutterites are in competition just as individual farmers are, because of the structure of land acquisition practices inherent in a private tenure system.

Colony 1, of the western group, was the first to come to the area. It began its negotiations for land in 1951, and completed its initial purchases (about 80% of its 1964 holdings) the following year. As we have noted, most of the farmers who sold out to the Brethren lacked heirs and successors and were ready to retire. Their lands were submarginal or barely marginal for agriculture, at least at the technological and economic level of relatively small operations. Until 1951, deeded land on the modest farms in this district was selling for eight to ten dollars an acre, as it was in most districts of the study region. This price was an advance on the five to seven dollars per acre prevailing during the 1930's and during the war. The Brethren of Colony 2 paid an average of eighteen dollars an acre for their land, or about twice the going price. As a consequence, during the first year after the Brethren came to this district, the land prices almost doubled. Other colonies began to set themselves up in the vicinity, already established colonies continued to buy land there, and the prices rose still higher. In 1963, when some colonies had nearly completed their scheduled purchases, the price leveled off to between $30 and $40 an acre. By the early 1960's this price had become about average for privately held properties throughout the study region.[8]

The most frequently encountered criticism of the colonies on the part of local residents was that their entry into the region had inflated land prices, and thus made it difficult for young men in the area to buy the land they needed to start out. This problem has several facets. In the first place, the initial sales to Colony 1 did mean an increase in land values in the district, through the "stick the Hutterites" mechanism. The Brethren had the cash and were willing to pay higher prices to obtain the land they needed, and the local people took advantage of this. According to Gentile informants, the land sales took the form of a "gold rush" in 1952, when the first colony indicated its willingness to buy land at bonus prices. A Canadian research organization that studied local attitudes toward the Brethren in the Jasper region in that year reported that the Hutterites themselves stated that their situation was becoming embarrassing: farmers were constantly stopping the Brethren on the streets or dropping in on them at the colony to offer land for sale.

In any case, most of the older farmers in the western district were without successors; or the young men operating farms were having a difficult time of it in the face of rising operation costs. In

[8] The new colony mentioned in Note 7 paid $50 an acre in 1966 and 1967. In 1967, the same price was being paid for submarginal land suitable for grazing in districts near Jasper town, primarily by outsiders interested in agricultural land speculation.

the early 1950's there were no buyers for these farms, for the young men returning from military service and the sons of local farmers were not interested in agriculture under the depressed conditions that prevailed. Hence in the early years the colonies did not constitute a threat to individual expansion. It was only in the late 1950's and early 1960's, when economic conditions had improved, that local people could make a case for their complaint that the Brethren's purchases were ruining the land market.

Those who complained that Hutterian purchases caused inflation ignored the fact that improved economic conditions, the emergence of the "expander" farmer, and the advent of young men interested in establishing themselves in agriculture would have increased land values in any case—or rather, that the development of the local economy eventually did contribute to this process, whatever role the Hutterian purchases may have played in the initial stages. It is impossible to distinguish clearly between the Hutterian influence and other causes of rising land values in the region, but some knowledge can be gained by comparing land prices in a region without colonies. In the region selected, about 100 miles away in southern Saskatchewan, land prices increased from about $7 an acre in 1950 to $30 in 1963—an increase comparable to the one experienced by the Jasper region. It would appear that the Hutterian presence had little independent effect on prices. Or put differently, the Hutterian entry into the Jasper region simply caused a sudden emergence of a higher level of economic activity and values, which in a few years made its appearance in the non-Hutterian sector as well, but which would have developed eventually without Hutterian stimulation.

Let us examine some typical cases of land sales, and look at the economic changes resulting from these transactions. Two of these cases were exceptions to the general rule that farms were sold to the Brethren by aging or retiring proprietors. In the first case, the seller was a farmer in early middle age who had been hoping to expand his operations, and especially to acquire additional land in order to establish his twenty-five-year-old son and the son's young family on a new place. However, the farmer lacked cash to finance the purchases. When the Hutterians approached him, he agreed to sell for $35 an acre. This sale was one of the last in the series of purchases for this colony, which was a late-comer. He sold them two sections of land for about $50,000 in cash. (The fact that nearly all colony purchases are for cash makes the Brethren almost unbeatable competitors in the land game, especially in the early stages of colony entrance into a region, before resistance develops.) The farmer then used about $25,000 of this money to buy another farm of two and three-quarters sections in an area where the soil and topography are largely unsuited to crop production, but useful for pasture if planted with domestic grasses. The farmer moved immediately into livestock production, using an additional $2,000 to purchase breeding stock to add to his existing small herd. With the remaining cash, about $23,000, and a loan of about $8,000, he purchased for his son a second farm consisting of one deeded section and a half-section of leased grazing land from a retiring operator without a successor. The son planned to repay his father on a crop-and-cattle share basis. This series of transactions meant that a farmer who had been confined to a two-section crop farm of relatively poor quality developed a family holding of three and three-quarters sections of deeded land and a half-section of leased land as a result of the cash made available to him by Hutterian purchases. The transaction also shifted the farmer's investment emphasis from crops to livestock. Moreover, the Hutterian purchase resulted in the additional removal of two other farms, although the number of farm families was reduced by only one. Finally, these various consequences of the initial Hutterian purchase were felt in a district of 200 square miles, since the two farms bought by the farmer were in an area of this size.

Hutterian techniques of land acquirement are based on the careful persuasion of likely sellers. We refer here to the purchase of farm properties after the colony has become established, when the initial "gold rush" described earlier has subsided. Usually the initial purchases will leave a number of farms partly enclosed by colony lands, or immediately contiguous. If the acquisition of these properties would permit completion of plans for cultivation or pasturage units, the Brethren will open negotiations with the owners several months or years before they actually expect to make the purchases. In one case, witnessed in part by the writer, the Brethren made it a point to stop by the desired farm on friendly visits and cheerfully ask the proprietor, an aging farmer, if he was interested in selling. Considerable subtle persuasion was exercised: the Brethren pointed out what the man could do with the cash they were willing to give, and offered to help him move his house into town if he wished to keep it for retirement. No hard-sell techniques were used, and after the friendly chat, the party of Brethren would leave with the remark that they would be happy to hear from him anytime, but that there was no hurry. In other cases the Brethren assisted the prospective seller with harvest chores, and charged him a rate below the going fee for custom machine work. These techniques are simply extensions of the policy followed by nearly all the colonies of establishing friendly relations with their neighbors.

In the Western district, portions of the land of each colony touched the lands of one or more of the other colonies in the area. This meant that a number of farms still owned by individuals were virtually surrounded by Hutterian lands, and access to these farms was along roads partly maintained by the colonies. (Most colonies owned a homemade or secondhand road grader, which they used to supplement the services provided by the municipality, because the colony trucks gave these roads considerable use.) The sale of these enclaved farms to the colonies was inevitable. Many factors entered into this situation: the persistent attempts by the colonies to buy these farms; the unease that many of the individual operators felt on being surrounded by efficient large-scale operators, or by what they perceived as "foreign" people; the unwillingness of sons or other relatives to succeed to farms in this vulnerable position; and of course the simple temptation of cash.

We spoke earlier of the strong local impact of Hutterian colonization. The inevitability of land sales in a district with several nearby colonies is another instance of this phenomenon. The colonies in the Jasper region selected their districts with considerable care, taking note of the facts already outlined: failing agriculture, farms without successors, and a scale of operations too small for the contemporary economic situation. That is, while such features, especially in the western districts, probably made these areas the only ones available for colonization, the Brethren also consciously sought out such situations because they knew they would face little competition in acquiring the remaining land once they had secured a foothold.

Relations between Colonies

In an unpublished manuscript, Verne Serl has described Hutterian social relations as consisting of three concentric circles.[9] The first is made up of all Christians who appreciate or follow the communal way of life, including all Hutterites and other Anabaptist groups who may retain some communal customs. The next consists of all the colonies of a particular Leut—Lehrer, Darius, or Schmieden—and the innermost circle consists of the colony parent-daughter pair. This concentric model illustrates the Brethren's concept of their own world, and helps to define the actual frequency of socially and economically instrumental relations. The most significant relationships usually are with the parent colony; the next most significant with the Leut, and the least significant with all other Hutterites and perhaps a few Mennonites.

This diagrammatic rendering does not, however, provide any indication of the frequency of inter-colony contacts. In the Jasper region, relations between all the colonies were frequent, no matter what Leut they belonged to. Because of the proximity of the western colonies to each other, the exchange of labor and ideas and the tendering of financial assistance on a small scale were common occurrences. The Hutterites are intensely practical, and if a nearby colony has something to offer, it will be investigated, whether or not there is a special intra-circle tie. Similarly, while the colonies were often rivalrous or in a state of mild feud, they generally extended help to each other when needed.

[9] Sere (1964).

The following table shows the frequency of two main types of contacts between one Jasper colony (Colony "X") and other colonies during an eighteen-month period preceding the study.

This table indicates the importance of proximity in inter-colony relations, and the difference between entirely practical and "social" reasons for visits. While the contacts with distant colonies of the same Leut were important for many reasons, frequency of all types of contacts with nearby colonies of different Leut membership was more common than with the more distant Leut brethren. It should be noted that in nearly all cases the "social" visits to colonies of the same Leut had definite causes or consequences—marriages, loans, disciplinary problems, and other vital concerns that would not usually enter into a colony's relations with those of a different Leut. Five of the "social" visits in the above table included the negotiation of loans to colonies in need of money because of crop failures or because they wished to make necessary purchases of land and new

Table 6—Involvement of Colony "X" with other colonies

	Type of Involvement	
Other colony	Technical (Labor or machine exchange)	Social (Including information exchange or business conferences)
Parent colony or colonies neighboring the parent colony (200 miles away)[a]	0	6
North Colony (about 80 miles away)[a]	0	2
Lake Colony (neighboring, but different Leut)	5	12
Colony No. 5 (in eastern group 30 miles away)[a]	3	5
Colony No. 6 (40 miles away)	2	4
South Colony (60 miles away)[a]	2	3
City Colony (about 60 miles away)[a]	2	5
Creek Colony (neighboring, but different Leut)	2	5
Oak Colony (neighboring, but different Leut)	3	4
Montana Colony (100 miles away)[a]	1	1
Totals	20	47
Involvement with colonies of same Leut	8	17
Involvement with colonies of different Leute	12	25

[a] Colony of the same Leut as Colony "X."

machinery. The relatively high frequency of contacts with Colony 6, 40 miles to the east, a member of a different Leut, is explained by the fact that this colony was being helped by Colony "X." Over a period of five years Colony "X" had extended Colony 6 about $6,000 in cash loans, and had given it several important items of machinery and a considerable amount of information on how to build hog barns, chicken installations, heating plants, and the like. The cross-Leut relationship between the two colonies was a matter of considerable comment in the region, since the fellow-Leut western colonies of Colony 6 had refused to help it because of complex stresses between the several parent colonies in Alberta. As noted previously, Colony 6 was located on the crestal plateau, and was engaging in various difficult experiments with the limited environment.

In addition to colony visits, the Brethren had frequent informal contact in Jasper and larger towns, where they met on the street or in places of business. In most of the western Jasper colonies, trips to town were made on an average of six times a week. On nearly every one of these trips, the Hutterites would encounter members of other colonies of the region, and matters of mutual interest and local gossip would be discussed.

In most colonies, each married man took his wife home to her parents and relatives once a year for a visit lasting a week to a month, and then returned at the end of her visit to pick her up. (These trips are not recorded on the table.) In Colony "X," all wives were from colonies of the same Leut, situated in the region near the parent colony in Alberta, 200 miles away. The wives' visits provided opportunities for the men to discuss matters of joint interest and concern. Another type of journey not recorded on the table is the annual meeting of all the ministers of the colonies in that Leut, which was held in rotation at different colonies.

The technical exchanges between Colony "X" and other colonies involved the loans of small and large items to colonies in immediate need. Typical items of exchange were cement mixers, refrigeration parts, corn and potato planters, trucks for gravel hauling, bulldozers, and powered swathers. Labor exchanges included house and granary construction, road, refrigerator, and roofing repairs, and the erection of a water storage tank. The colony examined was actually reluctant to exchange labor, even though it did so occasionally, for it felt that the mass labor sessions engaged in by some colonies were detrimental to the quality of the work. The young men and boys treated these sessions as larks, and the work was often done sloppily. For other colonies, a mass exchange of labor serves as an excellent excuse for a social visit, often for courting purposes.

While the actual number of visits to Gentiles was considerable, these contacts did not involve intimate matters or important labor or machinery exchanges. Because of the common economic frame of Hutterian life, inter-colony relations are of greater import than contacts with outsiders. Hutterites naturally tend to associate with each other because of their strong cultural and ideological ties. As we shall note in the next chapter, even under the best of circumstances their relations with Gentiles contain an element of strain, since Hutterites officially regard all persons who do not practice communal living as corrupted Christians, and persons who are not followers of the Christian religion as completely outside the pale.

It should be noted that this "consciousness of kind" and its social and economic implementation does not mean that the colonies are a closed group whose members refuse to criticize or judge one another. Once friendship or a close business relationship is established between Hutterites and Gentiles, the former show relative freedom in criticizing other Hutterites. Their criticism takes the form of candid comments on such subjects as farming techniques, business acumen, honesty in dealings, and literacy. But these manifestations of candor should not be taken as evidence of lack of cohesion in the brotherhood as a whole. Hutterites display a remarkable unity as well as cultural and religious uniformity, and this common pattern is created by constant watchfulness and admonition between colonies that may be experiencing tension as well as between friendly colonies. Moreover, whenever a colony is the target of Gentile hostility or otherwise getting into trouble with the local non-Hutterites, ranks will be closed and its neighbors, of whatever Leut, will offer help and counsel. Two colonies in the Jasper region whose Elders had been at odds for some time constantly exchanged ideas, tools and equipment, and social visits. In spite of tensions, the brotherhood was maintained.

FOUR

Hutterian Society
and the External World

Hutterian beliefs require avoidance of the external world—the world that the Brethren themselves call "the outside." Yet they must live with and in this world, while resisting its "corrupting" influences. For every modern Hutterian colony there are really two "outsides": the local social community of which the Brethren are to some degree functioning members; and the governmental "community" of agencies and bureaus that establishes the conditions of social and economic survival in a given area. For the Jasper Hutterites, the local "outside" consists of their neighbors the farmers and ranchers, and the merchants and wholesalers with whom the Brethren do business. The official community consists of the local and Provincial Government bureaus controlling access to water and land, Federal bureaus with similar functions, the Federal income tax agency, the Federal and Provincial agricultural extension services and medical services, and the local school units. Some of the external government bureaus have local representatives in Jasper, and thus the local and official "outsides" sometimes merge. Hutterites often prefer to conduct negotiations directly with external agencies, rather than through local representatives, since this helps them avoid overly intimate local contacts. In any case, all these official agencies establish the limits and conditions under which the Brethren do business, maintain health and welfare, and purchase land for new colonies.

The Hutterites in the Jasper Economy

How great a contribution have the colonies made to the economy of the Jasper region? On the whole, this contribution has been substantial. The entrance of the Brethren into the Jasper region meant an increase in economic values of several kinds. The sale of land to the Brethren at higher-than-average prices represented an immediate input of almost $1.5 million in cash, or approximately $250,000 more than these same lands would have brought in sales to individual farmers and ranchers. Some of the sellers left the region and took their money with them, but twice as many stayed as departed (see Table 5). The purchasing power of the Hutterian population was considerably greater than that of the original owners, although this power was (and is) concentrated in a few important commodities instead of being spread evenly across the retail market.

Table 7—Per cent of grain production of Crop District #4 and Jasper region provided by colonies

	Grain production for crop district #4[a]			*Wheat production for study region*	
Colonies	*Oats*	*Barley*	*Rye*	*Colonies*	*Wheat*
Western group					
1	3.3%	2.5%	0.9%	1	2.5%
2	17.9	8.9	none	2	3.2
3	5.4	4.8	1.2	3	2.5
4	3.6	6.9	0.7	4	1.5
Eastern group					
5	1.9	7.3	none	5	4.3
6	3.1	4.9	none	6	none
Per cent of crop district production by colonies[b]	35.2%	35.3%	2.8%	Per cent of study region wheat production by colonies	14.0%
Total for Crop District #4 . .	100%	100%	100%	Total for study region	100%

[a] Data from annual reports, Saskatchewan Department of Agriculture.
[b] Excluding one colony.

The diversified agriculture of the colonies has substantially increased the productivity of the region. The farms bought by the Brethren were all grain-cattle enterprises of limited output, many of them operated by aging men without strong interest in improving or even maintaining productivity (managers in one colony estimated that their land was producing about twice as much wheat and livestock as it had under individual management). None of the previous owners had raised commercial poultry, eggs, sheep, swine, or feeder cattle, hence the Hutterites' production of all of these constituted a net gain for the region. Table 7 summarizes available regional data for grain crops only; livestock data were considered unreliable. Since agricultural statistics for Rural Municipalities are not always available in Saskatchewan, we could not be certain of precise figures for the Jasper region. Wheat statistics for the region were available. We have used Saskatchewan Crop District #4 as a rough approximation of the region for crop figures for the other grains. This district is slightly larger in geographical extent than the actual region. The fact that Hutterian oats and barley each constitute 35 per cent of the total production for the District suggests the probable gain in productivity for livestock, for both of these grains are fed, and only small amounts are sold. Wheat production makes up only about 3 per cent of the crop production, but constitutes 14 per cent of the production of the Jasper region. If the ratio for wheat holds for the other crops, the regional percentages should be in the neighborhood of 45 per cent. These increases have taken place on land constituting four per cent of the total Jasper agricultural area. In 1964, the aggregate gross income of all six colonies in the study was about $700,000, and the computed gross for all the farms the colonies replaced was about $300,000.

Recognizing the fact that the local farmers view their advent with anxiety or resentment, the Brethren usually make a special effort to be good neighbors. In any case, the Hutterites' economic habits are such as to bring them into constant contact with their neighbors: picking berries, selling poultry and eggs for cash, and performing farm labor either openly, as neighborly help, or in secret, for extra money. Most colonies also furnished custom machine services for harvesting, planting, swathing, and fallowing to Gentile neighbors who lacked the machinery or labor to do a particular job at the right time. In the western district, such services had the effect of upgrading agriculture among the remaining farms. In spite of the general resentment over colony purchases of land, most farmers defended the Brethren as "good neighbors." Nevertheless the fear of being outnumbered was present: "They'll soon own all the land around here, if somebody doesn't stop 'em!"

The following summary of the economic exchanges between one colony and its neighbors for a period of about 14 months shows that the amount and value of such exchanges is considerable.

Custom swathing: 3 cases; cost to farmers: $150. In two of these cases, the swathing operation saved crops that might have been damaged if the colony services had not been available. Approximate saving to farmers, $3,500.

Custom harvesting: 2 cases; cost to farmers, $200.

Fencing: 1 case; no cost to farmer. The colony needed a good fence to keep their cattle in pasture; the farmer adjoining was in financial difficulty, and the colony paid the full cost of the fence, though the usual practice is a 50-50 split. Saving to farmer, $850.

Construction advice: A local farmer was asked by colony to advise them on the construction of a granary. This saved the colony the cost of a trip to a distant place.

Berry picking: The Brethren picked berries on the property of four nearby farmers and ranchers. These berries supplied the colony with most of its wine and some of its fruit preserves for the year. The hosts were given poultry and fresh vegetables in return for permission to pick the berries. Value of produce exchanged, $50.

Moonlighting: Three young men of one colony worked an approximate total of 2 days for their neighbors at the going wage of $1 an hour, thus earning $16 each.

The colony whose exchanges are examined here had the reputation of engaging in such exchanges more consistently than any of the others in the western district. All other colonies engaged in fewer of the activities listed for a comparable period of time, and one of the colonies, which was then at the apex of its development and possessed large holdings, had eliminated custom machine work completely. It was clear from our analysis that the intensity of these economic exchanges with the Gentiles varied with the economic position of the particular colony. However, it was also clear that the colonies recognized the public-relations value of these activities, and therefore maintained them whenever possible. The colony that had ceased to do custom work continued to exchange farm produce for berry-picking privileges, even though its members admitted in interviews that the berries, while useful, were probably less important than the "neighboring" aspect of the exchange. A third reason for continuing some of these practices was that they served to keep the younger women and boys of the colony busy during the slack seasons of the year.

The extent to which local retail business had benefited from the increase in productivity caused by Hutterian colonization is not clear. A frequently heard criticism of the colonies was that the Brethren did not make any real difference to the region's finances since they bought so little from local merchants. On a per capita basis this was true, especially in the realm of consumer goods; however, the Brethren's local purchases of food staples and farm machines did make an important contribution to the market. As can be noted from the data given (in Chapter 3) 271 Hutterites of the four incoming colonies in the western district replaced 67 members of farm families, 23 of whom had left the region permanently.

Two of these four colonies bought nearly all their condiments, coffee, flour, and the like in Jasper, and since Hutterites do not skimp on food essentials, this meant a substantial increase in the sale of these commodities. However, the colonies often bought bargain lots of items from urban sources, and this practice seemed to confirm the accusations made by the local merchants.

A colony of 73 persons in the western group usually purchased the following items locally:

Items purchased regularly:

Flour
Sugar
Coffee, tea
Salt, pepper
Yeast, baking soda
Margarine
Jams, syrups
Dried fruit, especially raisins
Canned salmon
Soft drinks
Candy, cookies, as special treats
Canned goods in small quantities, on sale
Toys and novelties in small quantities
Lumber
Hardware
Paint and painting tools
Many hand and power tools
All fuels
Welding supplies
Some soap
Some notions; most bought wholesale
Medicines
Some paper; most received in gift

Items purchased infrequently or at intervals:

Teakettles, plates, cups
Secondhand furniture
New furniture, esp. chairs
Linoleum
White goods
Springs, mattresses
Propane heating units
Electric grills
Electric floor polishers
Waxes and polishes
Pots, pans, cutlery
Pitchers
Meat grinder, meat saw, both powered
Dough mixer
Refrigeration equipment
Machine tools for repair work
Automotive vehicles
Tractors
Farm machinery of all kinds

Strictly in terms of substantial amounts of cash supplied to the local market, the most important items on these lists are farm machinery, tools, and construction materials. Over a two-year period, this particular colony bought tractors and trucks with a total retail value of $25,000; and over a period of 7 years they acquired vehicles and machines totaling $95,000, including some equipment acquired through trades rather than cash deals. The colony's automotive fuel purchases totaled over $5,000 per year in the 1960's. Nearly all the sales just described were made in the town of Jasper itself.

In one colony, the total value of all machines and implements purchased locally since the colony's establishment in the region was about $200,000 more than the total value of the machinery bought and owned by the farms sold to the colony. Because they are willing and able to utilize more and better machinery than the individual farmer is, the Brethren do not simply replace existing farm machinery in the locality, they add to it. An equipment and automotive dealer in Jasper estimated that his business had increased by about 15 per cent per year as a result of Hutterian purchases— and he was one of three dealers in town who traded with the colonists.

Clothing materials (Hutterites make most of their own clothing and shoes) are not listed here, because the Brethren bought yard goods in bargain lots in the larger towns of western Canada, and purchased only small items locally. Sewing machines were likewise bought in larger towns. Other items were rarely bought locally because Jasper stores usually did not stock them (e.g., secondhand furniture, noodle machines, hotel-type ranges).

There is an inter-colony trading system for many familiar items. Tools, hardware, building supplies of all kinds, furniture (handmade and refinished secondhand pieces), heavy equipment for food preparation, and other items are often exchanged for cash or barter. This practice is not necessarily an expression of Hutterian brotherhood, but is carried on mainly because all the colonies are in the same kind of business on the same scale. It is quite common for a well-established colony to give its outmoded equipment to a new colony hard pressed for cash, and to take this opportunity to buy itself new pieces; thus the fact that colonies obtain goods from each other does not necessarily deprive local markets of sales.

Many small items such as meat grinders and tools may be owned by the Brethren when they arrive in a district. Expenditures during the first year or so of colony presence in a region are confined to necessities and replacements in items that had to be left behind in the home colony. The amount of these expenditures varied considerably among the Jasper colonies: some started out with only the most basic equipment; others, who came from wealthier colonies, were better supplied. The colony whose purchases for the 1960's were indicated above had kept a careful record of its purchases during 1952, its first year in the region:

Land	$210,204
Crops on land	11,000
Sheep	5,450
Farm machines (tractors only)	3,850
Automotive fuel	2,000
Groceries	400
Hardware	670
Lumber	350
Coal for dwelling stoves	530
Miscellaneous	600
Total	$235,054

These expenditures used up the entire supply of cash brought by the colony to the area, and at the end of the first year the colony found it necessary to secure a loan from the local bank in order to continue in existence. In this case the Brethren had made a special effort to buy everything they needed locally, in order to counteract Gentile accusations that Hutterites do not support the local retail market.

In all cases, the pattern of purchases changes as the colony ages. During the first decade or so, land purchases are frequent, and the construction of new buildings necessitates continual purchases of building supplies. The development of repair facilities on the colony premises also means substantial purchases of equipment, although the Hutterian habit of buying secondhand articles and reconditioning them often means that the larger towns are used as sources of supply. As time passes, the Brethren usually develop permanent buyer-seller relationships with local dealers in various commodities, and much of the criticism abates. The colony used here as an example had such a relationship with a local machinery and automotive dealer who stated that while the Brethren were shrewd businessmen and sharp traders, they were honest, always paid their bills on time, and dealt in cash when they lacked an article for trade.[1]

A common sight in the Jasper region was the half-ton truck with boxes of eggs, cages or sacks of live poultry, that the Hutterites drove along the country roads and the town streets in search of customers. In addition to operating this peddling business, the Brethren sold dressed beefs, pork, butter, eggs, and poultry at the colony. After a colony had become established, it generally sold to a steady clientele. Cash sales were the usual procedure. In addition to sales to individuals, the more efficient colonies contracted to supply large quantities of produce, especially eggs and poultry, to the local restaurants. Contracts of this kind in one colony led to an investment in $3,000 worth of automatic chicken feeding machinery and egg-grading equipment. Gross annual proceeds from the local phase of this egg business were $3,000 out of an annual total egg gross of $18,000. Sales of garden produce and poultry for this colony, most of them contracted in the Jasper region, amounted to $1,500. Two of the remaining three western colonies sold about $2,000 each in eggs, poultry, and produce (though only about half of this was sold in the Jasper region as we have defined it), making a total of $8,500 in sales for these three colonies. In order to provide a standard of comparison, we may note that the two chain grocery stores in Jasper each sold about $35,000 in vegetables and fruits annually, so that sales of the three colonies were

---

[1] In two colonies, the writer was told that even though lower prices could be obtained in the larger towns, the Brethren there preferred to buy their machinery and vehicles in Jasper, in order to cement relations with the Gentiles and spike possible criticism. There is little doubt that prices are lower in the larger communities, but there is reason to believe that equally favorable deals can be made with the larger equipment dealers in Jasper, once a continuing relationship has been established. Most colonies had developed such relationships.

about 12 per cent of the supermarket gross. Figures on the Brethren's sales of dressed meat were not obtainable, but estimates showed that the colonies did a proportionately small share of the local business, since they actually had little surplus meat to sell.

Jasper supported two commercial poultry breeders who sold chickens and geese for meat and breeding stock. One of these businesses closed down in the late 1950's, partly because of inefficient management and partly because it could not compete with the Hutterites, who provided door-to-door delivery. The Brethren also cut into supermarket sales of dressed poultry, and after 1963 the third largest grocery store in Jasper, a privately owned market, bought its entire supply of poultry from one colony.

Underlying this local cash sale effort is a small-scale barter system. The Hutterites use certain spices and garden plants that they find it inconvenient or difficult to raise, and they obtain these from town or farm gardens in return for vegetables and poultry. Much bartering takes place during the berry-picking season: the writer once observed a party of Hutterites on a berrying expedition, and noted that in return for the privilege of picking the fruit, they presented sacks of green peas and bags of tomatoes to the ranch housewife. An effort was made to ascertain the monetary value of this sort of transaction in one colony, and it was estimated that $500 worth of produce (at retail sales prices) was distributed this way annually.

The Brethren are insatiably curious about how people live on the outside, and there are distinct practical advantages to maintaining contacts that provide them with local news of bargains, politics, and personalities. Since communal life makes it difficult for the Brethren to maintain normal social relations with local people, excuses are sought to make contact. Sales of produce provide this excuse. The immediate neighbors of the colonies benefit from this, since if a Hutterite wishes to find out about local sales or bargains in second-hand goods or breeding stock, he will stop by with a present in the form of produce. Some colonies utilize gifts as a means of furthering friendly relations with neighbors whose land they may wish to purchase one day. Thus even when a colony has reached its peak of development and does not need small cash sales (the local contract supply business aside), these sales may be continued because of their social value. Such sales will fall off as the colony has less need for the cash, but they will never cease entirely. Local people do not understand these secondary functions of the peddling business; they regard the Hutterites as penny-pinchers and super-salesmen, and are apt to comment cynically and humorously on their habits: "You can't beat them Hutterites! Here they are with more machines than any ten farmers around here and they go around selling chickens for a nickle!"

Social Relations With the Jasper Community

In 1952, the year the first Hutterian colony appeared in Jasper, a Canadian research organization conducted a survey of local attitudes and opinions toward the Brethren, in relation to attitudes toward the community and its problems. The study utilized a series of four open-ended interview schedules, two of which were used for the local people (one of these had "weighted" preference answer codes); a third for the Hutterites themselves; and a fourth, which was a "background" schedule intended for local leaders. The first of the community schedules merely solicited opinions; the second attempted to measure the strength of these attitudes. Samples were constructed in order to obtain representative coverage of town, country, and socioeconomic groups. The results of the 1952 study may be summarized as follows:

(1) The persons most disturbed by the Hutterites' entry were the businessmen, the younger farmers, and the local government representatives concerned with the economy. These groups feared that the Brethren would not contribute to the local economy in proportion to their numbers; that Hutterian success in acquiring land would raise land prices and thus keep young men from acquiring the property they needed to start out in agriculture; and that the Brethren would not wish to mix socially with the townspeople. (In preceding sections we have dealt with two of these issues, showing that the colonies did make substantial economic

contributions and would continue to do so. We also suggested that land prices would have increased anyway through growing competition for land among the local people.)

(2) Farmers in the districts close to that of the 1952 colony showed little fear and concern over the invasion, and came to view the Brethren as upright, God-fearing, and friendly, if a little frightening in their efficiency and determination.

(3) The respondents to the first schedule were given an opportunity to compare the problem of the Brethren's coming with other local issues. While a plurality felt that some kind of problem was created by the appearance of the colony, and that this problem would increase as more colonies entered the area, they also felt that other local concerns—for example, that a major new highway was probably going to bypass the town, and that there were insufficient recreation facilities available for teen-agers—were of greater importance.

(4) In the first schedule, 20 per cent of the respondents felt that the Brethren's coming would be of benefit to the district because it would add to the tax revenues and give the older people an opportunity to sell their farms at a profit; 27 per cent felt that if more Brethren came it would be very bad for the business of the community. There is some evidence that this difference discriminated between businessmen and businessmen-farmers on the one hand and local older farmers and retired persons on the other.

(5) In the second or "weighted" schedule, 62 per cent of non-business and 43 per cent of business respondents viewed the Hutterites in a favorable personal light, characterizing them as upright, honest, and capable.

(6) In the weighted schedule, 64 per cent of the business respondents and 28 per cent of the non-business respondents expressed the opinion that the Hutterites would not "mix in the community." For other "unfavorable" evaluations ("I feel badly about Hutterites moving in." "[They] aren't good citizens." "No economic value."), the percentages of "neutral" opinions were as great as or greater than those of favorable and unfavorable opinions.

We may conclude from this study that while apprehension and

resentment about the 1952 colony were present, these feelings were by no means universal, and varied according to the occupation, age, and place of residence of the respondent. A difference was noted between the respondents' attitudes with regard to the presence of one colony, and to the possibility that more were coming; this possibility was viewed with greater concern. However, appreciation of Hutterian personal and managerial qualities was evident in a majority of the respondents.

Because the 1952 study was made in the first year of the Hutterian migration, we attempted to reconstruct the attitudes of local people as more colonies appeared, in order to bridge the gap between that study and our own data for the 1960's. Our data suggested that as more colonies entered negative feelings increased, and that resentment finally broke out into the open in 1953. In that year, Colony 5 began purchasing land, and the local farmers sent a deputation to the Provincial capital to protest. In accordance with its announced policy of toleration of the Brethren, the government refused to take any action; and after a few meetings back home, the protests died out. The existence of such activities in this particular district was explained by the fact that the area contains some of the best crop land in the region, and while the Brethren displaced very few people, since they bought up uncultivated farms held in trust and farms without successors, the local men felt this fine farmland should not fall under the control of the colony.

However, by the 1960's negative feelings about the Hutterites were considerably less obvious, and in our interviews we found more liking and acceptance than hostility. These cordial feelings were concentrated to a great extent among businessmen who had dealings with the colonies and certain ranchers and farmers whose land adjoined the colonies. In all these cases the Brethren's honesty and willingness to extend a helping hand had convinced the local people that the Hutterites were good neighbors. However, this pattern was not always consistent. Many of the small farmers and bachelors in the vicinity of the colonies were violently opposed to the Hutterites, whom they saw as powerful and menacing competitors out for all the land they could get. Some businessmen in town, even though they enjoyed cordial surface relations with the Hutterites, disapproved of their ways. In any case, few local people were willing to take a vigorous pro-Hutterite stand. Despite this, the net direction of sentiment in the 1960's was acceptance—a general feeling that the colonies were there to stay, and that the Brethren were really not such bad people. Compared to the reports of consistent local hatred and difficulties in other parts of the Great Plains, the Jasper feelings seem remarkably accepting. This is consistent with the findings of the research project that the Jasper farmer-rancher culture is marked by unusually strong sanctions against the open demonstration of hostility toward others.

Jasper attitudes were compared with the attitudes encountered by a seventh colony upon its entry into a neighboring region (this was the same colony we excluded from detailed consideration because it lay outside the Jasper region). In 1952 the town that formed the center of this other area was more aggressive in business and civic development than Jasper was, and the agricultural economy of the surrounding area was somewhat more innovative. The 1952 study showed fewer negative reactions to the colonists on the part of the region's residents, a fact which suggested that general prosperity and economic security tend to reduce apprehension about the Brethren's presence. This must be set against the fact that strong resentment of the Hutterites has continued to grow in southern Alberta, even though the Gentile farmers there are prosperous. However, in the case of the Alberta districts, the colonies are numerous enough to constitute a serious competitive threat. Also to be considered is the fact that the people of Saskatchewan are unusually devoted to the principles of socialized tolerance and cooperation as well as to other values that tend to reduce hostility, whereas such values are not so strongly stressed in Alberta.

Studies of the Hutterites going back to the 1930's (see, for example, Deets 1939) report the same distinctive pattern of Hutterian informal relations with immediate neighbors that we saw at work in the Jasper colonies. This pattern consists of the following components:

(1) Frequent visiting of Gentiles by colony officials and the

bringing of gifts, sometimes in connection with the forms of economic exchange and land acquisition described previously.

(2) Informal and covert visiting by the young unmarried men of the colony, accompanied by requests to view television, listen to radios and phonographs, or smoke cigarettes. Often these visits lead to temporary employment for the young men, who sometimes work on Sundays and after working hours to earn extra cash—a practice sometimes tolerated by the Elders, but officially taboo.

(3) Rare visits by colony children, who come to play with farm or ranch children, gaze at their personal possessions, and pilfer small articles.

(4) Occasional thefts by young Hutterian men of articles left at a distance from farm premises, or of dogs used for sheepherding. (In at least two cases in the Jasper area, dogs were eventually found by their owners in a colony sheep barn, where one of the Brethren friendly with the dogs' owners had told them they would probably find the animals.)

(5) Formal visits to Gentiles by colony officials for the purpose of extending invitations to colony celebrations, particularly weddings and Christmas festivities. Personal contacts are preferred to telephone communication by the Brethren.

An effort was made to determine the frequency of these various contacts, especially ones involving visiting or petty thievery by children and young men, since these latter acts have caused much criticism of the Brethren by local people. One farmer whose land lay between two colonies stated that to the best of his knowledge he had received at least three gifts of food annually for five years from one of the colonies, had been visited by children five times in that period, had hired young Hutterites for odd jobs three times, and had attended two colony functions. Spot checks with farmers at greater distances from the colonies indicated that the frequency of contacts of this sort was very high, and was probably a function of proximity. The farmer in question enjoyed very friendly relations with both colonies.

Discussions with this man also indicated that the colony officials were well aware of the moonlighting habits of their young men, and tolerated them so long as they did not get out of hand. Young men in one colony agreed with this interpretation, noting that the pressure of temptation arising in an austere consumption economy in the midst of relative plenty is very great, and that minor and clandestine attempts to relieve it are recognized as a necessary evil. The question of theft was also discussed in some detail with the farmer, who stated that its frequency is probably very low, since he had run down several tales and discovered that they all traced back to a single incident.

Petty thefts by children seem to be a function of Hutterian exclusiveness, in that colony children regard anything "on the outside" as fair game. The same farmer told the following story by way of illustration. One day a man from a nearby colony, who was accompanied by several colony children, was helping him fix a flat tire. Meanwhile, two of the children picked up a hubcap and some tools and ran off toward the colony with them. The farmer and the Hutterite were forced to chase them to get the items back, and the child who had taken the hubcap had to be forcibly parted from it. The farmer observed that six- or eight-year-old Gentile children do not have this attitude toward the possessions of others, or at least would not dare to act this way in full view of adults. Somewhat similar stories were told by shopkeepers in the nearby town.

In any case, Hutterian leaders were aware of these undesirable proclivities in their young people, and did everything possible to curb them. They were aware too that life in the colony breeds an attitude of intense curiosity and wonder about the outside world, as well as a feeling that it is a vast, rich pile of loot ready for the taking. The enforced austerity sometimes leads young people to feel that outsiders are so comparatively rich that they would never miss a few small items. There is some evidence that the efforts of Hutterites to do favors for their neighbors and for the people of the town were in part compensation for the minor depredations of their young people. There was occasional friction inside the colony over matters of this kind: for example, in the incident of the sheep dogs, the Hutterite who "told on" his own colony brother was reported to have been extremely angry over the theft, and to have insisted on a discussion of the incident at a colony meeting.

The presence of Gentiles at colony celebrations was not common; usually only especially close friends were invited. Weddings were the chief occasions for celebrations and visits from outsiders. Hutterites celebrate these affairs with gusto, and considerable money is spent on refreshments of all kinds, including beer. The Brethren regard these events as opportunities to show outsiders the happy side of their life, and to counteract local misconceptions about their habits and standard of living. For the same reasons, the Hutterites are unfailingly hospitable to visitors who come to the colony out of curiosity. A guided tour of the premises is given to all.

Some of the Jasper Brethren, conscious of their alien status in the locality, took a special interest in the history and culture of their districts. This conscious effort to become identified with the local scene appears to be a relatively recent facet of Hutterian culture. In the background of this interest in the locality was the intense curiosity felt by Hutterites about the outside; and coupled with this curiosity were an awareness of "difference" and a borderline sense of inferiority—attitudes that are complexly interwoven with the Brethren's feeling of superiority at being the "truest" Christians and their pride in the obvious adaptive value of their way of life. Many Hutterites have a burning desire to communicate with outsiders in order to reassure themselves of their own superiority, or, conversely, of their lack of real difference. At the same time, they wish to show the outsiders that they, the Hutterites, are really the superior ones, in that they are following a better way of life. Attempts to communicate are often hampered by shyness or by a real ignorance of the rules of conversation and "presentation of self" in the outside world. Hutterites are particularly gauche with Gentile women, who simply do not fit their concept of woman as a submissive, loyal *hausfrau*. In this respect the writer was frequently reminded of the difficulties Japanese men had during the Occupation in dealing with assertive American women employees.[2]

The flavor of the Brethren's contacts and relationships with Gentiles is difficult to convey, since they include a number of con-

---

[2] See Bennett, Passin, and McKnight (1958, pp. 66, 248–49).

tradictory elements. While intimacy and feelings of equality could develop, there are inescapable limitations that restrict friendships or close relationships of any kind, for the Hutterian colony is not generally open to membership or to prolonged residence by outsiders, and even overnight visits, except in cases of emergency, are a rarity. Further, Hutterites must marry Hutterites, and so the whole range of contacts directly or indirectly concerned with affinal kinship and heterosexual relations are barred. The closest relationship possible between a Hutterite and a Gentile is that of a colony boss or manager with a local farmer, in which the former acts as a kind of adviser or friend in need to the latter, who is usually a small operator in need of assistance. The writer witnessed several occasions on which such relationships were implemented: in each case the colony man was friendly and direct in his dealings with the Gentile, but showed just a faint touch of paternalism. "The Hutterites take care of these little fellows around here," remarked a colony boss to the writer.

In any case, when contact was established between a Hutterite and a local Gentile, the Gentile was usually won over by the warm and perceptive personality of the other. He would generally discover that the Brethren were not the backward, old-fashioned, eccentric people they appeared to be, but were shrewd, aware farmers who somehow knew much about the world even though their contact with the mass media was minimal. The younger Hutterites were repositories of local Gentile gossip, because the Gentiles tended to confide in the Hutterites, whom they regarded as being outside the regional society. These young Hutterites were articulate about baseball and football, knew a good deal about international relations, had opinions on Communism and the Sino-Soviet quarrel, were able to discuss relations between the United States and Canada, and had heard of the Israeli kibbutzim and other cooperative communities.

In the years just preceding our study, the Hutterites had been making strong efforts to establish close and friendly relations with the townspeople of Jasper. In the case of the young male Hutterites, these contacts were most often jocular and informal, while the colony executives tended to act in a more formal manner. Cut off in many ways from the cult of Western folklore and tradition, the Hutterites relished especially those contacts with "local characters" that served to enrich their knowledge of the region's history and afford them at least a vicarious participation in the Western mystique.

Hutterites also developed fairly close relationships with businessmen who served their needs or bought produce from them. Nearly every colony in the Jasper region had contact with at least one businessman who regarded the Brethren as "good friends," or "good fellas," and who would visit the colony regularly whether or not he had business to discuss. The writer had several long talks with one of these townsmen, a restaurant proprietor who was in the habit of driving out to the colony almost any time of day or night in order to "get away from the damned town." (Alcohol may have had something to do with these visits; the Brethren are not abstainers, and they can be jolly drinking companions.) Sometimes such visits from townsmen would end in a quarrel, with the Gentile accusing the Brethren of bad faith in some business deal or other, and thereafter spreading tales of their alleged misdeeds. Usually these misunderstandings were repaired sooner or later, but the Hutterites came in time to distrust the weathercock nature of the townsmen's feelings about them. Most colonies have had the experience of having a local farmer or townsman patronize them for a while, praise their hospitality and efficiency, then suddenly turn on them and accuse them of theft, insincerity, and other breaches of law or ethics.[8]

---

[8] Some Hutterites advocated "turning the other cheek" when criticized or openly insulted; this seemed to be the fixed policy of the older generation, and it still characterizes the behavior of many Brethren. In one of the Jasper colonies the writer was told anecdotes by colony members exemplifying both this policy and its opposite. The colony had a very practical strategy when attacked: it assessed the merits of both policies and in the light of the demands of the particular situation, then reacted acordingly. In one instance, the Brethren were accused unjustly by a farmer of breaking down his fence and letting their cattle graze on his pasture. When they discovered that he had a reputation for inconsistent and erratic behavior, they decided to treat him courteously and to "let him holler." On another occasion, a town garageman tried to charge the Brethren twice as much as some slight damage to a farmer's car, caused by a colony truck, was worth. The Brethren refused to pay, and had firm, angry words with the garageman, who backed down.

At the time of our study, the Hutterites had begun to take a small part in civic and service activities, and there was evidence that this participation might increase in coming years. The more affluent colonies made cash contributions to the local hospital. When questioned about this practice, one of the Brethren explained: "This is a friendly place. We never felt much like helping out back in the old home (i.e., at the parent-colony location)." There were also instances of colonies volunteering to assist in the fire-fighting service for farms and ranches. One colony had an unusually talented, self-trained technician who volunteered to set up a telephone service that would serve a number of ranches and farms and one other colony. The presence of this other colony was not the reason for his offer, since the two colonies had rather distant and irritable relations. In explanation of his act, colony members said that they felt it their duty to help the local people whenever their special skills were needed.

The policy of increasing their contacts with outsiders is a relatively new development with the Brethren, and it suggests the beginning of a change in some aspects of Hutterian identity and in the "circles" of Hutterian social contacts postulated by Verne Serle. There is some evidence that the Gentile world is becoming a distinct outer "circle," and perhaps in some cases is even competing with the other three circles in importance. This development could be of considerable ideological significance, since Hutterian dogma contains two elements that the change appears to violate: the doctrine of election, which states that the Brethren alone are true Christians, and that all other "Christians" are corrupted by the world and hence to be avoided, and the belief that as true Christians the Hutterites must expect to be persecuted ("If ye were of the world, the world would love its own; but because ye are not of the world, but I have chosen you out of the world, therefore the world will hate you." John 15:19–21). Such exclusionistic aspects of Hutterian belief and behavior are difficult to maintain in North America, where pressures for greater participation in community and institutional life are very strong. At the time of our study, the Brethren in Jasper and elsewhere were giving way slightly on this point, and were expected to go further in the future toward contact with their neighbors.

In the town of Jasper, the Hutterites may be seen walking through the streets, looking into shop windows, and wandering through stores. The women carefully spend their *Zehrgeld,* or tiny monthly allotment of spending money. The men talk with shopkeepers, businessmen, and local government officials, linger in the local hotel lobbies or around the post-office or the bank, attend the cattle sales ring, and gossip with friends and neighbors on street corners. Occasionally a group of young Hutterites will visit a beer parlor. The Brethren are especially fond of inspecting machines and farm equipment, for in this way they are often able to memorize designs and then construct duplicates of the items back home in the colony shops. Though this practice sometimes irritates the townspeople, on the whole they are won over by the Brethren's genuine friendliness. In Jasper the Hutterites were accepted as part of the local scene, and their colorful dress was considered a part of the Western flavor of the community. One often saw a stray tourist staring at a party of Brethren on the street, delighted at having visited a "real old genuine Western town" full of Indians, cowpokes, Mounties, and Hutterites.

The Hutterites and the Official Community

In earlier chapters we mentioned the Brethren's involvement with the government, and noted that it has always been characterized by considerable strain because of the Brethren's refusal to accept public office, to participate in military service, and to pay certain taxes. Throughout the Brethren's history, governmental authority has tended to question the validity of their principles, and various forms of persecution, both subtle and open, have been practiced against them. At the time of our study, the Hutterites in Saskatchewan had experienced none of this. On the contrary, the Provincial Government had gone out of its way to give the Brethren a cordial reception, and had sought to assist (and discreetly to control) their purchase of sites for new colonies. The Brethren visited Regina, Saskatchewan's capital city, to consult with a special committee entrusted with the responsibility of advising on locations for new colonies. This had the effect of making them feel "wanted" and important, like the big ranchers who consult with officials of the Provincial land bureau about their large and valuable grazing leases. The Hutterites in Saskatchewan feel "wanted," but at the same time they remain somewhat wary; their long experience has taught them that officials can turn on them when political pressure from local farmers becomes intense.

The Brethren's dealings with Federal and Provincial water bureaus are of a different character. The water needs of all the agriculturalists in this semi-arid region are great, and the Hutterites, like other local people, are not always inclined to observe the water regulations to the letter. The ambiguity of the regulations themselves and the permissiveness of the authorities are of course partly responsible: Saskatchewan and the Federal Prairie Farm Rehabilitation Administration (PFRA) follow a policy of informal persuasion, and resort to legal penalties only rarely. In any case, some of the Brethren have built dams, pumped water from creeks and storage reservoirs, and engaged in other practices that violate water control schemes in the region. Not all colonies do this, and only two in the Jasper region are known to have engaged in such practices. However, most Brethren tended to avoid contact with the local water bureau offices, lest they be suspected of some violation. The officials viewed the Brethren with a mixture of tolerance and suspicion; they were aware that the water needs of these large enterprises were great, and that occasional violations were to be expected.

In line with their belief that governmental authority should be obeyed, the Brethren are usually conscientious with regard to paying taxes and other levies to local and external agencies. They frequently visit local government offices to consult with the officials and to learn about new Provincial policies in local government that may affect them. Some Rural Municipality secretaries viewed the Brethren as "pests" because of their habit of "smelling around" for information that would allegedly have been given to them freely if they had openly asked for it. Because of their deep distrust of officialdom, the Hutterites often ask questions in a vague and indirect manner, fearing that they will be refused an answer. A common view of the Brethren is expressed in the remark of a local official: "I've got to admit they are the best rate-payers around here, and they always settle up on weed-killers and such [chemicals for agricultural use are often distributed at low rates through Saskatchewan government offices]. But you never know how they feel about you, and I get tired of having them come in here and just stand around like foreigners."

The Hutterites are frequent visitors to agricultural extension offices in Jasper and in other towns where experimental farms and specialized services are available. In general, the Brethren prefer to deal with the agricultural colleges and the experimental farms, and not with the local extension agents, whom they feel are biased toward small-scale individual agriculture and hostile toward the colonies. At the same time, the Brethren are forced to deal with the local agent, since as the representative of the Provincial government he is in charge of many benefits the colonies can or must participate in: special financial inducements for hog production, loans for water and other resources development, plans for new construction, and similar matters. Here, as in the case of government officials, the Brethren are careful and often indirect: they must be friendly and personal since they are dealing with a local man; but at the same time they must be careful, since he represents the distant, impersonal, and potentially hostile government. Bad experiences with local agents of governmental farm policy have made the Brethren diffident and cautious—attitudes that outsiders often mistake for secretiveness and cunning. It must be remembered that the Brethren are barred by law from some benefits granted to other settlers and farmers—for example, from holding grazing leases—and their fear of recrimination or resentment prevents their acceptance of others. Few Hutterian families claim the allowance granted to families on a size basis by the Canadian Federal Government.

The Hutterites do make full use of Jasper medical services, and are as willing to take advantage of modern medical technology as they are to utilize the latest advances in farming methods. They fully accept the benefits of medical science; some of them read popular medical literature, and they all consult doctors when the occasion arises. All, or nearly all, Hutterian women in the Jasper colonies go to the hospital to have their babies; and, like their Gentile counterparts, aging Hutterites of both sexes spend a few days in the hospital "for observation" at regular intervals. The regional psychiatric service, part of the Saskatchewan Provincial medical program, has taken several local Hutterites as patients. Most of them were women suffering from the relatively mild depressive state known as *Anfechtung,* which we will discuss in Chapter 10. The Brethren's patronage of this and other medical services was more extensive in the Jasper area than it was in comparable districts in Alberta, a fact that can be explained as a result of the Saskatchewan medical program, which offers a variety of free and low-cost services. Though local Jasperites sometimes pointed to this patronage as proof that Hutterites will take advantage of anything free, in fact the incidence of patronage of the medical services by Gentiles also rose steeply after the Provincial program was introduced. In their relationships with medical personnel, whether doctors, hospital employees, or visiting health nurses, the Brethren displayed little of the wariness and diffidence that characterized their relations with government officials. This is probably because health functionaries do not come under the specific Hutterian taboos and injunctions concerning civil authorities (during the Moravian era several Hutterites were famous and skilled physicians).

The Brethren's relations with the local School Unit, the unit that supervises all the schools in the Jasper vicinity, are somewhat strained. The Brethren will only send their children to school on the colony premises, and although they are willing to provide the teacher with a well-built schoolhouse and dwelling, few teachers are eager to accept so isolated and demanding a position. The colonies often find difficulty in keeping the teachers they do get, for the older men often attempt to maintain surveillance over the teacher's methods, texts, and supplies. At the same time, the Hutterites respect learning and desire a basic education, and if the School Unit does not supply them with efficient teachers promptly, they complain. The School Unit, on its side, is inclined to blame the Hutterites for creating a difficult situation. Here, as in other matters, the Brethren's desire to live a life at once withdrawn from and engaged with the outside world leads to tension and misunderstanding.

While the Hutterites have worked out a careful, arms-length strategy of dealing with the external world, the fact remains that they must live within this world and to some extent assimilate its influences. In the most general sense, the basic pattern of a colony's economic adaptation is determined by the external society. The Hutterites have chosen to be farmers because they know that communal living can be carried on only on the basis of land ownership; however, in making this choice they have become subject to the forces and institutions governing agricultural economy in North America. Therefore, in order to survive they must seek knowledge of economic trends and opportunities, and of the many favors and inducements to increased productivity offered by organized agriculture. They must learn how to find bargains, how to deal for machinery, and how to sell their goods at the best price; and they must have close contact with the organizations and institutions of Gentile society and economy.

This means that Hutterites are no strangers to the economic sector of modern society, or to its governmental and quasi-governmental machinery. To an increasing extent, the successful colony is a sophisticated colony. One can discuss with its members trends in agricultural innovation, the best buys in machinery, advances in agronomic science, current costs and prices, and the political influences that govern all these matters. These discussions can be carried on at a much higher technical level with the Hutterites than with the typical Gentile farmer. This is especially true in the Jasper region, where there are a considerable number of traditionalized "seat-of-the-pants" farmers and ranchers. The Brethren's search for knowledge of the agricultural business has exposed them to a wide reading knowledge of the world in general; the sophisticated and affluent colonies are generally also those in which one may find copies of *Time* and *Life,* of business newspapers and magazines, and of technical manuals. These same colonies are also relatively free in their expressions of contempt for the "rough" type of colony, that is, the colony that does not keep abreast of events and consequently has an uncertain economic position.

At the same time, these gathering influences have not as yet resulted in true acculturation, in the sense of changing the basic Hutterian beliefs and institutions. The reasons for this will be discussed in greater detail in Chapter 11; here we need only state that the successful colony is generally also the deeply committed colony. We noted in Chapter 2 that wealth can be dangerous for the Hutterites; but in North America, the practice of colony fission has largely controlled the accumulation of financial surplus, and thus a colony can be "affluent" only in a relative sense. Such affluence simply serves to demonstrate to the Brethren the superiority, or at least the effectiveness, of their own institutions, and does not reflect the desirability of a change to outside systems. The Hutterites become effective modern agricultural businessmen by using the external world cleverly and with knowledge, rather than by assimilating its social program.

There are, however, some signs of a change in attitude that can be attributed to these influences. In the Jasper colonies, some of the younger men expressed their opinions of Hutterian life with considerable detachment:

"What do you think of this old Hutterite business? It's a pretty good deal, at that."

"Where else can you get a retirement scheme like this?"

"One thing we Hutterites know is how to make money. We got to—we have a lot of folks to support out here!"

"We got to be better than anyone else around here."

"One reason these people [the Gentiles] don't like us much is that we are doing better than they are at their own game. That's the big thing in the colonies these days."

These attitudes do not reflect alienation or cultural change in the extreme sense, but they do indicate an assimilation of the commercial, instrumentally oriented frame of mind of the modern farming business world that is a relatively new development in Hutterian thinking. Some key Hutterian institutions—efficiency, communalism, protection of the aged—are viewed by the speakers just quoted not as features of the correct Christian way, but as part of the practical way of life of modern farmers. It is significant that these remarks were made by some of the younger men; as we noted in an earlier chapter, conservatism seems to come with age. In any event, it seems to us that the assimilation of some influence from the outside is indicated.

The question of value influences goes even deeper. As we shall see in later chapters, the Hutterites are concerned over individuation and the social differentiation based on this process. They assume that men are tempted to assert themselves and demand separate treatment and rewards; there are passages in their writings that exemplify this concern. Since as young people the Brethren are taught the virtues of communalism and the equality of brotherhood, the question arises as to where they get the notion that men are inherently individualistic and separatistic. There are two possible sources: one is the tradition of Western civilization, which has always put considerable emphasis upon individualism in one form or another. The other is the contemporary North American culture, in which this emphasis is particularly strong, and to which the Hutterites have been exposed for the past seventy years. Both sources must be considered; the Hutterites are Western men, they are Canadian and American men, and they are close enough to the prevailing individualism of both the general and the specific worlds represented here to have acquired some of their basic ideas. Moreover, every withdrawal culture founded on the idea that there is something wrong with its larger milieu assimilates to some extent the frame of reference of that milieu. To be opposed to something means to think about that which you oppose, and to evolve your theory of opposition in part on the basis of the opposed doctrine.

As we suggested in the discussion of Hutterian dealings with water officials and other government agencies, the tentative approach of the Brethren to these organizations has led to misunderstandings. On the one hand, Hutterian Christian ethics require complete rectitude, honesty, frankness, and charity; on the other, the beliefs require distance from the world, and the conviction that all its denizens are corrupt and potentially, if not actually, hostile to the "true" Christian. In order to live communally in an individualistic society, the Hutterites must sometimes violate the rules of that society; and since it is deemed corrupt, they are often tempted to exploit it in various ways.[4] This situation has been the cause of considerable debate and tension among the Brethren themselves, and it is one basic cause of disagreements between colonies.

However, as a colony becomes established, there is some lessening of this tension (a development observed in the Jasper situation). The Brethren begin to move toward the external world more firmly and openly, and as they do the occasions of rule violation or of exploitation of the Gentiles become fewer. The Hutterites have begun to realize that they can make more intimate contact with the world and still remain pure—at least in the relatively tolerant atmosphere of contemporary Saskatchewan.

---

[4] With regard to external relations, the kibbutz differs greatly from the Hutterian colony. For example, the kibbutznikim are not barred from contacts with the outside; they are encouraged to participate in politics and other institutions, and in general are in touch with external society and culture. At the same time their community ideals require a degree of consumption austerity and selflessness not generally practiced in the individualistic Israeli society. These factors set the kibbutznikim apart from their neighbors just as the Brethren are set apart. In the kibbutz the combination of an open-door policy on cultural contacts with a degree of austerity and social differences has resulted in pressures to raise living standards, a steady loss of population to the outside, and a sense of confusion among the members as to the precise meaning of communal life in the midst of a modern world. On the other hand, the kibbutz is not the scene of such phenomena as moonlighting, smoking behind the barn, petty theft, duplicity, and other transgressions of the rule quite common in the Hutterian colony. Each form of communal existence seems to generate its own problems.

FIVE

Kinship, Family, and Marriage

Hutterian colonies are "intentional communities." That is, they have a charter for social organization that travels with them.[1] The rapidity with which most new colonies become well established is basically the result of their adherence to this plan. For example, at the time of our study the Jasper colonies were fully formed social systems, even though the oldest had been in existence for only twelve years. Rapid establishment is facilitated in most cases by the fact that the population pyramid of a new colony duplicates that of the parent group, and hence the same social factors of control and decision are present in the new colony and the old. Only one of the Jasper colonies (Colony 6) had a markedly younger population than its parent.

In this chapter we will examine the patterns of kinship, family

---

[1] The term "charter" is used here somewhat differently than it is in John Hostetler's *Amish Society* (1963, Chapter 3). By "charter" Hostetler seems to mean a particular set of moral values, or what we have called "beliefs" in Chapter 2 of this book. In our study, the terms "charter" and "social charter" are used to indicate a blueprint for social organization and social relationships containing not only values but also practical procedures for institutional structure and daily living. The Hutterian society is a "traditional" society in which values are extremely important, but it is also a pragmatic society that can adjust and confirm social arrangements by group decision, in a manner somewhat similar to that of English common law: i.e., by means of an accumulated "constitution." It is this cumulative body of definitions and practices that we call a "charter." The specific Hutterian doctrine that embodies many of these decisions is the *Ordnungen,* a book containing many recorded decisions of the Leut councils. We shall speak further of the Ordnungen in Chapter 11.

organization, and marriage in the Hutterian social organization, and will give special attention to the relationship of kinship to the problems of social maintenance and continuity in a communal society. In Chapter 6 we will continue with a detailed treatment of the instrumental organization of the colony, its systems of functional role assignment, and its decision-making mechanisms. The general objective of both chapters is to show how the collective system of organization confers adaptive advantages in the natural and economic environment of the Jasper region.

Since our study was based on six colonies, the question arises as to the nature of the differences between them in social organization. This question is a subtle one, due to the great uniformity among colonies. From one point of view, most of the differences are marginal, and a description of one colony can serve as a general portrait of them all. However, no two colonies carry out the social charter in identical ways, and there are always variations in their day-to-day functioning. Other differences can be found in the degree of rigidity each colony shows in following Hutterian norms, and also in the causes of strain and tension in colony life. Our treatment of the differences in social organization between the colonies will be reserved primarily for Chapters 7 and 10, where we will deal with the problem in terms of differences in economic management procedures and internal social tensions.

The major themes of this analysis of Hutterian social organization may be briefly summarized. To the Hutterites, values or ideology are given components of the social scene, defining the conditions and goals of social action, and the boundaries of all important institutions. Thus values, or religious principles, provide a rationale by which social life is organized with the greatest efficiency possible. Since the Hutterites regard their continuing existence as exemplars of the true Christian way as a major end in itself, they include efficiency as a goal in their scheme of values. Talcott Parsons has distinguished between "instrumental" (goal- or task-oriented behavior carried out with efficient means) and "expressive" behavior (behavior related to solidarity and belief). From the viewpoint of the casual observer, the Brethren's instrumental organization is more evident than their expressive behavior. A missionary of the Jehovah's Witnesses in Jasper remarked to the writer, "Them Hutterites are a case where religion is just something to keep the economics going." Grossly unenlightened though this view may be, it illustrates a point: the colony's religious activity is sometimes less conspicuous than its economic and decision-making apparatus. However, religion is not unimportant to the Brethren; on the contrary, it is all-important, for on it is established the basic frame of their existence.

The colony is a brotherhood not only in the formal sense, but also in the kinship sense. The most important solidarity groups in the kinship system are the various groups of blood-brothers, who, because of the patrilocality of Hutterian kinship, are associated together throughout life in the operation of the colony. These groups may be separated when the colony undergoes fission, but such divided colonies and their kin remain closely affiliated, and many decisions for both colonies are shared by the brother groups. The brother tie functions to promote solidarity and continuity, but it may also have the opposite effect when it results in the formation of cliques that threaten the colony's unity. To avoid this situation, the Hutterites have developed a system of institutions that replace kinship in the operational makeup of the colony. These institutions are complex and elaborate—possibly more so than any unit of local government in the Jasper region affecting a comparable number of people. The reasons for this elaborate institutional apparatus are to be found in the complexity of colony economy, in the Brethren's need to erect safeguards against schismatic tendencies, and in the fact that collective communalism always requires an elaborate decison-making and behavioral-control apparatus. The success of the Hutterian colony (and the kibbutz) does not prove that collective agricultural and communal living are somehow "better" than other forms of endeavor, but it does demonstrate that men can prosper under a communal system if a sufficiently ingenious framework is erected to protect it.

The Hutterian social system is one in which prestige status and the rewards that ordinarily accompany prestige are reduced to a minimum, even though functional roles are highly differentiated and fully elaborated. The colony is run as an egalitarian democracy in which no man, however important his contribution to the group, is given personal prestige or privilege over another. Respect, the deference due to age and experience, and a few small material rewards are all the compensation a Hutterite can expect. The ordinary laborer has the same vote and the same living quarters as the oldest executive; all make do with simple and nearly identical possessions, and live in the same condition of austerity; all have the same right to debate issues of concern to the colony. A man's job is not an end in itself, but only a way of contributing to the welfare of the entire group. This system is an ideal one, and therefore departures from it are inevitable; but the Hutterites have built up a set of procedures that inhibit, if they do not prevent, the development of hierarchical tendencies and self-seeking.

Underlying the structure of Hutterian social organization is a paradox: the paradox of a closed kinship society with egalitarian and brotherly ideals that nevertheless accepts a high degree of functional role differentiation, with its accompanying dangers of status, and an elaborate kinship system, with its dangers of factionalism. It is possible to view the Brethren's social organization as a series of institutions designed to bring these contradictory tendencies into adjustment—to realize the ideals while accepting the reality. We noted in the previous chapter that a related paradox accompanies Hutterian relations with the outside world. Many Hutterian institutions are designed specifically to cope with this particular problem.

Friendship patterns within the colony can follow age sets, individual interests, or random affiliations, as well as particular kinship ties. Wives of brothers are not necessarily friends because of the in-law tie, and brother-solidarity groups often joke privately about the fact that their wives are not overly compatible. The unmarried men as a group form one clique; the unmarried girls, another. The older men in executive positions constitute another natural grouping. The agricultural managers, mostly younger married men, may form another group, a very loose and variable one cut through by the solidarity bonds among brothers. The married laborers—men without executive or managerial roles—constitute still another grouping. However, none of these cliques are really well organized. There is colony pressure against clique formation, since the goals of the Hutterian social system are the welfare and equality of the entire colony.

One very important aspect of Hutterian social organization is the social education of the young. Like the *kibbutz,* the Hutterian colony has a remarkably detailed program of child training, the objective of which is to create human beings who can exist within a communal society.[2] Based as it is on insistent exposure of the children to the colony environment, it provides them with sustained interests, and offers them self-fulfillment within the functional role system. The success of this system of socialization is evidenced not only by the stability of the colonies as social systems, but also by the extremely low rate of defection.[3]

---

[2] However, kinship and family patterns in the *kibbutz* differ considerably from those in the Hutterian colony. The kibbutz is not a "kinship society"; that is, it is not a closed sectarian social system in which marriages must always be contracted with insiders. Though many *kibbutznikim* do marry within the movement, there is no rule against marrying outsiders, and there are plenty of spouses in every community who come from the outside. Moreover, the large population of the *kibbutzim* would make close reckoning of kin difficult. The kibbutz Federations bear some resemblance to the Hutterian Leute; however, they do not consider themselves marital or kin groups, but simply functional unions of politically similar kibbutzim. With respect to the position of the nuclear family in the community framework, the kibbutz resembles the colony in a number of ways. Like the colony, the kibbutz has chosen to rear its children primarily away from the nuclear household, and has experienced the social problems arising from nuclear family separateness. The different Federations follow somewhat variant patterns: some, like the Hutterites, allow the children to sleep at home at all times but keep them in school all day; others keep the children away from home all the time, except during the famous "children's hour" in the evening. The basic trend in family life in the kibbutz appears to be an increasing importance of the family, and a withdrawal from communal participation; see Talmon's papers, esp. 1965. On the basis of the data given in Talmon's papers, it would appear that the family in the present-day kibbutz is moving toward a compromise with the aggressive absorptive policy of the early kibbutz movement, and that its situation has begun to resemble that of the Hutterian family. This suggests that the Hutterites were first to recognize the need for a compromise in collective communalism with respect to the nuclear family.

[3] With regard to departures from the colonies, Arthur P. Mange (1963) reports

Men and Women

"Since woman was taken from man ... man hath lordship, but woman weakness, humility, and submission; therefore she should be under the yoke of man and obedient to him, even as the woman was commanded by God when He said to her, 'The man shall be thy lord.' ... The man, on the other hand, as the one in whom something of God's glory is seen, should have compassion on the woman as the weaker instrument, and in love and kindness go before her and care for her." This quotation from Peter Rideman's *Confession* defines the roles of the sexes in Hutterian life. There has been no significant change in this dominance-submission pattern since the beginning. Hutterian society might be described as a society of men aided and assisted by women. Since our treatment of Hutterian life emphasizes its agricultural aspects, we will concern ourselves mainly with the roles of the men, not the women. However, a word or two about the life of the Hutterian women may serve to place them for the reader within the scheme of the colony's traditions and activity.[4]

The formal status of women in Hutterian life is "low," insofar as the Brethren believe that women lack the "right" to make decisions in colony affairs. Women's duties are confined mainly to gardening, the preparation of food, sewing, and other domestic activities. They have less opportunity to leave the colony premises than the men do, since they are not permitted to drive vehicles.

---

the following figures for members of the Schmieden Leut in Manitoba and in South Dakota:

Decade of Birth	Male	Female
1900–1909	12	0
1910–19	11	2
1920–29	18	2
1930–39	47	2
1940–49	10	1
	98	7

During the period represented (1900–49) this Leut increased from about 500 individuals to nearly 4,000. Mange notes that most of those who left the colonies did so in their late teens.

[4] On the role of women, see Rideman (1565), in Hasenberg (1950, pp. 98–100); and Friedmann (1961, pp. 123–25).

However, as in all societies in which the formal status of women is restricted, their informal status and influence is considerable. Women have complete freedom on the colony premises, and even a certain irresponsibility when chores are light, which the men may envy. Most women have considerable influence over their husbands, and in the privacy of the nuclear family quarters, a couple may discuss colony affairs with considerable frankness and equality. Women are privately asked their opinion on matters of policy, but are never openly or collectively consulted.

Like all women, the Brethren's wives have many indirect ways of obtaining what they want. New kitchen equipment, new painting tools (in many colonies, the women are responsible for painting the buildings), new poultry and butchering equipment, and other items that pertain to the sphere of women's tasks, are bought on the advice of the women, who operate in most cases through the husband-persuasion method. When the women quietly agree to "convince" the men to buy a needed object, pressure mounts subtly but persistently until the thing is acquired. The Hutterites joke about this technique: "Oh, they know how to get what they want— they can do it better than us!" (By "us" the speaker meant the agricultural managers, who often have difficulty getting the Elders to invest in new equipment for their enterprises.)

The feminine Hutterian costume is a virtually unchanged edition of the dress worn by country women in sixteenth-century Europe: an ankle-length skirt, a separate bodice, and a kerchief or sunbonnet, the colors and details of which differ from Leut to Leut. The masculine costume is a version of the sixteenth-century Hutterian male dress of kilt, long hose, short jacket, and broad hat; however, extensive modifications were made in Russia and in North America, and now long pants are worn, the jacket is longer and resembles a suitcoat, the shirt is similar in style to a ready-made one, and the work hat or everyday hat is likely to be of the style worn by the local farmers or cowboys. The men's "dress-up" hat is a broad-brimmed black felt of distinctive cut. The general effect of the men's costume is not "peasant," but rather sober farmer style. This means that the women are much more conspicuous in town than the men are. They realize this, and it contributes to their feeling of "difference" when confronted with the gay, colorful styles of the Gentile women. Hutterian women often seem subdued and apprehensive when in town; on the colony premises, they are much more outgoing, personable, and witty. (Photographs follow p. 160.)

The obligation of the men to honor and protect the women is carried out faithfully. Hutterian men are polite and often deferential to their wives, though they do not show them some of the standard courtesies required by Gentile etiquette: e.g., they do not offer their women chairs, or remove their hats in the women's presence. In fact, a man who publicly defers to his wife, or is unusually polite to her, may injure his reputation with other men, and consequently not be voted into office. But Hutterian men are quite conscientious in giving their wives the little things they need, and in constructing home improvements. As a matter of routine, husbands relieve their wives of chores with the young children, although there usually are enough young unmarried women in the colony to "help out." The writer saw many a young Hutterian husband helping to bathe a new baby, or sitting with toddlers while his wife did other chores. No embarrassment was shown; it was taken as a matter of course. But in spite of the men's willingness to help out when necessary, the bulk of the domestic tasks falls to the women just as it does in any Jasper farm or ranch household.

The differences between Hutterian and Gentile inter-sexual relationships is symbolized in their feeling tone. The Hutterian women have an "air" about them—a shy yet assured womanliness that represents, perhaps, the ultimate result of their consciousness of their officially subordinate status, and their awareness of their ability to overcome it in indirect ways. However, in terms of the content of feminine personality, Hutterian women are as different from the Gentile girls as their respective worlds are. The Hutterian girl is shut off almost entirely from the vast, confusing consumption culture of North America, with its strident overtones of hedonism and narcissism. She may gaze on it from a distance, but if she evinces too much curiosity or detailed knowledge about it, she will be admonished by her parents, husband, or minister. (Men, on the other hand, are freer to participate vicariously in popular culture. They read magazines and comic books with relative freedom, although they are not allowed to buy them, and they are free to discuss sports and other aspects of outside culture among themselves or with male Gentile friends.)

The amount of emphasis given to the role components of the sexes in Hutterian culture may be expressed thus: Hutterian men are colony citizens first, executives and managers second, and laborers third; Hutterian women are housewives and mothers first, light laborers second, and citizens third. All facets of male and female role behavior follow logically from these role classifications.

Kinship and Marriage

Kinship ties may be used to define every important social grouping in Hutterian society. (It is a "closed" society: that is, the Brethren marry only among themselves, and marriage to an outsider means expulsion.) However, though kinship has a relationship to power, it is not assigned any formal role in Hutterian instrumental organization; instead, the chartered organization of the colony and the Leut provides for all instrumental jobs on an elective basis. Inheritance is unimportant, since personal possessions are few and colony property is divided at fission among the members of the old and new colonies. The few personal possessions of a deceased person are distributed as keepsakes among the members of his immediate family, except in the case of yardgoods and some furniture, which are usually returned to the colony pool of property.

Descent is traced bilaterally, and some informants have stated that the men have a tendency to feel more closely related to their father's side, and the women to their mother's. However, others deny any such consistent bias, and some say that if there is any alignment of filiation, it is toward the father's side in the case of both men and women. This would seem to be consistent with the strict patrilocality and the strong patriarchal patterns of the Hutterian social system. Marriages are allowed between second and third cousins on both sides of the family, but marriage between first cousins is definitely taboo. Because of the closed character of Hutterian society, marriages between cousins are quite common.

Kinship terminology among the Hutterites follows standard German usage, with no apparent exceptions. Some kin terms are used colloquially by children on an age-sex equivalence basis: for example, all men of the father's age may be called "uncle." Such usage is common in a closed-kin brotherhood.

The basic formal units of Hutterian society, which are ordered by kin and are perceived as being so ordered by the Brethren themselves, are the following: (1) the nuclear family; (2) the patrinomial family, which is often equivalent to the population of one colony and its daughter colonies (see Diagram 1 for an example of this); and (3) the intermarrying group of patrinomial families, usually equivalent to a specific group of colonies that consistently intermarry. This last unit has no name, but the Brethren informally recognize its existence. Each of the three Leute might also be considered a separate kin-ordered unit, since each is strictly endogamous; however, the Brethren do not conceive of the Leute as groups of kin, but rather as branches of the Brotherhood with different geographical loci and somewhat different customs.

Genealogies of the patrinomial families are kept by the Brethren, but such matters are of interest chiefly to elderly people, who keep "family trees" either as a hobby or as a duty to the community. The Hutterites are not especially preoccupied with tracing descent; the relations between the persons on Diagram 1 would be known to every person in the colony fifteen years of age or older, but only the oldest persons would be able to extend the diagram beyond the relatives shown. In our studies of kinship among the farmers and ranchers of the Jasper region, we found comparable phenomena: the extensions were imperfectly known except by older people who kept family trees as a hobby. Quite possibly the average fifteen-year-old in a Gentile family would not be able to do as well as the Hutterian child, but then the farm youth does not live with such a large group of relatives as his Hutterian counterpart does. It might be said that aside from certain obvious emphases on kinship arising

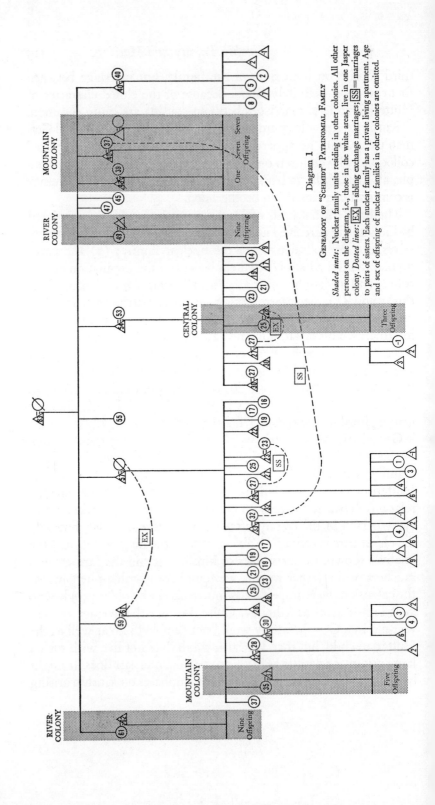

Diagram 1

GENEALOGY OF "SCHMIDT" PATRINOMIAL FAMILY

Shaded units: Nuclear family units residing in other colonies. All other persons on the diagram, i.e., those in the white areas, live in one Jasper colony. *Dotted lines:* marriages to pairs of sisters. Each nuclear family has a private living apartment. Age and sex of offspring of nuclear families in other colonies are omitted. EX = sibling exchange marriages; SS = marriages to pairs of sisters.

from the closed character of the Hutterian society, its kinship patterns are not especially different from those of the Gentile society around it.

The most important informal kin-ordered unit in Hutterian society is the group of male siblings, which has lifetime solidarity and therefore considerable functional importance in Hutterian instrumental organization.[5] In the lower age ranges, these groups constitute cliques with related interests and skills; among the older men, brothers may come to dominate the elected-Elder stratum of leadership in the colony. However, as age increases, the Elder group may develop as a group of male first cousins, which will function in ways similar to a sibling group.

There is no other significant generalization one may make about other loci of solidarity in the colony. Occasionally the young unmarried girls form an age-group, and show considerable recreational solidarity, but this is transient and in any case is controlled by the Elders. Tendencies toward solidarity formation among men and boys on an age-group or "horizontal" basis are limited or curtailed by the colony instrumental organization and on the early placement of the boy as an apprentice. In any case, the Hutterian colony itself is the main locus of solidarity, because any other form of solidarity is viewed with suspicion, or is carefully controlled as a threat to the commune. This appears to be in contrast with the situation in the kibbutz, where, according to Talmon (1965, p. 279), horizontal age-group solidarity has been highly significant, and has led to parental opposition to some aspects of communal child-socialization, thus contributing to the trend toward reassertion of the rights of the nuclear family group in kibbutz life.

The problem presented by kinship in a communal society is one of functionality versus dysfunctionality. Kinship offers the colony member the opportunity for close, emotionally satisfying comradeship; moreover, in a Christian communal society the nuclear family represents the fruit of a necessary and sacred union, and as such it offers spiritual security. On the other hand, kinship provides a

---

[5] Cf. Cumming and Schneider (1961) on the tendency toward sibling solidarity in American society.

focus for the development of a "personal community" in which the individual can find affection and sympathy when his brethren appear to reject him—a situation that may well be psychologically valuable for the individual, but is potentially dangerous to the society, since it sets up a barrier between the individual and his solidarity with the whole group. Therefore, though kinship in Hutterian society is a medium of early child socialization, a source of personal assistance and favors, and a model for the primary-group solidarity of the whole colony, it remains a source of cleavage between colony members.

The Hutterites regard the nuclear family as the basic social institution, but limit its function to domestic services and to the socialization of children from infancy to the age of three. Each dwelling house is built on a sixteenth-century "long house" plan, and contains several private, non-connecting apartments of three or four rooms each. These apartments are assigned to the nuclear family units on the basis of the number of children in each unit. Household furnishings are uniform and simple, but favorite pieces of furniture, ingenious devices made by the husband, and modest flowerbeds provide each dwelling with a marginal distinctiveness. (This trend toward individuality appears to be strengthening slightly, but is encountering resistance from the colony conservatives.) Visiting is informal and free, although there are certain subtle rules of privacy. Children live with their parents until marriage, but from the age of three on, they spend part of their day in the colony nursery, in the German School, or in public school classes.[6]

The Brethren tend to emphasize the domestic-group aspect of the nuclear family over its specific kinship features. That is, they often speak of the unit as the "home," not as the "family" or "kin group"—reserving these terms for the larger groupings. They appear to view the nuclear family as the place where the child can receive the basic and continuous early socialization needed to ground him in Hutterian principles. The nuclear family relin-

[6] Cf. Cooperstock (1961, pp. 267–69), on the importance of communal-sectarian child training, as compared with secular cooperative farm procedures.

quishes the child to the kindergarten and German school, which continue the teaching process on a colony level.

The casual visitor to the colony is likely to come away with the impression that there is little difference between the nuclear family units, and that everyone interacts in a more or less random manner on a communal basis. There is no doubt that in some respects nuclear family separateness is less distinct than it would be in a small town. The Hutterites attend church together, discuss colony issues together, send their young children to a central kindergarten, work as teams without regard for nuclear units, and eat at separate tables by sex in the communal dining hall. It is these public occasions of group organization that the outsider sees. However, at a less obvious level there does exist a degree of domestic-group differentiation and cleavage. (If one spends more than a few days in the colony, one begins to see that pronounced differences in personal interests and habits, personality traits, and views of "the outside" seem to run in nuclear families, and that soon one's own interactions with the members of the colony are following the cleavages between the nuclear families.) However, these differentiations are all in the private sphere; they are not allowed to reach significant levels of public social expression, because if they did so, there would be danger of a rupture in the colony's communal fabric. In general, such patterns are consistent with the Brethren's tendency to see the nuclear family less as a kinship group or "family," and more as a private domestic group.

Within the nuclear family, the most obvious bonds are those between brothers, and to a lesser extent, those between all siblings and between siblings and their parents. Generational solidarity appears to be molded by the electoral instrumental structure of the colony, in which the men of the parental generation are voted into the executive or Elder level of authority, and their sons between twenty and forty into positions in the agricultural management framework (see Diagram 2). Since the latter group must obtain their resources from their fathers, so to speak, a certain atmosphere of formality and even tension is created.

The writer witnessed a classic case of conflict in which the prin-

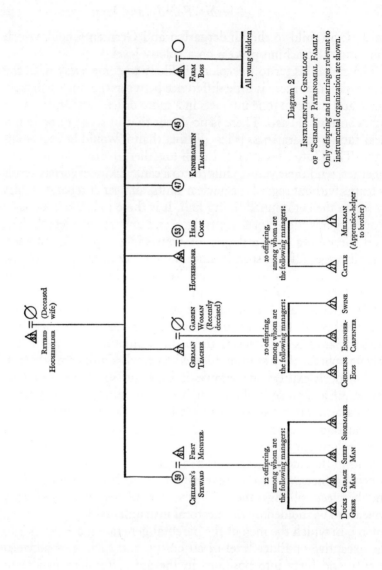

Diagram 2

INSTRUMENTAL GENEALOGY
of "SCHMIDT" PATRINOMIAL FAMILY
Only offspring and marriages relevant to
instrumental organization are shown.

ciples governing these bonds were displayed. The Householder, or business manager, of one colony proposed to construct a new dining hall, but the chief construction manager, his nephew, felt that the colony needed a new barn instead. Discussions proceeded for several days, following the usual Hutterian pattern of informally working through a disputed issue before bringing it to a vote. During this period, kin alignments developed: the Householder's sons agreed with their father that the construction of a dining hall was necessary, while the construction manager's father (an Elder-executive) and his brothers took his side and supported his demand for a barn. Thus two groups of brothers and their two fathers were opposed on the issue. In evening sessions the two sets of brothers met separately in their homes and discussed the matter; the fathers stayed away from these meetings. The two older men discussed the matter between themselves, since they did not wish to provoke a breach in colony solidarity by openly siding with their sons, and finally they worked out a compromise by which *both* the barn and the hall were to be built over a six-month period.

In colony life, the strength of the brother tie is everywhere apparent. As we will show later, the agricultural managers are in a de facto position of competition or rivalry. These men are in charge of the various agricultural enterprises and construction services of the colony, and must obtain their resources from the Elders. In spite of this, managers who are brothers tend to display kinship solidarity, and may take sides together in arguments against Elders or other managers who are not related to them. This solidarity pattern operates to prevent the formation of a general clique of all the managers, who might then solidly oppose the Elders. Such a clique does emerge from time to time, but its basic strength is weakened by the brother ties. By the same token, brother ties are prevented from becoming too strong, and thereby weakening the colony fabric, by the divisive tendencies emanating from the instrumental roles of management and the problem of obtaining resources from the "fathers" (Elders and executives). These patterns will be further explained in Chapter 6.

The Hutterites sometimes speak of the colony itself as a "family," even though a colony may consist of more than one kin group. The children often call many colony adults "Cousin" (*Vetter* or *Base*), but this term is never used indiscriminately between adults. The Jasper colony whose family genealogy appears on Diagram 1, had a single surname and was based on a group of second-generation male siblings and their unmarried sisters. All persons shown on the unshaded area of the diagram were residents of the "Schmidt" family colony. All the wives of the "Schmidt" men came from other colonies. The sibling group in the second generation from the top of the diagram included some persons in "Mountain Colony," the parent colony of the "Schmidt" group. The other colonies on the diagram were the marital destinations of "Schmidt" women, and several sibling exchanges between "Schmidts" and other members of the colonies are indicated by dotted lines. The four colonies— "Schmidt," "Mountain," "River," and "Central"—thus constituted an intermarriage group, even though not all of the "Schmidt" wives came from among the four colonies (two other colonies each furnished one wife).

One male member of the second-generation group, age 61 (he was the Church Elder, or First Minister, of the colony), is not a brother of the other men of this generation, but the husband of a female sibling of the other men. Since the Hutterian colony is bride-exogamous, his presence there seems to violate a rule. However, colonies often have more than one kin group (although one is always dominant in numbers) and if possible, they choose their Minister from a minority kin group in order to avoid accusations of majority discrimination. Such a choice also helps to keep internal family problems out of colony affairs, since the minority-group Minister can be expected to be impartial toward the disputes of the majority group. The Minister in question above was elected on the basis of these customs. He also happened to have the "Schmidt" surname, and was a member of a distant branch not thought of by the main group as being blood relatives. A small number of these minority "Schmidts" lived in Mountain Colony, but he was the only member of the minority group to come to the new colony. (One reason for his coming was that he had married into the "Schmidt" majority group.)

Marriage does take place infrequently between members of different kin groups in the same colony, but there is a strong overall tendency toward colony exogamy. Hutterians explain this in the usual fashion: people who grow up together generally think of each other as relatives, whether they are or not, and they are therefore disinclined to marry. There is also the feeling that pastures are greener on the outside; that some other colony may be better than one's own.

There are only twenty surnames among all the Hutterian colonies, and half of them go back to the Moravian period in the sixteenth century. A few names came from Mennonite families in Russia, and about eight names have been added during the North American period, mostly those of former Mennonite families who joined the Hutterian faith. All the original Hutterian patrinomial families have genealogies, and some of them extend back into the sixteenth century. However, no special effort is made by the nuclear unit in the surname family to keep the genealogies. The writer was unable to find out where the complete genealogies for several surname families were kept, although some informants knew that they existed.

Marriage patterns define the other two kin-ordered groups: the informal intermarrying group of colonies or kindred, and the Leut, or expanded affinal network. The three Leute—the Darius, the Schmieden, and the Lehrer—are endogamous groups. We discovered only one case of inter-Leute marriage in the six colonies in the Jasper region; and only one was found in a survey of a number of Alberta colonies of both the Darius and Lehrer Leute. The Hutterites say that such marriages are rare or nonexistent, although a certain number occurred in South Dakota, before the move to Canada. Originally the Leute were distinguishable from each other on the basis of a few minor differences in custom, dress, and time of entry into North America; as time went on, and after the separation of the Schmieden (Manitoba) and the Darius and Lehrer (Alberta) Leute, they ceased to intermarry, and developed their own separate administrations. When pressed for reasons for the lack of inter-Leute marriages, Hutterian informants stressed the differences in custom. A Lehrer man said: "We never marry outside the Leut, because the woman wouldn't know how to do things. She couldn't make our clothes right and she wouldn't want to wear our women's clothes." And a Darius man remarked: "It happens once in a while—there's no rule, like. It's just that it's a source of trouble. Well—there's a man over in [a colony in Alberta] who married a Schmieden girl, and she made those Schmieden men's clothes—the jacket has a collar, you know. And he wore this. The Elders had to warn him about it several times." Differences in the standard of living are taken into account when a marriage is contemplated: "Darius women wouldn't want to go into Lehrer dwelling houses, because they [sic] don't have any running water or sinks."

Since some of the differences mentioned above may appear marginal to the reader, it is necessary to explain that Hutterites make much of these small matters that have become symbols of tradition and the timeless, unchanging social system. There is no feeling of criticism: that is, the fact that Darius people install cold-water taps and sinks is not seen by the Lehrer as a breach of tradition— only as one of the differences which, with others, functions to define the divisions between Hutterian groups, and incidentally helps to limit the number of colonies from which potential mates may come.

The number of colonies from which mates are likely to be drawn is reduced even further by the tendency for a limited number of colonies within a Leut to form an intermarrying group, which we might call a "kindred." Among the six Jasper colonies, four had obtained all their wives from no more than four other colonies; one from three; the sixth from only two. (Diagram 1 shows some of these inter-colony marriages.) Comparable figures were obtained for the destinations of women marrying out of the six colonies. Two colonies had two marriages each within the home colony, owing to the presence of two patrinomial families in each of these colonies. In all cases, the colonies were members of groups of from two to four colonies each in Alberta and Saskatchewan between which there was much intermarriage. In the Lehrer colonies in Jasper there were two such intermarried groups or kindreds. Hutterian informants drew diagrams that represented these colonies in the form of a tree, with the younger colonies as offshoots from the older. In other words, many of the intermarried colonies were also parent-offspring colonies, and both of the intermarried groups tracing its colony lineage back to two original colonies that came from South Dakota.

Marriages did take place *between* the two intermarried groups, but not frequently. Repeated intermarriage between the same colonies means a high frequency of visits and considerable exchange of information. Consequently the closely intermarried colonies develop comparable management styles and modes of economic operation. To put this in the context of colony interrelations, we can say that the two most important social factors leading to relationships and similarities between colonies are marriage and the fission process.

It should be emphasized that this is a de facto pattern, not a system operating on the basis of formal rules. It resembles the patterns of intermarriage that develop among European farming villages more than it does those among tribes, where marriage rules are based on kinship regulations. There is evidence that the opportunities for exchange of information, cash loans, commodity exchanges, and socializing are at least as important as the marriage itself: "Of course there are a lot of contacts from marriage—it means you can help each other better." A wife is expected to transfer her kinship loyalties to her husband's family after marriage. If a colony mirrors the socioeconomic pattern of one's own, it is viewed as a favorable environment for one's women, or as an ideal place in which to find a wife. Consequently there is a strong tendency for the members of colonies with similar ideas and customs to intermarry.

The Leut itself is endogamous, and constitutes a diffuse affinal network linked together by marriage. This means that the Ministers who constitute the Leut council and who meet each year to discuss rules of conduct and colony procedure are all relatives, though they may be only distantly related. Thus all the basic functional groupings in Hutterian life are kin-ordered, even though favoritism is carefully guarded against in decision-making procedures. Kinship provides the desirable social atmosphere of the primary group, but bureaucratic instrumentalities furnish the actual procedures of community action.

Hutterites often prefer to marry siblings of their own siblings' spouses; that is, the "sibling exchange" marriage is a preferred form. This can take various symmetrical or non-symmetrical patterns: two brothers marrying two sisters; a brother and sister marrying a brother and sister. The complete exchanges can take place in one generation, or completion of the exchange can be made in a later generation. On Diagram 1, we show two cases of exchange in which a brother and sister married a brother and sister; and two cases of two sisters marrying into the same family.[7] There is no formal rule governing this type of exchange marriage; the Hutterites say that they like to be sure that their women will marry into a good colony, and if this has been determined by previous marriages, there is a strong tendency to repeat the procedure. Many of these sibling marriages result from the social visits that are occasioned by the original marriage; e.g., an unmarried brother has a chance to meet the sister of his sister-in-law, and a romance begins. The practice of sibling marriage is another indication of the solidarity of the bond between kinship brothers.

Marriage choices are expected to be free, and based on love; and parents and kin appear to exert no more pressure on the young people for preferred matings than local Gentile parents do, which means they exert strong verbal encouragement or discouragement, and arrange opportunities for courtship, but use no strong sanctions or force. As has been noted, young men and women have opportunities to meet each other on those visits that accompany such occasions as a marriage, the birth of a baby, or a harvest. Within the colony, the young unmarried people often get together at each

---

[7] Arthur P. Mange (1963) reports his data on sibling exchange marriages for the entire Schmieden Leut: "Out of 812 marriages there were 82 doubles (20 per cent of all marriages in this sample) in which the spouses of two sibs were themselves sibs. In 50 of these 82 cases, 2 brothers married 2 sisters—in the other 32 cases, a brother and sister married a brother and sister. In addition to these double inter-sibship marriages, there were 16 triples (6 per cent) and four quadruples (2 per cent). For both triples and quadruples one sibship supplied a single sex slightly more often than chance would predict, but the deviation from pure chance expectation is not significant."

other's homes to sing, eat, and enjoy themselves. Boys and girls in love can pair off and wander through the fields together for an hour or so, but a longer absence is frowned upon. Most Hutterian courtships last about a year. Once the young people have decided on marriage, the girl's parents must be consulted, and all disagreements cleared away. In the negotiations some go-between, perhaps the boy's father, will make the approach to the girl's family. At the time of their marriage, the colony provides the newlywed couple with the standard necessities of housekeeping. The couple may accept wedding presents from relatives, so long as these do not offend against the principle of austerity.

There is every reason to believe that most Hutterian marriages represent genuine attachments; and there is also evidence that the choice of a bride is influenced strongly by the interests and personality of the husband.[8] For example, in one of the Jasper colonies, the "intellectuals"—young men with interests in literacy training, philosophy, and scientific matters—had wives with generally similar interests, while the men with simpler interests chose wives like themselves.

The Hutterites do not practice birth control, for they consider it sinful, as do most fundamentalist Protestant groups. The woman bears children regularly throughout her fertile years, and the mature nuclear family units are quite large—the mean is about 9 children. The mother is relieved of a great deal of the daily responsibility for the children by the kindergarten and the German School. At the birth of a child, the mother is excused from most work responsibilities for a period of about six weeks. She is assisted at home during the first few weeks after the birth by a female relative—often an unmarried niece from another colony who hopes to use the visit as an opportunity for courtship.

Hutterian children are freely and firmly disciplined. "Strapping" is the usual method of corporal punishment. Loud warnings and threatening gestures are often used as deterrents, and affection can swiftly give way to sternness. Sibling rivalry is prevalent among

[8] Mange reports: "An individual whose parents had a given degree of relationship tends to choose a mate related to himself in the same degree; i.e., social, economic, and cultural values affect marriage choice."

the small children, and is dealt with understandingly but firmly. Under three, children stay at home; between the ages of three and six, they attend nursery school, where they eat lunch and dinner; between six and fifteen, they attend both the German School and the public school on the colony premises. At the nursery and the German School the child is inculcated with the Hutterian ideals of austerity and communalism; the writer was told repeatedly by children of ten and twelve that Hutterian ways were the "best" ways.

Hutterian child-training methods and the German School educational program are completely lacking in one feature commonly found in Gentile systems: the encouragement of competition between the children. In interviews, the public school teachers who come to the colonies on a daily basis stated that they had great difficulty "motivating the children" (i.e., getting them to compete with each other), and that if a teacher praised a particular child, the others would respond with embarrassed silence. This response is natural in a thoroughly egalitarian atmosphere, where differences in skill and intelligence are minimized. As the child grows up and becomes an apprentice, and later, when he is voted into a job, his skills are recognized, but not made much of. The Hutterites do not seek to eliminate differences in ability, but rather to prevent them from becoming the occasions of vanity or sources of differential prestige.

Fifteen is the age at which both boys and girls are considered adults insofar as work responsibilities are concerned. Baptism, which marks full adult status, is postponed until the age of twenty or thereabouts. At fifteen, a boy either becomes an apprentice to one of the enterprise managers or works as a machine operator. If he shows exceptional ability, he begins a more or less formal course of training that may lead eventually to his election as a manager. His interests here are his own; the Hutterites discourage father-son succession in jobs, for they have found that it fosters inefficiency.

At fifteen the girls begin their formal work assignments in the kitchen and garden, but they continue their domestic training in the home as well. Since there are few specialized roles for the women, the girl undergoes a more diffuse program of training than the boy does. This situation encourages the formation of those cliques of unmarried young girls that are the ornaments of most colonies, but which constitute a potentially distracting element.

Hutterian teenagers are relatively outgoing, and show an avid interest in "the outside." This interest often creates problems for the colony. The critical rite of passage in Hutterian life is baptism, which is regarded as an event marking the age of full self-awareness and consent, and the conscious affirmation of faith in the Anabaptist beliefs. It is expected that before baptism young people will be somewhat "wild," and a certain amount of oat-sowing is tolerated in and out of the colony. Some young men, and a few women, leave the colony for a year or so to live on the "outside," but most of them return to the colonies to wed (marriage with a Gentile would bar their return). Unmarried girls are expected to be somewhat forward and coy, and their little transgressions—such as listening to radios brought into the colony by visitors—are tolerated. The writer was visited nearly every night for a week during one of his colony stays by unmarried girls, who tape-recorded Hutterian songs and generally joked and enjoyed themselves. Usually one or two of the men were present; if the men were unmarried, the young women were much freer in their actions.

With conscious humor, the Hutterites sometimes characterize their own society as "a big retirement scheme." They have unquestionably created a solution to the problem, always difficult in an agricultural enterprise economy, of acquiring sufficient equity to finance the retirement of the aged. The young Hutterite can look forward to an absolutely secure old age—which is not true for the majority of Gentile farmers of the Jasper region. This expectancy of security is undoubtedly one of the main causes of the relatively high stability of Hutterian life, and the low rate of defection. As one outspoken young Hutterite put it: "Well, it's a pretty good life, you know. You go away from it once in a while, but you always come back. Where else can you get a good deal like this for a lifetime?"

Retirement of the aged is informal, but virtually mandatory

when a man can no longer maintain a full day's labor. This may occur anytime between sixty and eighty years of age; it may be delayed, since the oldest men can still perform executive roles until senility. An informal acknowledgment of retirement may be made: "Well, the young fellows, you know, they insisted I retire.... There isn't anything you can do about it." Although many retired men function as advisers, they lack job assignments, and hence have little to do but wander around the colony premises, chatting with the workers, watching the progress of daily tasks, getting in the way, and feeling left out. If he has scholarly interests, and his eyes hold up, the retired man can read, study, or copy the Scriptures and commentaries; or perhaps write his own historical reminiscences, which will be added to the centuries-old collection of such accounts. The situation is similar for the aged woman. When she is no longer able to do her part of the kitchen or garden work, she is eased out by the younger women. She may keep busy by sewing, babysitting, or helping out in the nursery school; or she may simply sit on a stoop and watch the colony activities go on around her.

Kinship and Instrumental Relations

Though Hutterian society is a kinship society, kinship relations are not utilized as a formal means of maintaining the social and economic order. This situation has some novel aspects.

After a stay of several days at any colony, the observer may find that kinship terms are rarely used as terms of address by adult Hutterites, although a number of extended-use terms are employed by the children. The avoidance of kinship terms is part of a tendency in Hutterian behavior to avoid kinship as a social context wherever the colony frame of reference is dominant. The writer tested this in several ways, usually by changing the context of the conversation from "family," or personal, to "colony," or public, while maintaining the reference to a particular individual. In all cases, as soon as the context switched to "colony," the informants ceased to use kin terms or personal references, and began to refer to the individual by his functional job title or by some other impersonal term. On many occasions it was impossible to determine whether a certain individual was a relative of the speaker or not. This can be bewildering if one happens to know that all the members of a particular colony are close relatives (as in the case of the family-colony in Diagram 2).

One test of the role of kinship in any administrative order is succession—the extent to which close relatives succeed the incumbents to offices or jobs. In the Hutterian colony, all offices are elective, and the vote ideally goes to the best qualified individual. There are frequent cases of a younger brother helping his older sibling in his job, but in no Jasper colony was there more than one case of father-son succession in the two mature generations represented, which shows that the majority of sons adopted trades different from those of their father. The Hutterites believe that "voting only kinship into office whether qualified or not, has led to serious harm" (Gross 1965, p. 62). Boys are encouraged to explore the various activities of the colony, and may informally apprentice themselves to any of the agricultural managers, or voluntarily study if they become interested in ministerial or teaching roles. There is some tendency for the intellectual and spiritual vocations to run in families, probably because the tradition of literacy cultivation is often best carried forward in a family context. Another de facto father-son or brother-brother succession tendency may appear when a colony divides: fathers will want to train their sons in their own jobs to ensure continuity of skills and efficiency; or will insist that they accompany them to the new colony—although the latter practice is not the rule, especially if the son is married.

Interviews with a number of Hutterites of both sexes verified the existence of certain customs with regard to the utilization of relatives for practical ends. In all cases the question asked was phrased as follows: "If you needed some help on———, who would you ask?"

Women most often stated that they would ask their sisters, usually the unmarried ones. If this did not work out, "anyone else" would do. If the task required two or more weeks of help with the children, they would ask a niece from another colony to come and stay. The nature of the task would, of course, influence the choice of relative, and if the two colonies had close ties, the niece would be asked directly if she were ready for marriage.

Most men said they would ask their brother to take care of their chores in case of absence or illness. If no brother was available, "anyone else" would be chosen; or the Farm Boss would be notified by the person involved, and would assign another man to the job. All informants placed considerable emphasis on this procedure: that is, they regarded it as the duty of a brother to take his sibling's place. This pattern and the "visiting niece" pattern were felt by informants to be the most highly formalized kinship obligations.

A father is expected to ask his son to help him before he asks anyone else. Informants stated that if a man whose own son was available asked anyone else to help him, it would be thought "peculiar." "There would be something wrong with the family if you couldn't ask a member to help you out," stated one informant. At the same time, the nature of the task was acknowledged as a variable. An unusually technical operation might require help from a non-member of the nuclear family; but since most adult men have a relatively uniform assortment of skills, this was not a usual occurrence. One other factor that might influence requests would be the Farm Boss's schedule of jobs, which in periods of stress took precedence over any other plans. One Farm Boss commented: "Yes, if we were harvesting or something like that, it wouldn't be right for anyone to ask one of the men on duty to help him out. Generally that kind of thing doesn't happen; but once in a while, if a father wants his son for something, I may give in. You have to be kind of careful about those things." He was referring here to the fact that father-son relationships can be close, and need to be respected. Granting this flexibility, it was clear that instrumental demands could take precedence over nuclear family obligations and reciprocities. This illustrates the tendency for the instrumental structure of the colony to take precedence over or to supplant kinship relationships.

In these interviews it was also noticeable that few respondents considered cousins and affinals in the same colony as second to nuclear family members in the task-assistance pattern. It was never

"If no brother, then a cousin," but always, "If no brother, then anyone else." "Anyone else" meant any other relative; and there was no evidence in these or other interviews of any special feeling of closeness among degrees of cousins or affinals.

Several informants commented that one should do one's own job whenever possible, lest one sin against the Hutterian concept of duty to the communal brotherhood. The individual is trained in, or assigned, particular roles and tasks; and these become his or her responsibility in the colony organization. During the writer's own visits in various colonies, he observed this pattern in operation. There were only four cases of job exchange, or requests for help, and these were caused by emergencies. The amount of minor reciprocal assistance was not recorded, but there was about as much as one might expect there to be on a big farm or in a village community.

Students of modern North American kinship have noted that in many social settings the ability to make claims for services or favors remains the only functional expression of the kin tie. We found this to be true for the distant relatives of the Gentile community of Jasper. In the case of the Hutterites, the question of claim is rendered complex by the emphasis on the religious brotherhood and autonomy of the colony itself: a special case of the problem of interplay between kinship and locality ties among agrarian peoples who live in nucleated centers. Studies of relationships between kin in one colony and its related colonies indicated that dependence on the help of relatives followed patterns similar to those in the Gentile community: i.e., some individuals made claims on relatives living in distant colonies more often than they did on those nearby or in the same colony. The writer himself experienced such claims: on a trip to related colonies in Alberta, taken with a Jasper Hutterian guide, most of the colonies visited were those with affinal and blood ties to the guide's colony, and beds were obtained by simply stopping at the living quarters of the closest or friendliest relative.

Within the colony, as within the local Gentile community, relationships between kin are more frequent but also more complex. As noted, one cannot exert kinship claims freely or automatically, because the colony as a whole has prior "claims" on its members.

The religious brotherhood of the colony is based on the conception of Christian unity, or the idea that actual kinship is second to Christian fellowship and colony membership. For this reason, every member is expected to contribute to the welfare of the whole. The image of the colony as presented to the outsider is that of a corporative organized brotherhood, and casual visitors are not told that it actually may be a single kin group. Hutterites simply do not conceive of kinship as a formal or instrumental bond.

A colony consists of a number of nuclear families living together in a cooperative "village" of about a hundred persons (John Hostetler says 94). Yet the majority of these people are relatives. They must function as a whole, not as a group of separate nuclear families. During the potentially divisive conflict between two groups of fathers and sons described earlier, care was taken to prevent a general quarrel or an open argument on a family basis. The young men of both family units maintained friendly relations in public, although in general there was a tendency among them simply to avoid contact until the affair was settled. In any case, it seems clear that the Hutterites instrumentalize kinship by making the group-decision process preeminent in the colony social organization. At the same time, kinship furnishes a primary-group atmosphere that helps to soften arbitrary features or tendencies in the instrumental system.

An example may help to illustrate further the relationship between kinship and the instrumental organization of the colony. On Diagram 1, the youngest sibling in the second descending generation is a man, age 40. On Diagram 2, he appears as the Farm Boss of the colony. This man is only three years older than some of his nephews in the third generation on Diagram 1; and some of these nephews are in managerial jobs, as shown on Diagram 2. When the colony first came to the Jasper region, this man, like his nephews, was a manager: that is, he was holding a job appropriate to his age level. However, the colony was in need of a new Farm Boss, and the man agreed somewhat reluctantly to be a candidate. He was elected, because of his skill and because he was a member of the second generation, the level at which the Elder authority is located in the great majority of the colonies.

Conversations with this man established the fact that he felt somewhat out of his age class; that in some respects he would have preferred to associate more intimately with some of his nephews on the managerial level, as he did before he was elected Farm Boss. His siblings and in-laws in the Elder generation were all older than he was by ten years or more, and he often felt he had little in common with them. "However," he remarked, "since I have been Farm Boss, I have settled down a lot." On the other hand, his wife, a woman in her thirties, still felt somewhat alienated from her elderly sisters-in-law, and she spent much time with the younger wives of the colony.

A comparison of Diagrams 1 and 2 shows that the instrumental organization of the colony described conformed to the sequence of generations: the Elder-executive group consisted of the second generation of the "Schmidt" family in the colony; the managerial group, of the third generation. However, other colonies mix second- and third-generation people at the managerial level. Since the "Schmidt" colony had a small population, every one of the second-generation men had to assume Elder responsibilities and leave the managerial jobs to the third generation. When, as in this case, the colony is small, the primary factor in assignment of jobs is not kinship but age, and the instrumental system of roles tends to approximate the kinship structure.

Living Together

To maintain an enclave of communal endeavor in the midst of a worldly and individualistic culture is not easy. The Hutterite is well aware that privacy, solitude, decision-making, and autonomy, the norms of the "outside," can, under the right circumstances, form the basis of a satisfying personal existence, but he also knows that they are forbidden to him. The demands of the Brethren's economic system, as well as the tenets of their faith, require them to live out their lives in the presence of many close relatives, to deny themselves even the most modest "luxuries," to avoid clashes of temperament, to obey the managers and the Elders, and generally to identify their own good with that of the collectivity. The Hutterites have many methods of ensuring behavioral conformity: for example, baptism can be conferred only if the candidate has no complaints against him. Every year, just before Easter, a church meeting is held at which persons involved in quarrels during the preceding months are required to rise and state that their differences have been settled. All colony members are expected to report serious breaches of conduct to the Elders. Strict sanctions are seldom resorted to, for the threat of their use is usually enough to control deviance. Public confession and the request for forgiveness, the standard Hutterian disciplinary procedures for adults, are regularly used, and are usually effective in promoting obedience. At all events, discipline is gentle and persuasive, not physical or drastic. Expulsion, the ultimate sanction, is rarely invoked.

The continued existence of every communal society depends to a great degree on the mutual forbearance of its members.[9] The "communal" person is one who does not habitually manifest "spirit," that is, a sense of his own rights, freely expressed. He does not *claim the right* to do this or that; he merely protests, or quietly resists, when he feels that the guarantees of equal treatment made to

[9] We do not know whether the term "communal society" has been applied to Japanese society, but seemingly such a concept would explain certain features of the Japanese social process. Achievement in Japanese society is obtained by maximal consideration of others; not, typically, by individualistic striving and competence alone. Achievement is a reward, by and large, for conformity to group norms and rules of procedure, not the reverse, as it is so often in American society. This is in essence the nature of the Hutterian achievement system. As shown in Chapter 6, the talented individual is afforded recognition by election to responsible office; he "achieves" this responsibility by behaving properly as well as by exhibiting interest and talent. But talent is not sufficient, and he must not openly seek office or other rewards, because to do so is to violate the rules of social procedure. If the Japanese case is similar, then a question arises as to the adequacy of this "agrarian" model of social organization for a modern industrial society. While some institutions of Japanese society are amenable to change, those that concern social relations are remarkably resistant. Material and technological changes are easily made, just as they are in the Hutterian case; certain social changes are more difficult, and have usually required extraordinary pressures, such as the defeat and American occupation. The communal aspects of Japanese society constitute an interesting paradox, in light of the fact that the millennial tradition in the West, which has repeatedly given rise to experimental societies and rifts with the established institutional system, has also produced one type of society that resembles the Oriental model of social stability. This is due to the fact that the utopian societies specifically react against individualism and competitiveness, and have as their goal the construction of a new *gemeinschaft*.

him in the chartered rules have been violated. (See Chapter 10 for descriptions of such situations). In other words, the communal person is not one who lacks a sense of individual "rights," but rather one who does not habitually claim rights; one who passively accepts the rewards due to him for respecting others and living up to the rules. It is the rules that define equality and individual achievement; these qualities and conditions exist only when members of the communal society obey the rules.

We recognize the paradoxes involved in comparing Hutterian with totalitarian or quasi-totalitarian sectors of modern societies. The Hutterite is a pietistic, egalitarian communalist—one could hardly find a more distant comparison to the modern totalitarian. But if any society, democratic or totalitarian, large or small, possesses a charter—a set of rules of social procedure to which adherence is required—it must have some means of enforcing these rules. (The charter, of course, need not be a recorded one.) The Hutterites seek to enforce rules that define egalitarianism and group decision-making, yet the very enforcement of these rules involves authoritarianism, which is accentuated by the patriarchal emphasis in the formal organization; an element of mutual suspicion; and what appears to an individual outsider as excessive deference to the wishes of others. The Hutterites, too, are aware that their methods of securing conformity are at least partial contradictions of the egalitarian spirit of their culture, and they therefore employ them with discretion.

"Awayness," or avoidance of interpersonal contact, is one means of resolving the contradiction. Hutterian life has its moments of freedom and self-expression, but they are relatively rare, and a social-emotional quietude or flatness is the everyday pattern. The lack of privacy and individual expression is felt more keenly by the men than by the women.[10] The latter, trained early to accept

---

[10] Nordhoff (1875, p. 410), writing on the utopian communalists of the American frontier, noted: "Some things the communist must surrender; and the most precious of these is solitude.... For in a well-ordered commune, there is hardly any possibility of privacy." Nordhoff also observed in the members of all of the religious utopias he visited the "dull and lethargic" or emotionally flat personality that many visitors note in the Hutterites. This observation is only partially correct.

much more severe restrictions on autonomy, develop many covert forms of self-expression and manipulation. On the other hand, most of the men can, from time to time, "escape" into town on an official trip, wander around the streets, loiter in the hotel lobby or perhaps even in the bar, gossip with Gentile friends, and vicariously experience the individualistic freedom of the "outside." The women have little opportunity for this; their visits to town are infrequent, and their movements are restricted to the streets and stores. There are no feminine gathering-places, and although very occasionally one sees Hutterian men and women together in a beer-parlor, most colonies frown on such visits.

The "awayness" in Hutterian interaction is symptomatic of a good deal of interpersonal tension and disagreement, some of which will be described and analyzed in Chapter 10. While the Brethren are thoroughly trained to feel and practice brotherly love, the vicissitudes of daily living and the conduct of a large enterprise inevitably generate tensions and difficulties. The techniques of avoidance serve to prevent these tensions from becoming open, public disputes; but at the same time, such techniques can promote an atmosphere of festering hostility. This is especially true of colonies whose leaders are inept at handling the tensions between families and individuals and internal disagreements over policy.

Hutterian life does have its moments of joy and release. The everyday atmosphere, with its avoidance of intimacy, its many unspoken commands and silent agreements and disagreements, gives way upon special occasion to festivity and spontaneity (often a little too much, in the opinion of the Elders). Religious holidays—Christmas, Easter, and Pentecost—are observed relatively quietly, but on the occasion of a wedding, the colony families enjoy themselves, both on a community scale and in separate *hulba* (dialect word for "party") sessions. Both wine and beer are served at these times. The Hutterites—at least the men—are not teetotalers; their Christian tradition is, after all, of sixteenth-century central-European origin. They make their own wine, buy beer in case lots, and relish schnapps (when someone else buys it; it is considered too expensive for colony purchase). Folk songs, both German and North

American, are a specialty of the women, who sometimes sing for visitors. The entire congregation sings a vigorous, seventeenth-century hymnal response during church services, at the top of its collective lungs. Christmas is a time for gift-giving: some of the colony's precious communal hoard of dollars is used to buy gifts; and the individual families may also spend their own small savings on gifts for special friends and relatives.

A general assessment of Hutterian society from the viewpoint of the Gentile community would emphasize the paradox inherent in the fact that while Hutterian life is lived in a total communal frame in which one's lifetime associations are predominantly with one's relatives, it is often lacking in spontaneous human interaction and open expressions of warmth. Life in a colony can be alienating and isolative, especially for the very old, for unusually "progressive" families, and for individual deviants. The Brethren's respect for religious injunction against open hostility tends to make them suppress all strong emotional expression. This repression creates the outward appearance of homogeneity and lack of familial distinctiveness already noted.

From the Hutterian point of view, the paradox of the Gentile community is that while it is individualistic and hence un-Christian, it is also more freely spontaneous and interactive. The Hutterites recognize that Gentiles are often more colorful and more interesting human beings than their own people; and the younger Brethren may seek out Gentiles as friends simply in order to bask in the warmth and expressivity of their personalities. This is why the Brethren welcome visitors—even resident visitors—although they are also constantly apprehensive of the "bad example" such outsiders may set the young people.

The Brethren's compensations for the necessary suppressions and avoidances of their daily lives are the familiar ones of institutionalized release and the normal interruptions of routine. Here certain "peasant" qualities in Hutterian life come to the fore: in the excitement over the return of the mother and her baby from the Jasper hospital; in family outings in the sparse grass near the houses, in the *schwatschmark* ("gabfest") and the song sessions.

"There is always something to look forward to," said one informant, referring both to these simple pleasures and to the fact that the Hutterite need not worry about the necessities of life. "No one has to want here; he can look forward to a long life and will always be taken care of, no matter what. A woman can go to the hospital for a baby and be sure her kids will be taken care of by the other women while she is gone. It is like that."

SIX

Instrumental Organization

The durability of the Hutterian social system constitutes one of its chief interests for the social scientist. Communal experiments generally are short-lived, but the Hutterian colony is in its fifth century. Since communal societies are difficult to organize and to maintain, the persistence of the Hutterian system raises important problems of social organization and process.

The reasons for the continued existence of the Hutterian communal social system can be found in its patterns of child socialization, in its ideologies and identity factors, in the balance struck between family autonomy and communal solidarity, and in its economic efficiency. In this chapter we will examine additional social factors that help explain the durability of the Hutterian colony: the organization of functional roles and task accomplishment, and the procedures of decision-making. Together, these factors constitute what we call "instrumental" or "formal" organization: that is, the operational or practical side of colony life. This organization is complex relative to the size of the population it serves. Its complexity derives from the needs of the diversified economy, and the institutional controls it must exert over disruptive and divisive tendencies among the colony members.[1]

---

[1] See the descriptions of cooperative communities of various kinds in Infield (1945). The basic structure of any communal or semi-communal settlement requires the following: (1) a set of institutional controls over individuating tendencies (which generally means devices to keep people interacting amicably with each other), and sanctions against hostile interaction; (2) specific decision-making ar-

The complexity and efficiency of the Hutterian system stand in contrast to the typical frontier communal sectarian society founded during the nineteenth century in the United States and Canada. Various studies (for example, Lockwood 1905; Bestor 1950) show clearly that the major cause of the disorganization and eventual demise of most frontier communal societies was their failure to evolve efficient institutional and managerial systems. In some extreme cases, ideals were expected to carry the commune to success; the practical organization of decision-making and economics was either neglected through ignorance or thought of as unworthy of attention. Even where a certain realization of the importance of organization was present, decay often set in before a suitable system of administration could be developed. In many cases, the difficulties were the result of the extreme heterogeneity and lack of preparation of the first recruits, who had not the slightest concept of the discipline required to live communally, and who were not shown how to do so by the leaders of the experiment. The case of Robert Owen's New Harmony community is a classic example of this situation: failure to control recruitment permitted large numbers of drifter types and failed farmers to enter the community, and neither Owen nor his lieutenants on the scene were aware of the difficulties that this implied. Moreover, the organizers of New Harmony were ill-prepared to deal with the highly technical needs of organized communal agrarianism; for example, during its first and only year, the New Harmony community had no qualified farming expert, and was even short of competent carpenters and craftsmen.

---

rangements that involve the entire community, not just a minority; (3) a diversified and intricate economy to support a relatively large number of people on what are usually relatively limited resources (i.e., few communal societies have ever been "rich," or have had unlimited resources, since they are almost always enclaves in larger societies, and must compete with individuals for what they have); (4) a commissary institution to provide for all the needs of all the members; and (5) a set of institutions to control the relationships of members with the outside, and protect the community against the influences of the outside world. These requirements constitute a larger administrative burden than would be found in the case of an equal number of individual farmers or residents of any rural or semi-rural district anywhere in the world, with the possible exception of certain agrarian areas of the rice-growing Orient, where institutional and organizational complexity also is great, owing to the nature of agricultural and resource-management tasks.

For the Hutterites, "the colony" is more than the settlement pattern of Hutterian populations; it is also the system of practical institutions that makes communal life possible. The structure of the Hutterian social system can be described in terms of three principal units. On one side, there are the kinship groups we described in the preceding chapter; these provide solidarity, but they are also potentially divisive, since the loyalties of nuclear families and other kin groups have the power to injure colony unity. On the other side, there are the economic activities, which support solidarity and continuity but also contain the seeds of disunity, since the separate enterprises technically compete for resources. In the middle lie the colony instrumental institutions—those procedures of role assignment and decision-making that control the differentiating tendencies of kinship and economic activities. This model is, however, not quite complete, since the colony instrumental organization does more than merely control individuation and factionalism; it also guarantees equal treatment to all. That is, in the light of Hutterian ideology, egalitarianism is a "right," not merely a sanction. ("Right" is our term—the Brethren do not use it.) Though an individual Hutterite has undergone discipline, at the same time he has the "right" to expect that others will be disciplined also. This guarantees his equal status. The dual aspect of the system helps to explain why it persists; it possesses important gratifications, and is not merely an efficient tyranny, as many of its local critics tend to believe.

Formal Organization

The present-day Hutterian formal organization—the arrangement within the colony of functional roles and tasks—is one expression of the colony's chartered social system; and it differs only in details from the system worked out during the Moravian era, when the Brethren were prosperous resident employees on great estates.[2] Diagram 3 was drawn with the help of Brethren in

---

[2] See Hersch (1931); Wolkan (1932); Loserth (1930); Smith (1950); Ziegschmid (1947); Infield (1945); and Friedmann (1961, Section IV).

Diagram 3

FORMAL ORGANIZATION OF THE HUTTERIAN COLONY

(All adult baptized males take part in the Assembly—the colony's group-decision body. Women do not participate or vote.)

GOVERNING ROLES

ELDERS, AUFSEHERN, OR CHIEF EXECUTIVES OF THE COLONY

1. CHURCH ELDER or FIRST MINISTER
(Spiritual leader; communications officer)
(Most colonies have a second minister)

2. HOUSEHOLDER or COLONY BOSS
(Business manager; financial officer)

3. FARM BOSS
(Personnel director; crops manager)

4. GERMAN TEACHER
(Teacher; mediator; counselor; often a second minister. Not always an executive—must be voted in. Often the Gardener.)

ADDITIONAL ELDERS or COUNCILLORS
(Semi-retired men not in executive jobs.)

(Authority principle: primus inter pares, but with slight gradation as represented by 1, 2, 3, 4.)

COUNCIL, OR VORSTEHEN DER GEMEINDE
(Made up of Elders, Aufsehern, or Chief Executives, in both elective and honorary positions.)
Membership: 4 Chief Executives; Councillors; plus 2 or 3 Farm Enterprise Managers, as below:

AGRICULTURAL MANAGEMENT ROLES

FARM ENTERPRISE MANAGERS (elective)
(Any number; varies with enterprise.)

TECHNICAL: BLACKSMITH MECHANIC CARPENTER SHOEMAKER ETC.	CATTLE (beef)	SWINE	SHEEP	CHICKENS, EGGS	DUCKS, GEESE	CROPS	GARDEN

(Authority: Over particular enterprises only—no gradation; no group organization.)

LABOR FORCE

A. LABORERS
(All men 15 years or older not in executive or managerial positions. When baptized, in voting group.)

B. ALL MEN IN EXECUTIVE-MANAGERIAL ROLES
(When available, or on call.)

FEMALE HIERARCHY

HEAD COOK
(Only executive position for women—not elective.)

GARDEN WOMAN
SCHOOL WOMAN
KINDERGARTEN WOMAN
(Workers, usually spinsters, rotate in jobs.)

C. ALL WOMEN
(Especially younger, unmarried.)

WOMEN DO NOT VOTE OR PARTICIPATE IN ASSEMBLY
→ ALL OTHER WOMEN

the Jasper colonies, and was checked against available published studies.[3] No significant differences were found in the accounts provided by these sources. The contemporary North American locus of Hutterian life is indicated by the English titles for some of the jobs; all titles in capital letters are those used familiarly by the Brethren today. The titles in lower-case are those used less frequently by the Brethren, and by analysts of Hutterian society, though many of the Brethren are familiar with such terms, since they read such sociological studies.

The system represented on Diagram 3 constitutes the entire formal organization of the colony. The church function has no separate structure; its only functional roles, those of the Ministers, are already represented on the diagram. This fact in itself indicates the synthesis of the practical and the spiritual in Hutterian society. The leaders of the church meetings are simply the men in the Elder or executive role category on the chart. At the church sessions, these men sit on a bench behind the lectern, facing the entire colony membership. The First Minister is in the central position, and it is he who conducts the services.

The placement of female roles on the right side of the chart mirrors the separation of men and women in the church services and in the communal dining hall. The women do not vote on colony affairs; and if a colony meeting is held after a church service, the women are excused before the business is discussed. The Hutterites do not emphasize this sexual role division, however, and there are no taboos against men and women associating or talking together in places other than the dining hall and the church. On informal eating occasions, for example, at a midnight supper after the return of berry pickers, or on mixed work details, the two sexes may eat together at the same table. The women are in sole charge of the kitchens and the food-storage areas; they may ask the men to leave these areas, or make it known that they are "in the way."

The women, with the possible exception of the Head Cook, are not part of the official organization of the colony; and it may

[3] See Clark (1924); Deets (1939); Infield (1945 and 1950); and Friedmann (1961, Section IV).

be technically misleading to include them on this diagram. The Head Cook, often the Householder's wife, is elected by the male voting body (one young man remarked that he would consult his wife before voting!). This office is regarded by the Brethren as a very important one, as well it might be for a population of hard-working outdoorsmen, and the Head Cook has considerable power and autonomy in her domain, which includes the kitchen and the other food preparation areas. The office is not, however, precisely an honor— in fact, no office is conceived as an "honor" by the Hutterites, since this would introduce an element of individuation contrary to the central dogmas of equal service and treatment. The Garden Woman and the Kindergarten Women are not elected, and really hold no official position; the latter are simply spinsters who entertain the pre-school children in the Children's House while their mothers are busy with other matters. The School Woman, often the German Teacher's wife, supervises the children at breakfast, which is served to them in the German School. In effect, the only consistent role for women in Hutterian society is that of wife and mother.

Diagram 3 shows two levels of authority. In the first, or "Governing Roles," are the chief executives, or Elders, who are in charge of colony affairs. Each of these roles contains both manifest and diffuse responsibilities: for example, the Church Elder or First Minister functions as court of last resort, guardian of tradition, and arbitrator of intra-colony disputes. He is also entrusted with the responsibility of disseminating information among the colony members on issues awaiting discussion or vote. The German Teacher is responsible for the education of the children, and is sometimes in charge of the colony garden as well—a dual role that places him on both the Elder and Agricultural Manager levels. He may also function as Second Minister, and be called upon to settle disputes. The Farm Boss is the agricultural manager in charge of field crops; but since this operation is the most demanding in terms of labor, he functions on the executive level as personnel director in charge of allocating labor. He is expected to be an agricultural expert, but usually the individual managers under him are more knowledgeable than he is about their respective operations. The Householder, or Colony Boss, represents the colony in dealings with officials in the Gentile community, and is in charge of financial management and bookkeeping as well.

There is a slight gradation of authority in the executive group, as represented by the numerical order of the functional roles on the chart. The Church Elder is thought of as the principal leader—the moral and spiritual paragon of the colony. Note, however, that the Householder—the chief economic executive—is next in authority. While in some colonies these two roles have much in common, the major difference between them is that the Householder's job is functionally specific, while the Church Elder's is more diffuse. The Church Elder can become involved in any phase of colony life he chooses, since he is the guardian of morality and tradition. Church Elders are likely to have held other executive positions, and may be skilled Householders as well as Ministers. A typical line of progression would be from Farm Boss to Householder to Church Elder. Evidence of the difference in degree of authority between the two positions emerges when advice is sought. On a particularly difficult issue, over which there is disagreement as to whether the matter should be considered formally by the voting body, the Church Elder will be consulted first; the Householder second. On issues of lesser moment, the Householder may be the only person consulted (although many Hutterites feel it is always wise to consult the Minister, or at least to check with him, on any and all issues).

The Council consists of all the executives and Elders, plus one or more of the agricultural managers. The Council meets whenever important business needs to be discussed, for example, major new machinery purchases, loans, inter-colony business, or construction plans. Older men without executive roles and semi-retired men automatically become members of the executive group and Council on the basis of age, although they have no specific executive jobs; and their advice is sought on most issues. The farm enterprise managers are expected to operate on their own, keeping their own books and solving their own labor problems, but reporting regularly to the Householder. These managers have no group organization, and while they may sometimes form functional cliques, they are prevented by certain competitive tendencies existing between them, and by kinship solidarity between brothers, from organizing any permanent bloc or "lobby" to represent their interests before the Council.

The principles of seniority are built into the Hutterian instrumental organization at several points, but they do not dominate it. The average age of job incumbents increases from the managerial to the executive positions, and up through the executive ranks to the role of Church Elder. The average ages of job-holders in the six Jasper colonies we studied were as follows. The mean age of shop foremen ("blacksmiths") was 31; the median age, 29. The mean age of sheep bosses was 32; the median age, 28. The mean age of Farm Bosses was 36; the median age, 34. The mean age of Householders was 44; the median age, 50. Finally, the mean age of Church Elders was 49; the median age, 52. (In this example, sheep bosses and shop foremen were taken as typical of the managerial group.)

The average ages of the Church Elders and Householders are younger than would be the case in a community of older colonies, where the Church Elders and Householders would be about 10 years older. This is because in the move to the Jasper region, several colonies had to elect new Ministers and Bosses. The considerable spread in the Householder ages also reflects the results of new elections in young colonies. This spread was assisted by the fact that one colony had an extremely young population, and a youthful contingent of executives and managers—all men in their 20's or 30's, except for one manager in his 60's. This situation is unusual, particularly in view of the fact that this colony included men in their 50's and 60's who were *not* in leadership roles. The colony in question is Colony 6—the one described in Chapter 3, which chose to contend with the difficult environmental conditions found at the 3,700-foot elevation in the Cypress Hills. This particular group was second to occupy the colony premises; the original group, from the same parent colony, failed to establish a viable enterprise. The second and more youthful group was encouraged by its parent group and by the Ministers of other colonies called for advice, to abrogate Hutterian seniority rules and to select its youngest and most vigorous men for critical executive roles. This policy paid off; the alterations in established routines necessary for adaptation to the habitat were carried through by the young group, often in spite of the objections of their elders. The writer served as a kind of agricultural consultant to this colony for a brief period, and thus was able to observe its social system and economy in detail; and he is confident that the chief reason for its relative success in this difficult district was that the colony was run by young men unafraid to adapt and innovate.

The Brethren often say that when two equally good candidates are competing for a managerial or executive position, the older will get the vote. A check on candidates in two colonies over a five-year period bore this out. However, there are no written rules that enjoin election by seniority; such preference seems instead to be largely a matter of job progression: a man is expected to move up through managerial and executive positions as he matures and accumulates experience. There can be little question but that the ministerial roles require the sort of perceptiveness and understanding that traditionally are believed to come with age and experience; and that the Householder and Farm Boss roles require the previous experience of enterprise management. It should be remembered that since the Hutterian Brethren's basic values and social structure change little or not at all, age *does* bring wisdom—that is, practice and experience in the chartered social system. It is only when a colony is forced to make a sudden change—as in the case of Colony 6, which had to adapt to new environmental parameters—that seniority becomes a liability. Generally, the Hutterites strongly emphasize the necessity for good leadership, and believe that if a colony has good executives, its social and economic well-being is assured (Gross 1965, p. 42).

In matters of seniority the Brethren can show the same flexibility that one finds them exercising in management contexts. Gentiles have been known to say of colony Elders, "Those old men really run the place." This is true in a sense, insofar as the Ministers are the chief officials, have great influence, and are usually the oldest non-retired men in the colony. Their main powers lie in the sphere of personal conduct and the religious traditions, and they do make the Brethren and their women toe the line. However, there are many spheres of decision and authority in a colony, and the "old men" are not necessarily influential in all of them. Their primary influence is moral and social; and they are not necessarily deferred to in technical matters, which almost everyone realizes should be in the hands of the most capable, regardless of age. The Hutterites thus combine rule by authority with democratic-functional leadership principles.[4]

The colony labor force (see Diagram 3) consists of all males over the age of 15. The executives and managers are prevented by administrative duties from assuming routine labor responsibilities, but at times of major effort, such as a harvest, they take an active part. The labor group proper consists of men without executive or managerial training. Generally these men are machine operators, highly skilled at running and repairing their implements. Most of

---

[4] The formal organization of the kibbutz closely resembles the Hutterian system. Differences appear mainly in the kibbutz tendency toward management by committee rather than by executive responsibility, a state of affairs that arises partly from the emphasis placed by the kibbutz on participative democracy, and partly from the large size of the kibbutz, which demands a large number of management personnel. The kibbutz has a general assembly made up of all members, including the women, which discusses and votes upon major issues and elects all officers and managers. There is a general business manager, corresponding to the Householder, who employs several assistants and a clerical staff. The duties of the members of this staff are rotated from time to time, although there is an increasing tendency to leave some of the bookkeeping functions in the hands of particular individuals indefinitely. The several enterprise branches are under the direction of managers, who also rotate positions, and who constitute an executive committee. This system differs from that of the colony, where the managers are more autonomous, and do not generally share executive responsibility. The colony Council resembles the kibbutz executive committee, but is not strictly comparable to it, since the Council is dominated by the Elder-executives. At the same time, many kibbutzim currently display tendencies toward more centralization of authority at the executive level (among the manager and his staff, and some branch managers), and a lessening of interest in management on the part of the assembly of members. Despite their differences, colony and kibbutz formal organization is basically similar in its structure, and the kibbutz system, despite verbal emphasis on democratic participation, seems to be moving toward the colony pattern of greater executive control.

them will be voted into managerial or even executive positions in time. When a new colony forms, new positions are created; and sooner or later almost all the Brethren get their chances to assume leadership roles. The colony fission process not only relieves the colony's economic and population pressures, but also provides opportunities for such personal advancement as Hutterian tenets will allow.[5]

Formal Decision-making

The Hutterian colony, like the kibbutz, has an assembly that debates and votes upon every issue affecting colony life. However, the Hutterites, unlike the *kibbutznikim*, do not permit women to participate in their assemblies, or to vote. Each man has one vote, and decisions are made on the basis of a simple majority. Voting is vocal, except during the election of executives and managers, when written ballots are generally used (voting procedures may vary slightly from colony to colony). Most assembly meetings are held immediately after church on Saturday night or on Sunday. Important issues may require a special meeting, in which case the big colony bell will be rung to assemble the men. Such issues are usually thoroughly discussed and analyzed by the executives and the Council, and by informal groups of concerned individuals,

---

[5] The Hutterites display concern over the incentive, or satisfaction, problem, and in compensation for the fact that the Brethren are strictly enjoined not to compete or to expect rewards, seek to give every man a rewarding job commensurate with his abilities. The kibbutz situation is quite different. Because of the large size of the community, there are many individuals who are not interested in responsible positions, and are quite content to work in menial positions, since the relatively high level of living is fairly uniform. Kibbutz executives told the writer that in recent years it has become difficult to attract young men into managerial positions, and that this is caused at least in part by the steadily rising standard of living in the kibbutz. The kibbutz policy on satisfaction and incentive has been developed for the purpose of making the community an attractive and comfortable "home," so that people will not want to leave permanently. The Hutterites discourage "homelike" qualities, for unnecessary comforts are regarded as "idolatrous"—that is, they constitute an attempt to substitute worldly joys for the love of God. Hence it follows that the Hutterites have been required to provide responsibility incentives.

before they are brought to a vote. If it is felt that agreement or consensus already exists, a decision may be made without assembly
action; but this procedure is viewed by most Brethren as dangerous,
and in any event it violates Hutterian rules, which require that all
issues be decided by formal vote. The majority of issues voted
upon receive affirmative votes, which indicates careful consideration before group action is sought (in one colony, over a period of
three years only five out of thirty propositions were voted down).
Considerable open discussion occurs at the assemblies, and the
laborer group takes part in them without embarrassment. However,
since most of the relevant information is in the hands of the executives and managers, it is usually they who make the most decisive
and cogent comments.

An executive or manager may, with good reason, resign from his
post. It is up to the colony to elect a replacement. As already noted,
there is a tendency for age to be the decisive factor when more or
less equally qualified candidates are available for a vacancy. There
is no formal submission of candidates before the assembly; the matter is simply placed before the group for a vote (it has already been
discussed informally throughout the colony), and the voters are
asked to write the name of the man they prefer on their ballot. If
there is a tie, the position is awarded by lot.

The election of Ministers usually proceeds on the basis of special
rules: among the colonies of the Darius Leut, the *Älteste,* or Leut
"bishop," officiates at the election. A slate of eligible candidates
is selected by vote of the Bishop and his assistant Elders, and the
colony must choose one of them. All votes for officers are recorded
in the colony minutes; the Brethren say they have found that it is
always better to keep a record of who votes for whom, since this
helps to protect the Minister from accusations of tampering with
the ballot count.[6]

---

[6] The Lehrer Leut executives are voted on by both the mother and daughter
colonies; in the Darius Leut, the new colony has sole right to vote on its own
bosses. The Lehrer pride themselves on their record of colony stability, and attrib-
ute this to the care with which they choose their Elders. The Darius experience
colony difficulties as the price of greater autonomy, but this autonomy also permits
them to vote younger men into executive positions.

Hutterian "democratic theory" (our term) is based on the idea that the voting process is really a means by which the will of God speaks through the assembly of Christians on earth. In elections, men must not seek out positions, but must wait until "God draweth them out and chooseth them."[7] The "lot" (vote) is the expression of the spiritual majority who, on that occasion, serve as "God's agents." A man is not looked down upon for having voted with the minority: Christians are imperfect servants of God, and they are not always in a position to feel God's will. This whole theory is, of course, held most seriously with regard to the election of the executives, especially the Church Elder, and least strongly for practical decisions about colony activity. It is the spiritual justification of a particular orderly procedure of conduct of the affairs of the group, and it is not on the same level with the major ideological commands of communalism and austerity. Still, voted issues of any kind have an almost sacred quality, since they bind the community to certain courses of action, and thus form the character of Hutterian life. The accumulated decisions made by the Leut Council of Ministers is called the *Ordnungen,* and can be regarded as the "constitution" of the Hutterian society.

The existence of this constitution-like basis of Hutterian life symbolizes the rational character of Hutterian society. In one sense of the word, Hutterian society is not "natural"; that is, it does not develop or function with complete spontaneity, but always according to rational plan and always under maximal control. The system's overt rationality makes it difficult to classify under social science terms based on a conception of a relatively freely-developing society, or a social system which is, to a large extent, a matter of interpersonal interaction outside of bureaucratic contexts. Hutterian social life is almost always part of a "bureaucratic" situation, due to the high level of rational decision-making and planning. Thus the social-science concept of "role" often must be replaced with a term like "job" or "assigned function," since the individual's role in the system is really an elected position. However, there are relatively

[7] Rideman (1565, 1950, pp. 80–81). The passage also reiterates the dangers of ambition.

autonomous spheres in Hutterian life, particularly in the privacy of the nuclear family, where the usual social-science concepts can be applied.

Though the Hutterites do not allow women to vote on colony affairs, and maintain a body of privileged Elders, we regard their overall system of decision-making as democratic in emphasis and operation. The face-to-face quality of colony life makes it difficult for anyone to assume arbitrary authority. Moreover, all important decisions are thoroughly aired and talked over before they come to a vote, so that a clear understanding of the issues is obtained by all. One of the Church Elder's most important duties is to see to it that every adult colony member is kept informed of impending decisions and matters of concern to the community. The conduct of work is equally democratic: the Farm Boss is careful not to issue arbitrary orders, and he allows his workers considerable latitude. "You have to be careful with these fellows. You get too bossy with them, and there will be trouble. We don't try to push too hard." (In Chapter 10, we will comment on a few instances when arbitrary authority was used by colony leaders.)

The Israeli kibbutz offers a contrast to some of these patterns. Descriptions of kibbutz procedures emphasize "idealism and free will" (Darin-Drabkin 1961, p. 95) as the basis of kibbutz democracy—elements generalized from the distinctive history of the kibbutz as a community formed by voluntary memberships. In this same passage, the author paraphrases an Israeli researcher, Y. Shatil, who remarked that there is no democratic principle inherent in collective living. "History has known ... forms of communal life which were based on government by the 'Elders of the Community' as a stratum of privileged persons." Presumably the Hutterian system would be undemocratic from this doctrinaire point of view. Actually the Brethren combine government by the Elders, who maintain the symbolic unity and solidarity of the community, with genuine group decision for the resolution of everyday issues. The kinship basis of the colony structure is so effective a safeguard against the establishment of autocratic rule by any group within the instrumental organization that the Hutterites are often heard to complain of "inadequate" leadership. They seek to balance the authority of the Elders with primary-group egalitarianism and permissiveness, but they have no wish to operate without competent leaders and mentors in both the spiritual and the practical sphere.

Still, the viewpoint from the kibbutz ideological perspective raises a question: to what extent could order and obedience to the communal norms be maintained without a patriarchal body, without the charismatic authority of the Minister? Would Hutterian social order be possible with a less stratified, more completely egalitarian system? The question is really impossible to answer, for the Hutterian system has already adjusted to a hierarchal system, and finds paternalistic authority necessary and useful. The Brethren do not perceive a conflict between the norm of an egalitarian brotherhood and that of a patriarchy; they rationalize and accept this apparent conflict by Biblical references and by reference to patriarchal tradition in Judeo-Christian history. There is a distinct Old Testament air about the Hutterian system which is an echo of their obvious similarity to Jewish sectarian communalists like the Essenes, who likewise had strong patriarchal and hierarchal traditions.

Incentive, Recruitment, and Competition

According to many students of industrial society, the basic problem of communal and collective economies is their apparent lack of the factors that are believed to provide the individual motive power for economic effort. This problem has been fundamental to the endless debate over socialist and communist ideologies, and it has been dominant in the historical analyses of American utopian communities, particularly New Harmony, which had troubles of this kind (Bestor 1950, pp. 164–65).

In the exposition of capitalist-industrial incentive, as developed by Barnard, among others, a distinction is made between the job, and the prestige or rewards conferred upon the individual by the job.[8] A man works hard to acquire a position because this will bring him material or non-material rewards. Another element of the theory holds that competition spurs the individual onward. While this may be a more or less accurate description of incentive in industrial society, it does not apply to the Hutterian situation. "Incentive," in colony terms, is difficult to understand, for there is no pay, no prestige, no status to speak of, and no visible competition between individuals for positions. Among the Hutterites, labor is not an end value; and no matter what job a man has, he receives exactly the same subsistence support, comforts, and recreation as all the others. The ideological goal of Hutterian life is to maintain true Christian identity as an example to mankind; the major practical goal is the maintenance and continuity of the particular colony as a social and economic entity. The activities of all the members of the colony are expected to contribute to these goals, and therefore a job is not a personal end but rather a social means. The performance of the job role is viewed as its own reward, and such performance has the function, as well as the sanction, of furthering the welfare of the colony. Ideally, the selection of certain individuals for certain jobs is not based on competition, and overt praise of talent is avoided; there exists only the recognition implicit in a majority vote, which in Hutterian ideology is a manifestation of the will of God. It is felt that there is no need for public recognition of a man's personal excellence; the continued performance of the task is itself recognition, since this performance enables the colony to exist. There is a complete lack of "incentive" as defined in terms of occupational success.

While this is an accurate description of an ideal Hutterian situation, it is necessary to qualify it in certain respects. In the first place there *is* a hierarchy of jobs in terms of authority and respon-

[8] Barnard (1950). See especially Chapter 11 and p. 145. Lincoln (1951) is a useful "folk" document on incentive, full of such aphorisms as "Man is always in competition with his contemporaries"; "Recognition is real incentive"; and "Pride is a fundamental urge." Actually, Barnard (1950, p. 148) has recognized "communion" as a factor in incentive, but this is added to the competitive factors, and is presented as part of the desirable atmosphere of the organization—something to keep people contented, and to ameliorate the destructive effects of material incentives.

sibility, and some of these jobs *do* possess small elements of material privilege. In the second place, there *does* exist a special form of competition between the agricultural managers. With regard to the differences in authority and responsibility, it is clear that the executives and Elders have the responsibility of guidance and policy-formation. Agricultural managers are entrusted with the maintenance of the colony economy. Both these levels are recognized by the Brethren as being of utmost importance to the colony's welfare. These two levels of elective roles are hierarchically arranged, and when asked, the Hutterites will draw diagrams that place the executive roles above the managerial. However, they will never verbalize the functional difference as reflecting a difference in privilege or prestige, and in fact there is considerable interchangeability and progression of jobs as the colony matures.[9]

Some Brethren remain in the ranks of laborers throughout life, but the present ecology of the colonies requires nearly every man to work at managerial or executive jobs sooner or later. In a colony of about 75 persons, almost half will be fifteen years of age or younger; about seventeen men or less will do all the farm work and management. Perhaps ten of these will be unmarried or unbaptized. As a colony grows older, the number of mature men without managerial or executive positions increases—when the population reaches about 130, seventeen men of the forty or so who are eligible will hold all such jobs. It is usually at this point, however, that colony fission occurs; and when it does, men who wish responsible positions generally find it possible to obtain them. In all the Jasper colonies we studied, only two men of middle age were still in laborer positions.

Hutterian roles carry slight differences in privilege. The Ministers are permitted to eat in their own quarters, but the other executives eat in the communal dining hall with the colony. Even this privilege is marginal: many Ministers would really prefer to eat with the colony, and the "privilege" is more a matter of form

[9] The only overt evidence of dissatisfaction with a particular role was displayed by a few of the managers, who indicated that they were "tired of the same old job year after year."

than of personal preference or gratification. The managers, by virtue of the fact that they control the farming enterprises, may drive vehicles to town. Depending upon the enterprise, they may be excused from many types of manual labor (although every man is pressed into service for the major tasks, such as harvesting and planting). Laborers are aware of these differences. When asked what he would do if he became the Farm Boss, one of them said, without hesitation, "I would put on a white shirt and go to town!"[10] In remarks of this kind one may see aspiration, or at least a hope for privileges. However, Hutterian men never *consciously* aspire, or consciously and openly prepare themselves for managerial or executive positions. The seniority tendency in the executive roles limits such behavior, and the broad informal training given from childhood on in a variety of tasks equips every man reasonably well for almost any job. Skills and increasing maturity bring their own "rewards."

There is some evidence that young men who wish to do so are allowed to prepare themselves for the intellectual jobs in the colony by reading and study. The writer associated with some of these young men, and is sure that they realize the likelihood of their eventual selection as Teachers or Church Elders. However, they did not verbalize this as a personal aspiration, and did not appear to understand questions by the writer designed to uncover ambition. The tone of their behavior was simply that of routine expectancy; that is, if a man makes a special effort to read Hutterian history and to study the Bible, he may expect to be chosen as a Minister. One remarked simply that it is the duty of a man who can read well to spend time on Hutterian literature, in addition to his other duties. In fact, however, only a very few really follow this admonition to read, and those who do are obviously the ones who will be considered for the jobs that require such knowledge.

With regard to competition, further detail will be presented in

---

[10] A very curious remark, incidentally, since Farm Bosses never wear white shirts to town! Like all other Brethren, they wear white shirts only at the colony, at church and on ceremonial occasions. The remark is indicative of the Hutterite's assimilation of "outside" prestige symbols.

Chapters 7 and 10, but we can provide a summary here. By "competition" we do not refer to active, overt competition between individuals for positions, because there is no evidence that this exists among the Brethren. However, the managers are in a de facto competitive position for resources: each must ask the executives for money to finance the development of his enterprise, and each must be prepared to accept refusal in the interest of the common good. The rather surprising autonomy of the individual managers, and the fact that they rarely constitute a social clique, suggests that there are adjustments built into the instrumental structure to accommodate the pressures of competitive stress. Evidence from colonies that have experienced difficulties indicates that while such stress usually starts at the executive level, one of its secondary symptoms is the tendency for individual managers to begin operating their enterprises as private affairs—pocketing proceeds, floating their own loans, and so on. Gentile cooperative farms in Saskatchewan have foundered for similar reasons: the individual members of some co-ops began to seek to appropriate for themselves community proceeds and land.

It is possible, therefore, to characterize the colony social system as functionally differentiated, but only marginally differentiated on prestige principles, and lacking in overt competition. There does exist, however, a degree of personal hope for or expectation of acquirement of the privileges that accompany official duties; and because of the structure of the economy, an indirect form of competition does exist between the managers. The Brethren seek to eliminate personal ambition and competition by emphasizing communalism and egalitarianism, and the executives are expected to watch carefully for signs of anti-social tendencies. Men in managerial or executive positions who manifest such tendencies will be called to account in the colony meeting, and "talked to" informally by the executives.

These aspects of status and achievement permit some observations concerning the role of the Hutterites in the development of Western civilization. The Hutterian social order provides a fresh perspective on the key elements of the "Protestant Ethic," a configuration of values and social-emotional patterns proposed by Max Weber (1904) as the ground for the development of the capitalistic spirit. According to David McClelland (1961, pp. 55–56), the individual need to achieve has its origins in the "independence and mastery training by parents" characteristic of Western family life. The Hutterites seem to feel little need to achieve, but they certainly are given strong incentives to do well for the good of the group. Moreover, they are trained in self-mastery; they are taught to control their impulses and forgo their desires for the good of all. The result is almost a caricature of the classic Weberian type of the Protestant businessman who, ideologically barred from spending money on his pleasures, reinvests it in his business.

The Hutterian case illustrates the fact that very strong incentives to produce, and, if not to "achieve," at least to perform well, can arise in a social system that negates individualism. One is therefore inclined to believe that the early capitalist spirit was really a combination of two things, achievement motivation and individualism; and that the two are, in fact, separable. The Hutterites exemplify the theory that strong incentive can exist in social systems that suppress individualistic competition and aspiration.

The Jasper region from the Cypress Hills.

Stone houses built by South Dakota Hutterites soon after their arrival from Russia. A similar "row-house" design is used today in wooden structures.

A typical Northern Plains colony.

The men's side of the dining hall.

Women at dinner.

Using the last rays of daylight.

Group labor: men from several colonies cooperate in constructing a new barn.

Group labor: men pouring the foundation for a new grain storage building.

Hutterites repairing machinery with modern equipment.

Hutterian women painting a house from the bucket of a tractor.

Hutterian children in everyday costume.

Boys learn to drive tractors early. Toys are almost nonexistent, and children are allowed to play instead with farm machinery.

Women and children working in the garden. Male supervisor at right.

SEVEN

The Hutterian Economy

The economic implementation of the Hutterian withdrawal from the "World System" is the production, on the colony premises, of food and material objects needed in domestic and economic activities. The original ideal was one of total self-sufficiency, although this was never fully realized in the past, and is even further away today. However, the original economic image of the colony was that of a self-sufficient island in the midst of the interdependent economy of "the outside" with its specialized production and commerce. This concept had its historical antecedents in the medieval monastic community, and in the manors and estates of the nobility of the sixteenth century.

Economic Ideals and Objectives

Communal self-sufficiency means diversification, and the colony was founded on this concept; agriculture was originally only one of many economic activities. As we noted in Chapter 2, when Hutterites reached their first peak of prosperity and numbers during the Moravian period, they practiced nearly every important sixteenth-century craft, plus the arts of estate-management, bookkeeping, letter-writing, medicine, and other professional services. They were, and are, barred by their beliefs from trade and commerce, which is inherently individualistic and competitive; hence their crafts were generally used only for colony needs, although in Moravia the Brethren did engage in some sale of their products. Various crafts and professional skills were practiced by large numbers of artisans and other professional men who had become converts to Anabaptism. Peasant converts were apparently in the majority, but the lack of available land, and the soil exhaustion in most of the regions inhabited by the early colonies seem to have encouraged the development of crafts over agriculture (Gross 1965, p. 30). The remarkable versatility of the Hutterites was what led the Moravian lords to invite them to their estates, and later persuaded Catherine the Great to invite the Brethren and other German sectarians to teach the Russian peasants by example their methods of production.[1]

The move to Russia reversed one prevailing trend, and encouraged agriculture over craft industry, because while the Ukraine was lacking in markets and resources for craft production, it abounded in good soil and available land. By the 1870's, when the Brethren moved to South Dakota, they had ceased to engage in craft production, and had become agricultural producers, although they still made most of their own tools and household articles. Since the resources in South Dakota closely resembled those found in the Ukraine, the colonies were able at first to duplicate their Russian farming program in the New World. However, the growing commercialization and specialization of North American agriculture soon required a more intensive agricultural regime, and hence correspondingly less time was given to home manufactures. To meet the need to support a relatively large colony population on a relatively limited land area, the Brethren inevitably tended toward the development of labor-saving devices and mechanization. This was supported by Hutterian traditions of expertise and efficiency. With regard to diversification, the Hutterian economic system could be said to be preadapted to the evolving form of Northern Plains agriculture.

By the 1960's, the garden remained the only substantial area of home production in the Hutterian economy. Those articles still made by hand included most clothing, shoes, most furniture (espe-

[1] See Friedmann (1961, Section 11), and Klassen (1962).

cially chests, cabinets, and hatracks), and a few traditional types of children's toys. Some tools and farm implements, and a few kitchen items are still manufactured in the shops of the colony with modern equipment, but such items are duplicates of factory-made articles. The Brethren also build their own dwelling houses and farm buildings in the North American style (though the dwellings are still built on the ancient European row-house plan), and use modern construction materials.[2] Clothing, with the exception of some underwear and heavy outer garments, is still made at home on sewing machines, from factory-made fabrics and findings (it is more profitable for the Brethren to sell their wool than to spin it). Most colonies bind their own hand-copied books of sermons and commentaries; some make stainless steel utensils; some repair clocks; others knit socks by machine. Not all of these pursuits are financially important: many are engaged in to perpetuate the "self-help" tradition, and others supply recreation, especially during the long winter (see Table 8). A typical Hutterian living apartment may have as much factory-made furniture as home-made, although the commercial articles are usually purchased in secondhand stores and are stripped of paint and decoration to conform to the Hutterian taste for varnished natural wood finishes. We noted in Chapter 4 the extent to which the Brethren rely on local stores for their basic food staples; they no longer grind flour or make sugar, but like most Jasper farms and ranches they produce their own vegetables, dairy products, and meats.

---

[2] Despite modern methods and designs, Hutterian craftsmanship is traditional, in that the trades are learned on the colony premises and transmitted by apprenticeship. The Hutterites very rarely send their young men to trade schools, but prefer to keep up with new methods by self-teaching. Carpentry patterns and techniques are handed down by colony craftsmen (in one colony, the writer was shown a shop attic containing models going back to the sect's days in Russia). Moreover, there is considerable interchangeability of skills; nearly every man is capable of making the traditional chests and cabinets, as well as doing his part in automotive repair and farm implement manufacture. Versatility seems to be the rule in most of the religious communal societies: compare the description of craftsmanship in the Shaker communities (Andrews and Andrews, 1937, pp. 35–38) "The skill of the more talented individuals was more widely distributed [than in a Gentile community]." The Shakers deliberately rotated jobs among the male members of their communities. The Hutterites do not strictly follow this principle, but the result is nearly the same.

Table 8—Handicrafts in the Jasper colonies

Craft	Colony					
	1	2	3	4	5	6
Furniture making . . .	3	2	2	2	2	1
Tailoring	1	1	1	1	1	1
Shoemaking	2	2	2	3	2	2
Simple toys	X	X	X	X	X	X
Rug weaving	X	X	X	X	X	X
Wool spinning	X	X	X	X	X	X
Winter sock knitting (by hand)	X	X	X	X	X	X
Winter sock knitting (by machine)	X	X		X	X	
Quilting	X	X	X	X	X	X
Tin and stainless steel utensil making[a] . . .				1	3	
Clock repairing				1		3
Bookbinding	2			1		

Key:
  X = Unimportant economically, but routinely done.
  1 = Highly developed; economically significant.
  2 = Moderately developed.
  3 = Poorly developed or newly developed.

  [a] A new Hutterian craft, developed in the 1950's and '60's.

It is conceivable that if Hutterian population had remained static, the colony might have persisted as a self-sufficient "island"; an exotic sectarian establishment insulated from the market; an enclave of sixteenth-century peasants in the modern world. However, the Hutterites do not believe in practicing birth control, and so they continue to increase and thus to create the need for additional colony sites. The colonies need more and more cash in order to buy more and more land. This reduces the amount of cash available for other things, and makes efficient production a necessity. Consequently the Brethren's entrance into the modern agricultural market and their adoption of labor-saving mechanization were inevitable.

At the same time that the Hutterian population has been steadily increasing, land has become progressively more difficult to find—which has meant that in recent years the colonies have had to seek out submarginal areas and northern frontiers in order to find the large blocks of acreage they need. Such land is productive only in the presence of agricultural methods of high efficiency; and these methods become even more of a necessity when the number of persons to be supported on the land is relatively large.

Young colonies starting out, or any colony unable to realize the levels of productivity needed for saving, will be helped by other colonies. In extreme cases of need, the colony may be dissolved and its members absorbed by others. However, dissolution happens rarely, because of the efficiency and industriousness of the Hutterites, and also because of the profound sense of shame felt at the failure of a colony to manage its affairs successfully—a circumstance that is seen by the Brethren as not merely an economic failure, but also as a failure of the "true" Christian way of life. Neighbors may envy the Brethren their seeming prosperity and accomplishments, but they are usually unaware of the fact that Hutterian determination and activity are survival necessities, and not simply a manifestation of strong character. The careful saving, and the strenuous efforts devoted to planning and self-help, particularly in the garden, are not just quaint Hutterian customs, but are necessary for the reduction of expenditures. In one Jasper colony, the value of home-produced food at current retail prices was almost exactly $10,000, which is incidentally the average amount of annual savings required to accumulate $200,000 in twenty years, or the period many colonies take to progress from establishment to fission. In the 1960's, $200,000 was also the typical price for about 11,000 acres of submarginal farmland in most Northern Plains districts— a desirable quantity of land for a new colony to have.

The Brethren's abandonment of total self-sufficiency, and their reliance on cash, represent adjustments to the market economy, in which the cost of manufactured articles is low in comparison to the value of the human labor needed to make them at home. Labor yields greater returns when it is used for the production of agricultural commodities that can be sold for relatively high prices. By virtue of its land area and population the Hutterian colony is and always has been a large-scale diversified enterprise; therefore it has been better equipped to adjust to the modern form of agricultural production than its Gentile neighbors with their smaller farms. Generally speaking, the larger the size of the enterprise unit, the lower the per-acre or per-capita costs of production will be. Thus the decision of the colonies to mechanize was not merely an ideological decision but also an economic necessity. Our informants stated that the use of machines came, as it did among the Gentile farmers, when large-scale production required it: "We have all the latest, the best—you know, the modernest stuff. Why not? You spend your money, you might as well have the best. We stayed with the old things [i.e., cheaper equipment and horse-drawn machines] as long as we could, but you couldn't make no money with them; and you just couldn't get around on the roads with them old wagons fast enough. We changed, like everybody."

The history of mechanization in Hutterian agriculture, as gained from informants at the Jasper colonies, suggests that it followed a pattern well-established in both North America and the British Isles (see Meij 1960, p. 147). The first stage, begun in South Dakota and completed in Canada in the 1930's, involved the replacement of horse-drawn equipment with tractors and trucks. However, some cultivating implements of the old horse-drawn type were still used, and a few of these can be seen today in the older colonies in Alberta, where they remain available for the use of the offspring colonies, if they lack sufficient funds at the outset to buy all the equipment they need. The second stage of mechanization, reached by most colonies in the 1940's, involved the replacement of the old implements by powered and mechanical devices. This second stage was marked by an emphasis on capital over labor. The third stage, reached by colonies in the late 1950's and early 1960's, involved the purchase of highly specialized labor-saving devices like hydraulic post-pounders, automatic milkers, automatic bale-stackers, and forage harvesters, and thus furthered the shift to a capital-oriented agriculture. For all six colonies in our study, the move to Saskatchewan meant an inevitable rise to this third stage, since it became clear to everyone involved that establishment in this high-risk environment could be attained most effectively by investing in such equipment and thereby permitting the labor force to work more productively on machine maintenance and high-income products like eggs and swine. Generally speaking, the younger colonies are more highly mechanized than the older, since very little second-hand machinery is transferred to new colonies at fission.

The Ideal of Austerity

The Hutterites are the only group in North America who enforce consumption austerity on a collective basis. Old Order Amish and conservative Mennonites also live austerely, but enforcement is not communal. Their rejection of material values alienates the Hutterites from Gentile society, even though that society too in its early days held out goals other than prosperity for its own sake and the pursuit of pleasure. But the Brethren go further than expediential frontier austerity; they have always rejected, and still reject, personal possessions, perceiving them as hindrances on the Christian path. For them, austerity is not merely a positive virtue—it is a way of life.

In studying the austerity customs of communal societies, it is necessary to distinguish between personal and communal, or collective, consumption. The former concerns expenditures for goods used only by individuals; the latter, goods used by the entire group. The Israeli kibbutz, for example, has a very high communal consumption level, expressed in such things as swimming pools, motion-picture projection equipment, paid vacations for every member, and the like. However, the individual consumption level of the kibbutz, while higher than that of the Hutterian colony, is lower than that of comparable socioeconomic class groups in Israel, owing to the small monthly stipends allotted the kibbutz family units for spending. The Hutterites limit *both* collective and personal consumption: openly, on religious grounds, and covertly, on financial grounds, for the savings provided by general austerity are vital to the colony economy.

However, the Hutterites are not poverty cases, even though the per capita or per family income of the typical colony is quite low in comparison with that of the average individual farm or ranch. Other measures of wealth—gross income, efficiency of production, savings, capital values, and income per laboring man—are all relatively high. The austerity of Hutterian life shows up in the uniformity and sparsity of possessions and furnishings in the various households, and in the remaining areas of self-help such as the production of food and clothing. As noted, the savings effected by self-help are substantial; and the same can be said for austerity. There is no doubt that in the young colonies the economic balance is sustained by consumption controls. This is not, of course, the case for the older and wealthier colonies, who could afford to spend more on possessions; but even in these cases, capital savings are used in loans to impecunious new colonies, and unusually large bank balances are not maintained.

Our experiences with the Brethren left no doubt in our minds that the average Hutterite is inclined to want more in the way of personal possessions than the colony allows him to have. There is, of course, a degree of habituation to austerity and a general acceptance of it; and on a value-attitude scale, the Hutterites would probably be at the low end, as compared to the Gentile population. However, the general level of desire is higher than the general level of possession. This is reflected in the frequent statements in Hutterian literature to the effect that it *is* difficult to live apart and differently from the Gentiles, and not to share in the rich and interesting world of commodities. The Brethren are able to acknowledge their human desires, and to recognize that they themselves do not perfectly follow the way they have chosen. Austerity is a highly conscious dogma and procedure, not a symptom of a conservative or ignorant peasant mentality.

The explanation of the relative success of the austerity system is to be found in the communal basis of Hutterian life, and in the relatively small population of the typical colony. The low consumption of the individual Hutterite is maintained not entirely by will power, but also by the face-to-face quality of life, and by the specific instrumental procedures of colony finances, such as the absence of a wage payment system, the control of all the funds by the Householder, and the small monthly expense allowances for family units; as well as by constant reminders, in sermons and on other occasions, of the need to save and to live austerely for both economic and religious reasons. The existing level of living thus becomes a standard which all must follow; the force of the system is to be found in its communal pattern. If the individual breaks with it, and begins to acquire possessions, he does so by illegal means. Any change in the level of consumption is voted on by the entire group, and its results are shared equally by all. We will note later slight tendencies toward a rise in the level of living when colonies enter their affluent-plateau stage, or when they divide; these are usually the consequence of deliberate decisions to give the people more goods. However, the rise has a very definite ceiling, at least for the present. By any outside standard, the improvement is very slight; it generally does not go beyond such items as electric razors for the men or electric floor polishers and the like for the women. Personal adornment or purely functionless possessions are still officially taboo, and commercial amusements are forbidden.

In cases where austerity is violated, one usually finds trouble in the colony. In fact, acquisitiveness is one of the first signs of colony breakdown. When leadership is weak and disorganized, the Hutterite may begin to feel that he might as well indulge his ever-present secret desires, and use some of the colony money to buy what he wants for himself. He may steal colony property and sell it, or otherwise tap colony funds. To do so is an act against the group as a whole, and is therefore a symptom of a weakening of the colony social fabric.

Seeds of possible change in the austerity program are not only found in the average Hutterite's desire for more than he is allowed to have, but also in the attitudes toward individual consumption and gratification found among members of North American society. These attitudes are closely associated with enterprise economy. The Hutterites are surrounded by agricultural enterprisers whose general goal is to increase production so that they can have a better life. The Hutterites also seek to increase production, although for collective or communal ends. However, the point is that a desire for better living can be contagious. The Brethren must strive to avoid feeling proud of their relative wealth and stability when surrounded by enterprises less wealthy and secure. The Jasper colonies represented the most prosperous farms in the entire region; the Brethren's resultant sense of pride in their inherent power and strength was evident in many contexts, but was always carefully played down. To live austerely in the midst of abundance is not easy, and they seek substitutes: beautifully varnished and painted home interiors; carefully handcrafted furniture and small conveniences; hand-bound books; colorful hand-sewn shirts, and other things that appear to the Gentile eye inconspicuous or unimportant. To the Hutterites, these are functional substitutes for expensive consumption; they represent the economic security of the Hutterian system, but without displaying the customary abundance factor so prominent in Gentile culture. Collective ritual and enjoyment is often substituted for individual consumption, for example, in songfests, wedding banquets, and religious holidays.

The Hutterites are not devoid of an esthetic sense, and indeed their homes and costumes show definite style. "Simplicity" is perhaps the most relevant term here; like the Shakers, whose craftsmanship and architectural design have influenced modern stylists, the Brethren have definite standards of functionality and beauty. These standards may be invisible to their neighbors, who follow the overstuffed-furniture and plastic-plant style of interior decoration; paradoxically it is the urban intellectual who can perhaps best appreciate the Hutterian love of plain woods and symmetry. The few personal possessions of the Hutterian man or woman are placed in little cabinets and chests, out of sight and reach of the children, but carefully and lovingly arranged with neatness and order. Thus the culture, while morally condemning self-conscious estheticism, contains its own definite esthetic standards—another of the paradoxes of the Hutterian way.

A Hutterite's possessions come from four general sources: he may make them by hand; receive them as gifts or "find" them (in waste materials and the like); receive them through collective distribution by the colony; or purchase them with his monthly *zehr-*

geld, or allowance. Every Hutterite has possessions gained from all three sources. It is sometimes difficult to differentiate the strictly personal sphere of possessions from the familial, as it is in any Gentile family. For example, if a Hutterite husband makes a hatrack for the family apartment, but uses it exclusively for his own hats, is it a "personal" possession or a "family" article? Similarly, if a man makes a folding table at the request of his wife, who uses it almost exclusively, is it "her" property or the family's?

The Hutterites themselves do not consider questions of this sort relevant, and are usually at a loss to answer them objectively. The ideology of communal property is so pervasive that queries assuming an ideology of ownership are not clearly understood, and when understood, are avoided. This does not mean that the Hutterite owns no truly "personal" property; that is, articles which he himself views as "belonging" to him and to him only. As in all communal social groups, there is a last-ditch sphere of personal autonomy that centers around articles deliberately acquired by one person and used by him only. This is "personal property," and is recognized as such by the Hutterites—although, as noted previously, they often avoid overt recognition of its existence in discussions, since the ideology of communal property is supposed to apply absolutely.

Some idea of the relative importance of the source categories of personal possessions is shown in Table 9. This list includes all the "personal" possessions owned by one male Hutterite, age 34, whose colony job is that of an agricultural manager. It excludes all clothing made for him by his wife or received by him from colony disbursement.

Most of the items listed were kept by their owner in his bedroom, inside a locked highboy-type cabinet he himself had made, which also contained the family linens. The cash retail value of all purchased items on the list—$50—is a little above the average value of such items owned by most Hutterian adult males. As a manager, the owner had need of special items such as drafting materials and technical books. However, it is interesting to note that the single most costly purchase—the $20 electric razor—had nothing

Table 9—Selected personal possessions of male Hutterite

Item	Made by self	Gift or found	Purchased	Received from colony
Electric razor			×	
Wallet	×			
Coin purse			×	
Pocket watch				×
Work shoes (1 pr.)			×	
House slippers			×	
Western-style summer hat			×	
Shop cap		×		
Pocket knives, 2				×
Small hand lens		×		
Assorted tools, about 10			3 or 4	Remainder
Pocket slide-rule type calculator . .		×		
Drafting instruments (simple, crude)		Pens, ruler	Compass	Pencils only
Drafting and note paper (simple materials)		Most	Some	Graph paper
Technical books, manuals, 20 . . .		Most	One only	2 or 3
General books, 5		All		
Books on Hutterian history and religion, 5		2	1	2
Assorted general magazines		All		
Cabinet for small articles	×			
Flashlight			×	

to do with managerial needs, but was instead a pure gift to the self, a reflection of a basic acquisitive residue in its owner's thinking. This is typical: almost every Hutterian male known intimately by the writer owned a few such unnecessary possessions.

It should be noted that a number of substantial interests—not necessarily desires or wants—are represented in the "Gift or Found" category. Most books and magazines of general interest are acquired as gifts; Hutterites who like to read must satisfy their craving by literally begging or borrowing printed matter. In the case of this manager, cash value of these acquisitions was $29—more than half the value of the purchased items; for men lacking in specialized needs, the value of the "Gift or Found" source items would be equal to, or exceed, the value of those purchased.

Regardless of source differences, the total value of this man's personal possessions (including an approximated value for his clothing) was about $225. An estimation was done for a Gentile male of similar age and responsibility on a neighboring ranch: a low estimate of the total value of the Gentile's personal property is $2,500. Such comparisons show that Hutterian austerity is very real indeed.

The "culture of austerity" is a way of living with less, and doing so with dignity and purpose.[3] It involves the substitution of sentiment for objects: most of the Hutterian hand-crafted furniture is made to be given to a sister or brother upon marriage, and it is not the object but the gift that is significant. The writer was the recipient of numerous gifts, always hand-made objects or agricultural products. His own presents to the Brethren, sometimes specified after the writer had asked for a suggestion, were in the nature of books or serious magazines, pocket knives, razors, cloth, or kindred items of practical use. These were always received with deep gratitude, and invariably were taken as a token of the donor's love for the Hutterites and their way of life.

So long as the Brethren can find satisfaction in simple possessions, and in valid emotional meanings of objects, they will remain invulnerable to the inducements of advertising and the "American way of life," at least with respect to personal possessions. They are perhaps already overly inclined toward the expensive farm machine and the ingenious labor-saving device in their technology. Here, too, functional substitutes for personal consumption are probably evident: "You don't really need those tractor cabs, but it makes the men feel a lot better. It really makes a difference in their work." There will be limits set to spending, however, for the Brethren recognize that the accumulation of objects can easily become a goal in itself. Increasing wealth is a danger; and the Brethren are currently striving to spread this wealth as evenly as possible, so that no colony will find itself in a position to spend money on unessential things and thereby compromise the Christian way.

The apparent basic paradox of Hutterian economic organization is that while the culture maintains a traditionalized and static con-

[3] Cf. J. W. Bennett, "Communal Brethren in the Great Plains," *Trans-Action*, Winter 1966.

sumption level, production is, to a degree, rational and maximizing.[4] Moreover, the Hutterites have a "redistributive economy" of a type associated with pre-industrial societies, insofar as they hold to communal ownership and ration goods and cash to the family units. At the same time, the Brethren sell their products for cash on the capitalist market. While they have a phased plan of economic development and expansion, they limit their investments after a certain level is reached, and use accumulating savings to finance new colonies and to support the retirement of the aged, rather than to increase the colony's standard of living. The maximization of output and income is pursued for the purpose of sustaining a traditional style of life. While capital requirements are increasingly emphasized over labor, Hutterian agriculture still benefits from an abundant labor supply, and hence is both "labor-intensive" and "capital-intensive."

This economic configuration is a mixture of static and dynamic features. Limitations on productive investments and the maintenance of a traditional culture represent static goals; yet the means utilized to attain the desired levels of productivity are fully rational and follow dynamic maximizing patterns. It is in this combination of apparently contradictory features that the Brethren differ from peasant societies, and from the conservative entrepre-

---

[4] The rationality and prosperity of Hutterian economic organization in the sixteenth century and later have been noted by many writers, who point to the efficiency of their craft industries; their extensive use of money as capital, and their understanding of credit—all in an age when money was still not widely used. Also noted are the Brethren's efficient educational procedures, under which the stewards, craftsmen, and agricultural managers were trained. See Correll, in Horsch (1931, pp. ix–x); also Horsch (1931, pp. 22–24, 30–31; 37–38; 67–68); Friedmann (1961, pp. 115–22); and Klassen (1962). The point is that Hutterian economic rationality did not develop in North America under the stimulus of a cash economy, but was present from the beginning. This is brought out clearly when the Hutterian system is compared with the economic adaptations worked out by the nineteenth century utopian communities on the American frontier (Bestor 1950 and Nordhoff 1875 are the best accounts). Few of these groups had a clear conception of the social and economic adjustments necessary for the success of a communal experiment. Most of them failed to resolve the tension between egalitarian ideals and differentiation of economic function, and it was this tension which, in varying ways, wrecked most of these communities. The Hutterian experiment benefited from its choice of a supremely practical model: the prosperous noble estate, with its diversified activities and need for efficient management.

neurial agriculturalist who limits his rationality and efficiency extensively by adherence to traditional cultural practices. Tradition in Hutterian life is not an important obstacle to relative rationality —although there are certain minor anti-rational effects. The Hutterian system was planned in the sixteenth century, and it has not departed from its basic tenets; its sophistication derives from the ideas and skills of the founders of the Hutterian movement: experienced artisans, stewards, and religious intellectuals, with a clear understanding of the problems of communal life. In the subsequent centuries, this system has had the opportunity for thoroughgoing test and revision, although the "miracle" of Hutterian existence is that very little change has been necessary. The basic structure and objectives of Hutterian society have remained the same; only the content of the economy has changed; and these changes are not perceived for the Brethren as dangerous, since they serve the group-approved goal of maintenance of the system.[5]

Because the Hutterian colony is a large enterprise, and because the support of a large number of persons, combined with the need to save large amounts of money, requires high efficiency, the Brethren frequently demonstrate greater knowledge and ability to manage their enterprises than their Gentile neighbors do. This is no secret in the districts where colonies have been established; farmers and ranchers are commonly amazed at the efficiency and activity of their Hutterian neighbors—their seeming ability to take advantage of every economic opportunity, their shrewdness at bargaining, and their ability to stretch a dollar by repairs and clever innovations. Often the ultraconservative farmers, of which the Jasper region has a large number, are, in their unwillingness to take chances or to maximize output, and their readiness to accept a low level of living, more "peasant" than the Brethren, with their antique clothing and Middle-European rural customs. In the most general sense, the Gentiles and the Hutterites share the broad objectives of a market and cash economy characteristic of North American agriculture. However, in the Jasper region we found considerable difference between farmers in their acceptance of the

---

[5] See Serl, n.d., for a discussion of this point.

full range of these economic values and goals; and often it was the Brethren who occupied a position at the extreme rational end of the distribution.

The Regime of Diversification

The conduct of Hutterian agricultural operations is characterized by full acceptance of diversification, or "mixed farming." As this mode has developed in Hutterian hands, however, it resembles more closely the structure of a large company-type farm than it does the limited cattle-grain diversification of the typical small Jasper farm. In fact, the Hutterian system of extreme diversification resembles that attempted by certain early land-grant farms of the Jasper region, such as Sir Lester Kaye's enterprises, a group of separate farm enterprises owned by one man.[6] The colony is far more efficient than farms of this type in its conception of balance, investment, and financing; and in its efficient use of labor, which concentrates all activities in one location. In any case, the Hutterian system thrives, and the ill-conceived diversified enterprises of the early settlement period have long since perished.

Diversification for Hutterites therefore means producing anything that will either provide cash income on a balanced basis, compensating for price fluctuations, or help reduce expenditures by furnishing home-produced food, seed, breeding stock, or raw materials (the last are now very rare, being confined to a few items like straw). Because of their large-scale operations, adequate labor supply, relative self-sufficiency in food, and available capital, the Brethren can "afford" beekeeping, extensive horticulture, dairying, wine-making, keeping ducks and geese, and other activities that would drain the individual farmer. Hutterites ideally value each enterprise equally, regardless of the income it yields. Field crops and beef cattle are their most lucrative sources of income, but since they seek diversification for reasons of self-sufficiency as well as to avoid one-crop instability, and since they also wish to maintain the

[6] Morton (1938, p. 83); MacEwan (1963, p. 255).

motivation of their agricultural enterprise managers, they are against letting any one activity absorb capital to the point of forcing the cessation of others.[7]

This ideal, however, is not always encountered in practice. As we shall see in Chapter 8, some "relaxed" colonies permit profitable activities to move ahead without control, and some "pushing" colonies deliberately seek out profitable enterprises and abandon unprofitable ones. The conservative Hutterian ideal is a balanced program in which all enterprises are sensibly developed, even though some require more labor and capital than others. The Jasper colonies emphasize livestock more than most Alberta colonies, since grain production is much riskier. But the ideally balanced colony tries to keep grain production high as well, and build up other enterprises as a cushion against falling livestock or grain prices.

Table 10 provides data on production and values of selected commodities for the six colonies in our study. Three of the six colonies did not raise sheep; in two cases this was because the colonists disliked sheep-raising, and in the other case, it was because they lacked adequate pasturage. Two of the six colonies did not buy feeder cattle in addition to their own calves and steers; in both cases, this was because they considered cattle feeding risky and unprofitable (a well-founded belief during the early 1960's). Considerable range in egg production is evident: from 10,000 dozen annually in one colony to 90,000 in another. The returns from the sale of cattle vary from about $11,000 to $70,000 annually. The number of swine sold annually varies from 430 to 1,800. Colony 2, the one with the largest acreage, stands out as a very large producer of all the commodities listed; but Colony 1, with nearly as much land, has a well-balanced but far more modest production schedule. Colony 6, a newly established colony at a high altitude, omits cash grain crops

[7] There are ideological controls at work here as well. As we noted earlier, the Brethren are admonished to guard against ambition, the substitution of material things for God, and activities that are rewarding only in a material sense. Cf. Rideman (1565, 1950); Hofer (1955); Arnold (1940). Thus the Brethren cannot give the cattle boss more overt respect than the beekeeper, even though the cattle boss's activities furnish half or more of the colony income. This avoidance of differential prestige constitutes one of the key differences between the Hutterian colony and modern "utopian" communities like the kibbutz.

Table 10—Acreage, production, and returns for selected items produced in 1964[a]

Colony	Total acreage	Pasture acreage	Crop acreage[b]	Wheat (in bushels)	Value of wheat sold (@ 1.40 per bu.)	Barley (in bu.), all fed	Rye (in bushels)	Oats (in bu.), all fed	Hay, all kinds (bales)	Number of cattle sold	Value of cattle,[c] sheep, lambs, and wool	Eggs sold (doz.)	Value of eggs sold (@ .31 per doz.)	Number of hogs sold	Value of hogs sold[d]
1	13,000	9,000	4,000	25,000	35,000	18,000	3,000	30,000	30,000	165[e]	31,550	55,968	17,350	600	24,000
2	14,240	5,140	9,100	32,000	44,800	65,000	none	160,000	23,000	362[f]	72,000	90,323	28,000	1,300	45,000
3	10,000	3,500	6,500	25,000	35,000	35,000	4,000	48,000	15,000	175[f]	30,500	57,143	17,714	430	15,000
4	8,000	3,000	5,000	15,000	21,000	50,000	2,400	32,500	20,000	325[f]	64,000	19,000	5,890	1,000	35,000
5	10,400	2,900	7,500	42,900	60,060	53,000	none	17,325	24,000	136[f]	23,350	10,000	3,100	1,800	79,200
6	6,000	3,000	3,000	none	none	36,000	none	28,000	8,000	75[e]	15,250	22,857	7,085	667	25,000

a Value given in dollars.
b Includes summer fallow and hayland.
c Includes yearlings and cows, with yearlings averaged at $181 and cows averaged at $120. The heaviest yearlings were sold by Colony 4 and Colony 2, at $200 per head.
d Price averages $34. Range is from about $45 to $35; Colonies 5 and 1 raised the heaviest animals.
e No feeders.
f Includes feeders.

and has a relatively small and, from the standpoint of the Hutterian ideal, an unbalanced production schedule.

The ratio of crop acreage to pasture acreage varies greatly from colony to colony, even in the confines of the Jasper area. Of the western group in our study, Colony 1 had 4,000 acres of crop land and 9,000 of pasturage, a ratio of 4 to 9; Colony 2 had 9,100 acres of crop land and 5,140 acres of pasturage, a ratio of 3 to 2; Colony 3 had 6,500 acres of crop land and 3,500 acres of pasturage, a ratio of 2 to 1; and Colony 4 had 5,000 acres of crop land and 3,000 acres of pasturage, a ratio of 5 to 3. Of the eastern group, Colony 5 had 7,500 acres of crop land and 2,900 acres of pasturage, a ratio of 5 to 2; and Colony 6 had 3,000 acres of crop land and 3,000 acres of pasturage, a ratio of 1 to 1. The crop land of all the colonies combined totaled 35,100 acres, and the pasturage 26,540 acres—an overall ratio of 12 to 11. The ideal ratio, as defined by the "balanced" colony, Colony 1, is its own—1 to 2—or, at the most, 1 to 3. This ratio guarantees a good income at low cost. A colony with less pasture, but with a need for the extra income derived from livestock, must feed cattle or raise sheep: Colony 4, without sheep, fed cattle (60 per cent of its total of 362 cattle were feeders). Other colonies criticized it for not raising sheep, since sheep provide large returns on a rather small investment of labor and pasturage. Colony 6, at a high altitude, devoted all its cropland to forage crops for its livestock, and consequently it had a 1 to 1 ratio of crop to pasture land.

While it is evident that the colonies do differ in their production schedules and emphases, they are all engaged in large-scale "mixed farming," and even the least diversified colony, Colony 6, has a wider range of production than the largest Gentile mixed farm in the region. Large-scale diversified farming requires considerably more labor than can be supplied by the individual farmer relying on his family members and an occasional part-time worker. The superior position of the colonies with regard to capital has also been mentioned; they start out with more money than the Gentiles, and hence have a firmer base from which to expand and develop production. Theirs is an economy of scale; therefore they can afford to experiment, and to endure occasional losses or extensive indebtedness that would ruin the average individual operator in the region.

Comparisons were made of the productivity of the various colonies, in terms of per-bushel yields of crops and per-pound dollar values of livestock. The results of the crop analyses were not conclusive, because of the great variation in moisture conditions and hence in crop yields. Ten bushels to the acre for wheat is considered a good average in this part of Saskatchewan. All the colonies were close to this average, but differences relative to colony age were noted: the younger colonies tended to fall below this level, but were catching up as they refined their field practices. More significant differences were noted in livestock production. The Alberta colonies had tended to emphasize crops over livestock; the move to Saskatchewan meant a reversal of this emphasis, and the Jasper colonies were still in the learning phase. The average price of hogs sold by the colonies ranged from $35 to $45 per animal (although most colonies were in the high range), a spread attributable to differences in the quality of feeding regimes and general care of the animals. Less variation was found in the price of cattle. Efficiency of poultry production varied, largely relative to differences in equipment. Since colony agricultural economy is always large-scale economy, differences in productive efficiency are not as significant as they might be between low-capital individual farms; and in any event, information transfer between colonies is so great that sooner or later the less productive colonies catch up by copying from the adapted senior colonies.

More data on productivity for one colony with average-to-high yields is presented in Chapter 9, where it is compared with that relating to a large Gentile-owned farm in the same area.

Economic Development

The Hutterites have had considerable experience establishing new colonies: in four generations, the number of colonies has grown from eight to more than one hundred and sixty. This growth experience has enabled the Brethren to formulate certain basic rules for the success of a new colony. Some of these involve ideal conditions that are not always present, and for which substitutes or alternatives must be provided.

The first of these requirements concerns the size of the population. The Hutterites say that 150 persons is considered maximum size for a mature colony, at which point it must divide. However, a sample consisting of the six Jasper colonies and ten others in Alberta showed that the mean size at division was about 130. A few Brethren stated that in recent years the colonies were finding it desirable to split sooner, because of income problems; but the majority of informants did not appear to be aware that a tendency toward earlier division might be developing. In any case, the Hutterites regard from fifty to seventy-five persons as the ideal size of a new colony, since this number is large enough to furnish the labor force so badly needed in the early years, but small enough to be supported on the 6,000- to 10,000-acre spread typical of new colonies in the Alberta-Saskatchewan region. However, many colonies begin life with more than seventy-five members—100 seems a fair average for the contemporary period.

If a colony began life with 100 persons, it could reach the 150 mark in about ten years, and a new division would be necessary. Obviously a decade between establishment and division would not be long enough for a colony to accumulate the $200,000 or so in cash that is the going price for 10,000 acres of cropland and pasture in the Jasper region. This sum could be saved in a period of twenty years, providing the colony saved at the rate of $10,000 a year, and added two or three thousand acres during that time. Fifteen to twenty years is the amount of time required for a colony to grow from around 70 persons to 150. Colonies that split on reaching 130 members usually do so after ten or fifteen years. (The average colony age at fission in the Jasper area was seventeen.) Thus under ideal conditions a colony would be able in twenty years to finance completely the establishment of a daughter colony—or at least to buy the requisite land, which is the most important item. If fission occurs sooner, supplemental financing is generally needed.

Actually few colonies follow the ideal twenty-year pattern. In the first place, a relatively long interval (fifteen to twenty years) between establishment and fission seems to be more seriously adhered to by the Lehrer Leut, whose members place great emphasis on orderly establishment and growth and an adequate financial basis for settlement. The Darius are more willing to form new colonies sooner, and do not mind starting out with a small labor force and marginal resources. Also to be considered is the presence or absence in the district of related colonies willing to help out. However, the most critical factor in all cases of colony establishment is the role of the parent colony, as expressed through the nature of the agreement made between the old colony and the new one. This agreement, of course, is worked out by the entire parent colony membership before the choice of nuclear families for the new colony is made. The Hutterites generally feel that the parent colony must give as much aid as possible to the "new farm" during the first year or so. To give inadequate support to a "new farm" is regarded as dangerous to the entire Hutterian order. The fact that a number of Darius colonies seem to have neglected their duty in this regard during recent years has created tension between the Lehrer and Darius Leute.

The various types of agreements between the parent and the daughter colonies in the Jasper area fall into three categories; (1) outright cash grants, with the remainder of the new colony finances being secured by loans from other colonies or from banks; (2) term financing by the parent colony, with a sum of money given each year for the first few years of the new colony's existence; and (3) special financing, over a period of years, of particular items, like machinery or land. It should be remembered that the new colony is actually established as a farm before its human contingent is selected by lot, hence the earliest stage of capitalization takes place before the new colony is a reality.

The Brethren often observe that a population of 150 persons is the most that can be handled easily within the Hutterian patterns of social organization. Beyond this size, the number of men employed in menial or laboring positions becomes too large: the Brethren like to keep this laboring force to an efficient minimum, lest discontent with what appears to be an exclusive managerial-executive elite develop within its ranks. However, other factors can influence colony division. Financial difficulties in the parent colony may encourage early fission (this was the case in two Jasper colonies); or schisms in the parent colony can lead to separation of the factions by fission, as happened in the parent group of another Jasper colony.

The Hutterites believe that a colony must not attempt to save money by reducing initial land purchases. Their experience in the more arid parts of the Northern Plains has taught them that between 10,000 and 15,000 acres is sufficient land to support a growing colony and carry it up to the point of division; much of this acreage must be acquired at the outset, if possible. If the colony wishes to reserve some of its cash for other purposes, then the land must be paid for by the first crop, or by shares on the livestock acquired with the land. If this is not possible, then the Brethren depend on cash loans. Some of the most common informal inter-colony credit operations are loans for the purchase of land by new colonies; the Brethren prefer colony loans since they do not require interest, and terms of repayment are flexible. One-year bank loans on land carry between 5 per cent and 6 per cent interest, an amount that can be difficult to bear in the early years.

Colonies sometimes show considerable hesitation over certain aspects of credit financing, especially the interest ratio. The Brethren in one Jasper colony admitted that in some of their early credit transactions on machines and stock they were unduly cautious because of their fears concerning interest repayment. In one instance, they took over, on the usual half-share basis, the cattle on one of the farms purchased as colony property. This sort of arrangement is standard in many parts of the Plains, and is unquestionably in the interest of the seller, for though the buyer must pay for the raising of the cattle, he receives only half of the proceeds. In later years, the Brethren calculated that the arrangement had actually cost them more than a bank loan to buy them outright would have. (Furthermore, the cattle were not healthy.) Many colonies refuse this type of deal, preferring to build up their own herd slowly. The Hutterites are not alone in their distrust of commercial lenders. This is the feeling characteristic of most farm and ranch operators of the region, and to some extent it reflects relative inexperience with credit operations. Like the more conservative farmers, many Hutterites tend to boast of their reliance on cash, but nowadays they are rapidly learning the rules and advantages of credit, and are ahead of the more conservative farmers.

Another important condition of colony establishment is proper equipment, livestock, and seed to begin operations. Here, as in the matter of cash, a colony that is formed from a wealthy parent is in a better position to start out than one that has come from a relatively poor one—providing, of course, the parent colony is willing to make a good agreement. Since there is never enough cash even in the best of circumstances, the colony that can bring some equipment and agricultural materials to the new site will be able to put more into land purchase and other necessary expenditures. The problem confronted by the parent colony is simply that often there is not really enough of everything for an equal division. This may be especially true with regard to machines, since the loss of half of the colony labor force means that more machines, not less, will be needed by the reduced parent colony. Similarly, since the parent colony retains all its land, it is not inclined to give up more than the standard 50 per cent of its seed and breeding livestock. Therefore the burden tends to fall on the new colony: *it* sacrifices, *it* is expected to take the brunt of the economic shock, which means that it is required to begin life with minimal equipment and stock and with the burden of loans. It is usually better supplied with livestock than with machines. (New colonies often have better and more machines than the old, after a few years, for they are forced to buy their own.)

Let us describe briefly the beginnings of a new colony in the region—a colony from a relatively wealthy parent group, which was able to begin operations with about twice as much cash as that available to at least three of the other colonies. (The process of growth described here is shown on Diagram 4.)

The decision to divide was made by the mother colony in 1951.

In early 1952, representatives of the proposed colony toured the Jasper region, and selected an area west of town (already described in Chapter 3). An agent was hired from a larger town, and land purchases began. Construction parties arrived on the site in the summer of 1952, and by the spring of 1953 the first essential structures had been erected, the crops had been planted, the stock installed, and the entire colony moved into residence. The physical move was made easier by three or four of the neighboring colonies in Alberta, which provided trucks and drivers to transport property and personnel.

The new colony was given $270,000 in cash by the mother colony as an outright terminal grant. This amount was larger than average—$70,000 more than was required for sufficient land. The colony spent $200,000 of this cash on land, acquiring 11,000 acres at an average price of about $17 an acre (as noted in Chapter 3, this was higher than the current price, and represents a manifestation of the "stick-the-Hutterites" mechanism). After 1951, an additional 2,200 acres were acquired little by little. With the balance of $70,000, the colony purchased most of the supplies needed for construction, as well as a combine, a powered swather, a hay baler, a power mower, and one tractor. The parent colony supplied one tractor, two old trucks, some ancient cultivating implements unsuited to the Jasper region, several teams of horses, and an assortment of shop and kitchen equipment in poor condition. The drilling of two wells was paid for out of the $70,000 also. This cash balance was completely exhausted by 1953.

A good amount of breeding stock for poultry was supplied by the parent colony, but it had to be supplemented by additional purchases later on. During 1952, the colony bought 400 sheep and 150 swine with money loaned by other colonies. Some lumber and other building supplies were bought on a promissory note during that year also. About fifty head of cattle were brought from the parent colony, and more cattle were taken over from one of the land sellers on a half-share basis. The first year's crop was used to pay some of the bills. In 1953, the second crop was completely hailed out, and since cash was exhausted, and the colony members

Diagram 4
COLONY AND KIBBUTZ PATTERNS OF GROWTH

Colony: Controlled growth

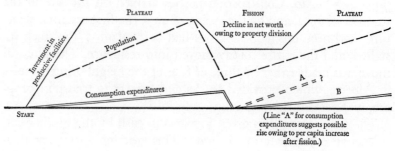

Kibbutz: Theoretically continuous growth

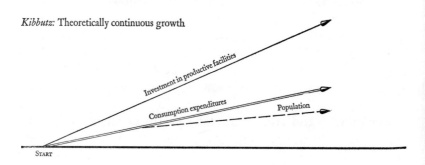

owed approximately $15,000 to various creditors, it was necessary for them to negotiate a considerable cash loan. Technically, the colony was bankrupt at the end of its second year of operations. They had assumed a degree of indebtedness that would be sufficient to destroy most individual operators, whose smaller scale of operations would not permit them adequate credit. (In contrast, the colony scale of operations provides it with an advantage, since it is able to give banks the collateral and repayment guarantees they want. An efficiently run establishment of, say, 11,000 acres, can obtain loans relatively easily.) The colony approached one of the Jasper banks, but was refused, largely because of community resentment. The Brethren thereupon phoned the home office of the bank, which instructed its Jasper branch to provide the loan requested. The colony received $25,000, with which it financed its third-year crop and paid some of its bills.

During the first three years this colony received from other colonies the occasional loan of a truck, one load of seed wheat, four breeding boars, and one load of seed barley. Labor for construction and maintenance was also donated. By rough calculation, the total value of this aid was approximately $20,000, an amount close to the size of the bank loan, which means that the colony required credit of at least $45,000 in addition to its $270,000 to gain a firm footing during its first three years of operation. At least $20,000 of this indebtedness was caused by the total destruction of its second-year crop by hail. The adaptive advantage of the colony system is clear: few individual operators, plagued at the start by crop failure, could have made it beyond that point.

After the starting phase, the typical colony enters a period of intensive buildup. The initial phase of colony development is marked by concentration upon the large income-producing activities of grain and livestock production, with emphasis on extensive modes of operation; that is, grain and forage crops may be produced on more than half of the available land, often at the risk of soil blowing and lower yields. The land is often in poor condition, since the Gentile farms purchased are usually substandard. This makes it difficult to be certain of a permanent crop plan, and hence much cropping is done primarily for experimental reasons. The pasture may be grazed without cross-fencing and without adequate watering, even at the risk of temporary injury to the grass cover. Swine and chickens may be raised in substandard accommodations. During these buildup years, when the major objective is to boost cash income in order to repay creditors and finance needed developments, the Brethren may seem to the outside observer to be rough, careless farmers with a slapdash frontier style, who are able to make money and obtain credit solely because of their very large acreage. Such observers have erroneously concluded that the colonies are only partly attuned to modern methods, and are ignorant of the proper use of machinery and agronomic methods.

As its debts are retired and its income reaches a point where substantial savings are possible, the colony ceases to spend large sums on equipment, and invests modestly in intensive methods and labor-saving devices. Usually no additional enterprises are inaugurated, and a plateau of development is reached. Cropping is reduced to the standard 50-50 annual rotation of crop and fallow, fertilizer may be used on some tracts, and pasturage is more carefully fenced and allotted.

Water resources on the colony grazing lands are carefully developed. Swine and poultry are housed in standard, scientifically designed accommodations, and automatic cleaning and feeding devices are installed, thus reducing hand labor. After sufficient basic machinery such as trucks and tractors has been acquired, money is spent on nonessential labor-saving devices such as post-hole pounders, automatic stone-pickers, hydraulic lifts for the cultivating instruments, air-cooled cabs for the field tractors and combines, and expensive shop tools (e.g., turret lathes and hydraulic presses). With such devices, the colony is in a position to redirect its labor force into a different pattern of activity. In the earliest phase of growth, all available manpower is used to the fullest extent; but as the number of machines reaches its maximum and labor-saving devices are acquired, the working hours are reduced, and the men are retrained to operate other equipment, or to learn shop trades so that the colony can become more self-sufficient in the matter of machine and automotive repairs. For example, in the colony whose first years were described earlier, fencing operations at first involved four men, a tractor, and a pickup truck. When the growth plateau had been reached, the two men not employed in fencing were used instead in the shop, to repair machines and engines, and were trained to operate and repair the new combines as well. At first the colony had two combines, which were run on 24-hour shifts; in the later phase, after the crop area had been increased through land purchases, four combines were operated on 10-hour shifts. The women, too, benefit from colony prosperity: in the early days of a colony's life, all garden cultivation and poultry preparation is done by hand by the women; but in the later phases, a garden tractor, cultivation tools, and improved poultry processing equipment is usually purchased.

While austerity remains the guiding principle of colony life, certain differences in its application can be noted as colony wealth increases. At first the typical apartment will have rough wood ceilings, one chest, one cabinet-bureau, old curtains, a chair or two, and an old pot-bellied stove. Later on, when the women are freed by labor-saving devices for household work, and the men have more time to work on household items, the typical apartment may be furnished with three or even four cabinets and bureaus, ingenious hatracks and clothes racks, folding washbasin contrivances, shelving, inlaid linoleum floors, an efficient propane stove, attractive curtains, and painted ceilings. There is little accumulation, but much improvement in order and quality. Increased cash allotments to the nuclear family households permit the purchase of small conveniences: electric floor-polishers, thermos jugs, and even electric grills to be used on the rare occasions when the family is permitted to eat privately at home. The communal kitchen may acquire stainless-steel hotel-type ranges, powered meat saws, patented noodle-makers (often improved upon by the colony mechanics), and new and improved refrigeration equipment. Community hot showers in stainless-steel housings may replace the old washtubs, and sprinkler irrigation systems take the place of crude ditches in the garden.

At this stage the colony gives a different appearance to the visitor. The thinly-painted buildings, the old barns left over from the original Gentile farm, the ancient tractors and horse teams have all been replaced by orderly, neat, well-painted buildings and new, specialized equipment. The furious activity is replaced by a more measured tempo. At this stage, outsiders frequently give a different appraisal of Hutterian life: "These Hutterites—they don't work half as hard as we do. Why, they have more damn time on their hands! I don't know how they get so rich. It must be because they never spend any money." Such comments are made in apparent ignorance of the fact that the Brethren's relative prosperity is brought about precisely by the spending of money on labor-saving devices, and rests on the increased productivity that these innovations permit. To give a single example: in one colony, during the starting phase, egg production yielded only $10,000 a year and demanded the full-time labor of two men. Later on, with the installation of automatic equipment, only the three-quarter-time labor of one man was required, and the yield was increased to $17,000 a year. The cost of the new equipment was amortized in two years.

Actually, improvements in the dwelling houses, in the kitchen and in the garden usually come about long after the agricultural facilities have been improved. Quite possibly it is advisable to regard the advent of non-agricultural improvements as a fourth stage in colony development, which is entered when all necessary improvements in the basic economic activities of farming have been accomplished. However, there is usually a considerable overlap. The Hutterites are keenly aware of the stresses that the austerity program creates in a culture completely surrounded by "poor" neighbors with a much higher level of consumption, and they introduce home improvements as soon as possible, or whenever they perceive a certain restlessness or dissatisfaction in a majority of the households. In any case, such changes are always a matter of group decision, and any innovation is discussed by all the men before the expenditure is made.

Thus, the third, or "plateau," stage of colony development could be said to begin when the level of operations and the standard of living have reached the highest standards current in the Hutterian system, and when the annual rate of savings is maximal (in a good year, a colony sometimes puts away as much as $30,000). At this point, the colony has acquired all its land, has worked out as perfect a system of land use as it can, and is within a few years of fission. In the present pattern of colony division, this plateau of relative prosperity lasts between five and ten years, at which point any cash reserve is turned over to the daughter group at fission, and the colony must rebuild its savings. However, this can be done with relative ease, since the colony owns much or most of its needed equipment and housing, and has a relatively efficient ongoing agricultural regime.

Colonies differ to some extent in their development strategies. Some colonies build houses and barns first, and delay the purchase of machinery until after their debts have been substantially cleared. Others buy machines first, and build slowly. Most colonies are able to lend money at least by the end of the first decade of their establishment, although some can do so sooner. In any case, development is, to a considerable extent, a conscious, planned affair among the Hutterites—at least to a degree greater than that of the typical small farm or ranch of the Jasper region. In these small enterprises, the vagaries of moisture, the price squeeze on cattle feeding, the uncertainty of succession, and many other factors make programmed development very difficult.

The colonies themselves are not entirely free from the uncertainties associated with a variable habitat and dependence on a market economy. While size and diversification tend to lessen risk, there are the usual effects of bumper crops and failures. If a colony has bumper crops during its first few years, it may be able to pay off most or all of its debts very quickly. Colony 1 was hailed out during its first year and as a result its indebtedness doubled and repayment of loans was delayed. Such events directly affect planned development, even though the relatively large size and excellent credit position of colony enterprise reduce risk.

There is, however, a special form of risk associated with Hutterian colonies: that of increasing population. A colony is wealthy in the sense of its large returns and investment value as compared to the individual farm. However, it is "poor" in terms of *per capita* wealth. As population increases, *per capita* returns and investment tend to fall. If shortages of land or government discrimination should prevent the establishment of new colonies, a greatly increased population would have to be supported by the existing regime, and if efficiency did not increase production, an even lower level of living would have to be adopted.

The possibility of increased rational efficiency is limited by several factors, one of the most important being the present level of education and knowledge. Hutterian agriculture could benefit by a number of improvements based on a careful management study of labor output and productivity, and on a shift of production emphasis. At present, their low educational level does not provide the Brethren with the mathematical skills and managerial know-how necessary for this type of study. The Hutterites are extremely efficient farmers within the context of trial-and-error management and simple accounting skills, and they have not sought or permitted specialized studies of their methods by outside experts. Their religious ideology prohibits overly precise accounting, which might undermine the ideal of free and equal contribution. If they were to educate their young men beyond the eighth grade level, they would be forced to send them to town high schools, thus precipitating a general exodus from the colonies. This they would avoid at all costs, since it might well mean an end to the Hutterian way of life. As the population increases and the possible sites for new colonies become more difficult to find, these problems will be felt more keenly. Hutterian economy cannot remain static: it must change, and experiment, and seek out new forms and procedures.

During the early 1960's, however, there was no question that the colony form of agriculture was free of most of the built-in uncertainties of individual enterprise in the Jasper region. There was absolute certainty of succession at the colony, whereas the individual enterpriser is rarely certain of his son's plans. Retirement income was assured; there was no need to require a son to finance his father's retirement as well as his own growing family. Large size and abundant land provided the colonies with the opportunity to acquire funds for expansion and investment. The colonies, in their relative security, represented the furthest extreme reached in the adaptive process of enlargement of the enterprise unit in a resources-variable agricultural habitat.

Colony and Kibbutz: Patterns of Growth

The strategy of Hutterian economic development emerges as a case of controlled growth, in which economic expansion and productive investments cease or are restrained after a certain level is attained. In the early years of the new colony, investments in productive equipment and facilities are heavy and frequent, resulting in a relatively steep climb in productivity and solvency. As soon as a desired rate of return is reached, the colony ceases to invest large amounts, and saves a maximum amount against the time when part of the colony population will leave to establish a daughter colony. Modest improvements in the level of living also are made, most of them involving collective consumption rather than the amount of cash allowed the family for personal expenditures. However, in general the colony ceases to grow economically, and stays on what we have called the "plateau" of affluence. This is not only because of the need to save cash, but because of Hutterian beliefs, which accept practical economic efficiency but discourage commercial orientation. The Hutterites are forbidden to invest in stocks and bonds, or in any other form of speculation, just as they are forbidden to buy and sell goods at a profit and to enter into competitive manufacturing. A few colonies have invested in securities, and a few colonies do increase their productive investments indefinitely, but they are criticized and censured by other colonies for it. Colonies with cash savings in excess of their scheduled savings must lend money to others who need it; a great deal of moral pressure is brought to bear on a "rich" colony to use its surplus to help others.

The practical side of the Brethren's consumption austerity, then, is the need to save for fission. At the same time, consumption austerity as an ideal is functionally reinforced—perhaps even sustained—by the fission process, since this requires a high rate of cash savings that must be withheld from potential consumption uses. In the background of this process is the high rate of population growth, which creates the need for fission—a need based, of course, on the Hutterian definition of the ideal size of a colony. Yet even this conception is importantly conditioned by the facts of Northern Great Plains agricultural productivity and rate of returns. It is doubtful that the colonies could support very many more than 150 persons on each of the areas of land usually available to them.

These factors are summarized graphically in Diagram 4, where they are compared with a schematic representation of the situation in the Israeli kibbutz. The reader should be warned that this comparison is highly generalized, and lacks concrete quantitative documentation. However, a fairly close study of the two types of communal economies has led the writer to have considerable confidence in this interpretation.

Diagram 4 shows that though the Hutterian population rises steeply, the consumption curve generally remains low and nearly flat throughout the history of the colony, from inception to first fission, and through the subsequent rebuilding phase. At the point of fission, the consumption level may drop slightly because of withdrawal of cash and other facilities. However, since the colony is relieved of half of its population at this time, the possibility of a quick recovery and even an additional rise, owing to the higher per capita consumption made possible by reduced population, is present, as indicated by the dotted line. Very few, if any, colonies submit to the temptation to take advantage of reduced population in this way, and to consume at a higher rate. Moreover, in the usual fission situation, the reduction in resources is sufficient to control undue expenditure. However, it is a possibility, and there are reports of a few colonies indulging in this practice.

The curve of productive investment rises steeply, then levels out as the colony ceases to grow and heavy savings begin. Thus the fission process creates a distinctive shape for the whole Hutterian assemblage of growth curves. It is the fission process that controls the economic development of the individual colony.

The typical kibbutz pattern differs. The number of kibbutzim is very large, and there is considerable variation in their size and style of enterprise, but the economic forces playing upon the kibbutz, as well as the distinctive beliefs of its members, push it toward the expansive pattern shown on the diagram. The kibbutz does not undergo fission, but encourages its population to grow indefinitely (though more slowly than the colony, since the goal of a stable, growing communal society is basic to kibbutz values). The kibbutz does everything possible to keep its members and their offspring from leaving the community. The mean population of contemporary kibbutzim is around 300; a few have as many as 1,500 members.

Since the kibbutz population increases indefinitely, so must its productivity. Hence kibbutz investments for increasing production continually rise. The kibbutz continually experiments with new enterprises, and intensifies production by every scientific means available. It has recently introduced non-agricultural forms of production in small factories, in order to increase and sustain income. The kibbutz is an exceedingly well-planned enterprise—far more so than the Hutterian colony. The future of kibbutz population growth and productivity patterns are not known in the technical sense; that is, it is an open growth pattern, and if it levels off, it will be because of inherent limitations, not the mechanical force of fission that affects Hutterian growth.

The level of consumption rises steadily in the kibbutz, although emphasis is placed on collective forms of spending. The overall level of living, while higher than that of the Hutterian colony, is relatively modest by "outside" standards, owing both to the need to use money for productive investment, and to the effect of religious beliefs. However, kibbutz collective consumption has been rising relatively rapidly in recent years, as the members of the older pioneer generation, who sacrificed their urban, middle-class standard of living in Europe in order to settle Israel, demand a degree of gratification in retirement. Consumption rise has also been dictated by the need to make the kibbutz attractive to the younger members, who have been leaving in increasing numbers. (Swimming pools, movies, and paid vacations are now common, and dwelling units become more commodious with each new construction phase.) These needs for increased consumption expenditures have competed with the need to reinvest surplus funds in production. There has been considerable controversy in kibbutz communities over this problem.[8]

Though the population of the individual kibbutz is flexible, whereas the colony population is never allowed to exceed a certain maximum without fission, the population growth rate of all the kibbutzim is much lower than the Hutterian overall growth rate. In the 1960's, kibbutzim population in Israel was barely holding its own, while the Hutterian was doubling every twenty years. This indicates that the Hutterites are forced to control consumption as a practical financial measure; and it also suggests that the kibbutzim may increase consumption at less financial risk than the colonies.

Both communal systems display a measure of functional homeostasis as a practical state of affairs; that is, in the 1960's, during the period of observation, both the Hutterites and the kibbutznikim were succeeding in maintaining desired levels of living at existing levels of production and population. However, these conditions could and will change. The kibbutzim may cease to grow, and may even experience a population drop—in which case, assuming that prices and costs remain stable, consumption can continue to rise. The Hutterites are approaching the limits of expansion. In a few years it will be exceedingly difficult for them to locate sites for new colonies, and they will need to find ways to limit population growth or to increase productivity, or both. Hutterian consumption

---

[8] In 1966, the writer witnessed a case illustrating this situation. A particular kibbutz was required to decide whether or not to purchase refrigerators for the family dwelling units (the issue had been proposed by some of the older members). At a long assembly meeting, the issue was voted down, largely by the younger managerial element, who felt that the community economy needed further productive investment, and could not afford to buy sixty refrigerators. See Darin-Drabkin (1962, Ch. 8).

will probably not rise, not only because of their austerity principle, but also because of economic necessity.

The policy of the first kibbutz, Daganiya, was to take care of population growth by fission, since it was believed that communalism works best in small communities. Daganiya actually did divide: it was the only kibbutz to do so. The policy of retaining population developed because of pressures from the outside to increase production. This increase required a large labor force. Moreover the great majority of kibbutzim were founded by colonists and refugees, rather than by members of already existing communities. The kibbutz was a refuge, a home; no one wanted to leave. The consequence has been growing community populations, but a static or declining overall population. The Brethren's case is the reverse; consequently they can control the economy of the individual colony.

We have seen that the level of economic rationality in the kibbutz is considerably in excess of that in the colony. The kibbutzim have been thoroughly integrated into the national economy of Israel and its export business, which requires versatility and complete control of production. In order to maintain such detailed control over the economy, the kibbutz is required to study its own financial picture in great detail. This is done by constant scrutiny of efficiency and productivity of the individual enterprises, or "branches" as they are called. The analytical procedure consists of the following steps (here somewhat simplified). (1) Each branch is assessed in terms of its contribution to the consumption and service expenditures of the kibbutz, usually by dividing the total per capita consumption and service expenses by the number of days of work in the branch, which gives the value of one day's work in that branch. (2) Each branch is studied as a separate enterprise in terms of its ability to pay for its own costs and realize a profit. This is done by standard bookkeeping methods. (3) The sales of agricultural products in each branch are studied with reference to Israeli national quotas, and production for the following year in each branch is adjusted accordingly. The precise financial position of each enterprise branch in the kibbutz can be calculated, and its activities curtailed, increased, or even terminated as necessary. All this implies a high degree of involvement of the kibbutz with the "outside," and a minute interlocking of its economic activity, and much of its consumption patterning, with external standards and requirements. The individual kibbutz has become, therefore, a functioning unit of the overall economy of Israel.

The Hutterian colony, on the other hand, is a relatively isolated, independent farming community or farm enterprise that takes its chances in the general North American market, like other individual enterprises. Its operation does not require the degree of rational planning and analysis exhibited by the kibbutz, nor does it have at its command the skills to perform these operations. There are signs that pressures for more rational control are building up in the colony economic system, primarily because of the ever-increasing costs of agricultural production. It remains to be seen how the Brethren will cope with these pressures within the framework of their traditional economic and religious principles.

EIGHT

Labor, Management, and Farming Techniques

Labor is a major preoccupation among agrarians. The socialist or utopian-socialist tradition in communalism, beginning with the *fouriériste* phalanxes of the eighteenth century and culminating with the Israeli kibbutzim in the twentieth, has always given work an important emphasis, and in extreme cases, an end-value. In these movements, which were for the most part conceived by urban intellectuals, the agrarian life was idealized as a means of escaping from the corrupt influences of capitalist society, and the communal farm was seen as a haven from effete civilization where the "working man" could really work with his hands and his body.

In the religious-communal tradition, labor has always held an important place, but on the whole it has not been seen as an end in itself. The Hutterites consider work important, but they do not use it as a source of discipline or measure of achievement as the kibbutz has done. There the individual's capacity for work is a prime factor in the community's evaluation of his worth.

All Hutterian colony members, including the children, are expected to work.[1] Labor is expended not only on the major tasks of

---

[1] The work routine of the typical Jasper colony is a steady but relatively relaxed one. The morning bell rings at 6:30; breakfast is at 7; work begins about 7:30. A mid-morning snack is served. Dinner is at 12, and work resumes about 2, after an hour's siesta has been taken. Supper is at 6, and the colonists are free for the rest of the evening, except for certain routine tasks like milking and egg packing. Dur-

farming, which produce income, but also on construction, maintenance, the garden, and other activities that sustain life. Labor is occasionally hired, and the Hutterites themselves sometimes "work out" for wages when a colony is in financial difficulty. However, the official or inside view is that labor is not a commodity one purchases, but rather a basic human activity.[2] The Brethren supply nearly all their own labor; it is their personal contribution to the colony economy, and a significant means of saving. The colony does not keep an account of time spent at work, nor does it measure its productivity by the "man-hour" technique, as the kibbutz does, for measurement of the rewards brought by labor would violate the Brethren's principles of assumed equal contribution. This attitude toward work permits the colony to avoid some of the contradictions felt in the kibbutz, where the emphasis placed on work as an ideal occupation often leads to competition for status and concern over seniority.[3]

Most of the Brethren simply look upon work as a necessity. However, underlying this attitude is the secondary concept of work as a general value. Among the Hutterian beliefs is the idea that the individual must contribute to the general welfare; that his own

---

ing slack seasons, snacks can be obtained in the kitchen at any time, and rest periods are more frequent. Although there is no rule against talking, meals are eaten quickly and silently. The main reason for quick meals seems to be that the women need time to clean up the dining hall and kitchen and prepare for the next regular meal. In general, the work routine gives an impression of relaxed efficiency, not furious or grinding activity.

  [2] In both the Hutterian colony and the kibbutz there is anxiety shown in the debate over the advisability of hiring labor. In the case of the colony, heavy construction activities, especially in the early stages of colony development, occasionally make it necessary or desirable to increase the available labor force by hiring outsiders—although usually some nearby colony will furnish extra labor. In the case of the kibbutz, extra labor has been hired in recent years for the small industrial activities carried on by many kibbutzim as a means of boosting or leveling income, or for the new central service depots established by some of the kibbutz federations. In both the kibbutz and the colony, the hiring of outside labor is viewed as a violation of basic principles of self-help, and also as a source of potential trouble, since the outsiders seldom understand community customs, and can be disturbing to the young people, who often find them fascinating. Both the kibbutz and the colony are established on the self-help principle, especially in the high-cost area of human labor; and to hire outsiders is, in a sense, a confession of inadequacy.

  [3] Cf. Spiro (1956, pp. 75–76, 11–15).

pleasures and wants are unimportant, and that in any case they must be kept in control lest the system of communal ownership and consumption austerity break down. Work is the physical manifestation of the individual's assent to the group purpose. While working, the Hutterite is expected to be conscious that he is making his contribution, and to take "joy" in it; therefore he is expected to work steadily and regularly. The Hutterian values concerning work thus seem to strike a balance between two extremes: on the one hand, the utopian-socialist concept of work as a desirable end in itself; and on the other, the urban-cultural concept of work as a meaningless burden to be eliminated.

Although their rationale is unique, the Brethren's attitudes toward work are not radically different from those taken by most of the farmers and ranchers of the region. While these individual enterprises are chronically short of help, and hence must objectify the concept of work as a commodity, in their own labor they seem neither to elevate work as an ideal, nor to regard it as an unnecessary or meaningless burden. Instead, their attitude is utilitarian: work is simply that which one does in order to survive and to carry on agrarian life.

Division of Labor

In the colony, work begins with "play" in early childhood. The Brethren give their children very few toys, either homemade or factory-made, but instead allow them to play with the tools and devices of the farm. The writer witnessed several sessions of such play involving the children of farm managers. These children were encouraged by their fathers to use tools in constructive ways, and also to take apart and put together complex devices like the transmission gears of a poultry feeding channel. Children of all ages learn farm routine by performing such tasks as garden harvesting, housepainting, chicken slaughtering and plucking, and dairying. The Brethren give the children a minimum of formal instruction on such tasks, but permit them to explore each learning opportunity. Control is exercised only when the play becomes dangerous for the child or when the destruction of an important tool or other object seems possible.

When a child is about ten years old, his play activity is gradually replaced by regular work assignments carrying some real degree of responsibility. The male labor force between the ages of 10 and 15 is important to the colony economy: these boys take over many small tasks and thus free the older men for heavier or more important duties. Among jobs assigned to adolescents are cattle herding, pen maintenance, egg collecting and sorting, livestock and poultry feeding, and some tractor operation. Girls of the same age mainly babysit, help with household tasks in the nuclear family, and learn the communal kitchen and food preparation routines.

In a typical Jasper colony there is a distinct division of tasks between the men and the women. Gardening, housekeeping, clothing manufacture, and the tasks performed in the communal kitchen and food storage areas fall to the women, while the men are responsible for all the farming operations. In the colonies we studied, the women were divided into three groups: the young unmarrieds (girls 15 and older), the married women, and the spinsters. The first group constituted the only true "labor force" so far as manual labor was concerned. In general, the women cease to do heavy work like gardening, at the age of 42, but continue to help in the kitchen. The spinsters sit with the children, run the kindergarten, and work in the kitchen.

Among the men, the three basic groups are the managers, the field hands, and the young boys. The field hands may include men who were managers at one time, and who resigned or were voted out, but the majority are men who have never enjoyed a managerial position. In all the colonies studied, there were men in their late thirties who had never held a managerial position, but who expected eventually to do so. However, the fission process means that sooner or later all men will be given responsible positions. "We must give them a chance, otherwise they feel left out," remarked a progressive young manager about several men in their late thirties who had not yet been managers. However, even if they work as field hands or laborers, such men are not in strictly menial positions, for each is responsible for the operation and routine repair of his own farm machine, whether it be a tractor, cultivator, or combine. While highly technical repairs on these machines are performed by the so-called "blacksmith" (the shop foreman or chief mechanic) and his staff of young assistants, all the men are encouraged to work in the shops if they have the time to do so; and any man with the requisite skills is free to use the colony tools and machinery at will.

While the men are responsible for servicing the machinery with which they work, the women are not expected to repair their kitchen devices. Women are occasionally seen operating garden tractors or repairing small household items, but the men take care of the larger pieces of equipment such as meat-slicers, laundry devices, ovens, ranges, and refrigeration units. In most of the Jasper colonies the women paint the buildings, partly because painting is considered a routine, low-skilled task, and partly because the men are busy harvesting during the dry, warm days of late summer, when it is best to do painting. Elderly men sometimes join the women at this task.

In their traditional occupations of gardening, painting, food preparation, sewing, laundry, and so on, the women show considerable initiative and consciousness of their economic value. The men sometimes compliment them, but generally do not interfere or give them orders. The routines of colony life are usually so well established that all the members know what needs to be done, and when. There are few announcements or orders given at gatherings like meals; if a job needs doing, the word gets around quietly, and a task force mobilizes on the spot. (This differs, of course, from the major farming operations, where the Farm Boss supervises; these are planned in advance and executed according to schedule.)

In the work performed by the women, the level of mechanization is not as high as it is in farming activities. This is partly because of the nature of the tasks themselves, but also because there is a silent understanding that the young unmarried women need to be kept busy lest they become discontented or distract the men. The major female labor force consists of the unmarried girls; and many colonies have more than they really need to perform the routine tasks. The problem of "unemployed" young women has become somewhat more urgent since many colonies have invested in garden tractors and cultivating attachments, for in the past, hand cultivation kept the girls busy most of the day. Moreover, in the old days the women also cared for the poultry and were responsible for many more tasks connected with food production. However, the reasons for keeping the young girls busy are not openly discussed, at least with outsiders. At one colony, housepainting was done by a team of fifteen young women, while all the field farming activities were performed by five men and their machines. The women painted by hand. The writer asked why the colony had not bought a paint sprayer, and the answer was a deadpan "We don't need one."

However, if current trends continue, eventually the colony *will* buy a paint sprayer—partly because many Brethren cannot resist gadgetry, and partly because the productive principle is deeply ingrained in the culture. This acquisition will shorten the amount of time spent in painting, and something else will have to be found for the women to do. As the colonies slowly acquire more and more basic conveniences, they are required to make adjustments in their division of labor. The move toward labor-saving procedures, even for the women, is made possible by the Brethren's utilitarian attitude toward work; but at the same time, the traditional system whereby each person contributes to the welfare of the whole group is endangered by the substitution of machines and labor-saving methods for hand labor. The Brethren are conscious of this—perhaps more than they show—and hence move more cautiously in certain spheres of mechanization, particularly those having to do with the work of women.

The women's tasks, like cooking and sewing, are organized on an informal basis, with little supervision. For example, the women choose the fabrics used for clothing, but the Elders sometimes step in to caution them against fabrics with patterns and colors too far removed from the traditional. Some observers have noted a tendency toward greater personal autonomy and forwardness among women than among men, which might be the result of the fact that the men generally do not interfere very much in the activities assigned to the women. On their psychological tests, Kaplan and Plaut (1958, pp. 34–44) found a different pattern of responses among women to the communal milieu, which indicated that women had a somewhat greater autonomy and independence. However, other observers, including the present writer, are not inclined to make too much of this, and feel that the observed autonomy of behavior is largely an age-grade phenomenon, and is characteristic only of young girls up to the age of 19 or 20. Moreover, the pattern is more marked in the Darius and Schmieden Leute groups than among the Lehrer, where all the women are quite reserved.

In terms of task-accomplishment, Hutterian efficiency is great. But the pervading egalitarianism of colony social life prevents firm, overt direction or "bossing." "You have to be careful with these men; if you tell them what to do too often, they won't do so well," stated a Farm Boss, who backed up this observation with the comment that "it is the same on these big ranches—I know—I worked as a cattle boss for a while in Alberta." The writer observed the methods of cattle handlers in this particular colony at some length, and noted their clumsiness; yet the speaker, who obviously knew better, rarely corrected his men, and when he did, did so in a casual manner. Such relaxed practices matter little in the long run, because the overall direction is competent. (This sort of delicate control is also found, as the Farm Boss noted, on most of the big farms and ranches in the West.)

Farm Management

It will be recalled that each of the colony's farming activities is under the management of one man. Overall direction is provided by the Farm Boss and the Council, and financial management by the Householder. The entire colony constitutes the labor force, although in each colony there is a group of men who do only farm work, and do not hold managerial or executive positions. The allocation of labor is under the direction of the Farm Boss.

The system of incentive and competition for resources that exists between the several agricultural managers is a de facto consequence of Hutterian economy. From the point of view of the colony as an enterprise, this pattern of indirect or covert competition functions to promote efficient and profitable modes of operation. Each manager is expected to become an expert in his own field of agriculture. The typical manager obtains farm information from many sources: from agricultural extension services (local and Provincial), commercial companies, visiting experts, other colonies, and local farmers. In order to run his enterprise efficiently, he must thoroughly investigate costs and varieties of equipment before proposing investments. He must be able to figure cost-price ratios, and to determine whether a labor-saving device will pay for itself easily; to keep up with the advances made by other colonies, and to evaluate their innovations in terms of the needs of his own colony. Above all, he must be prepared to forego his own plans in the face of a decision against him by the rest of the colony. Vital interest in his job, rather than personal identification with it, is the ideal goal of the Hutterian manager in his approach to his endeavors.[4]

This pattern of activity is indirectly competitive, though competition is rarely manifested by open argument or striving, but more typically appears as the personal cultivation of farm skills and literacy. The managers avoid charges of ambition, self-seeking, or over-identification with the project or the job assignment, lest they be accused of "idolatry," i.e., of substituting a material interest for the Christian way and for the general welfare of the colony. Overt

[4] The writer witnessed these modes of managerial behavior during his close association with several of the agricultural managers in one of the colonies. He spent many hours with each manager over a period of three months, and became the personal friend of several of them. These men made great efforts to secure the latest information on their fields, and spent hours in technical preparation while planning and advocating improvements. In several cases, the writer assisted them in their search for literature on specific problems of technical development. Comparable participant experience, but over a briefer period, was engaged in with the members of a kibbutz.

competitive behavior is suppressed, and the emphasis is placed on extreme objectivity and rationality: the manager is expected to advocate the interests of his enterprise only in the most objective, neutral, and dispassionate terms, and with full awareness of the general economic picture.

The managers often show persistence and ingenuity in developing successful strategies. When a manager is convinced that he needs something, and that the colony will benefit from it, he will launch an intensive though circumspect campaign to obtain it. In one colony, the swine manager and the chief construction engineer worked out a plan for an elaborate manure disposal system capable of handling the hog-barn and feed-lot manure. The scheme involved the construction of a large concrete tank, elaborate piping, carrier-belt mechanisms, and cleaning devices, the total cost of which would have amounted to about $5,000. The initial proposal was made informally, through discussions with the other managers and with the Elders, and the scheme was debated in the colony for six months before it came to a vote. During that period, the two proponents worked out their arguments in detail. They showed that the cost would be amortized in three years, and that the ease of final disposal of the residue would greatly reduce the laborious job of shoveling raw manure.

Opposition to the project was not, however, confined to those with practical arguments concerning costs and labor. The most serious criticism came from a group who were opposed to the idea on the grounds that it was new and untried, and that it involved spending money to lighten a burden—in their eyes, a morally dangerous act, since the Brethren were already far too prone to accept the values of the majority society. According to this group, disagreeable labor is the Hutterite's lot. These arguments are representative of the thought of the ultra-conservative faction in every colony. In this particular instance (as in many other cases during the 1960's), the conservative faction "lost." The two proponents of the project persisted in their informal arguments, and eventually, when the issue came to the vote at a meeting, the majority decided in favor of the plan. The tank and other equipment were built and installed over a period of three months, and all the members of the colony exhibited considerable pride in the layout, never failing to escort visitors to it and to explain how it worked.

This example does not imply that determined young managers always win. Indeed, they often lose, especially on routine requests for equipment that they and everyone else realize they can easily get along without. One elderly executive summed it up this way: "Sometimes these young men [the managers], they want everything, you know. But they can't have it. They will ask for it whether anyone else needs something or not. The only way it can be settled is for the Elder [First Minister] and the Householder to get together and work it out and make it clear how things should be divided up. There has to be a balance." That is, the competing advocates are shown what is best even before the issue is brought before the voting membership, since it is wrong that competition be openly displayed at a meeting. If possible, conflicts are worked out in advance of the meeting; but sometimes the competing advocates dispassionately present their cases to the assembly, and the voting members are asked to choose.

In large-scale enterprises, where recurrent crisis situations require immediate action, managers must have a certain flexibility, and be able to deal with problems that challenge established routines. Furthermore, they must be able to deal in a diplomatic yet effective manner with the factors of authority and senority. The case of Colony 6 and its youthful staff, described in the earlier chapters, is one example of the judicious avoidance of conservatism. The Hutterites show their recognition of the need for flexibility by giving the individual managers a certain degree of autonomy. Each manager is permitted to keep his own books, and to develop his own enterprise as he sees fit (subject always to colony approval). In the case of the Brethren, the very tight control exercised over funds by the Householder and the executive group in general can create tension, but this control is not only economically advantageous to the colony as an enterprise, but is also ideologically necessary because of the principles of communal property ownership and consumption austerity. In most colonies it is felt that all expenditures of more than a dollar should be approved by the Householder, but no great attempt is made to enforce this as a rule. Expenditures of more than a hundred dollars definitely require discussion and vote by the membership.

A study was made of various types of decisions to determine the degree of rigidity that control may create in the Hutterian management system. The results of this inquiry can be summarized briefly. Any decision involving a serious emergency such as the complete breakdown of a wheat combine during harvesting can be made on their own by the men in charge of the operation, without a meeting being held or even, in some cases, without detailed consultation with the Householder. Complete flexibility is indicated in these cases, and the normal rules of permission and vote are suspended. In large, mechanized agricultural operations, decisions of an emergency character are common enough, and the Hutterites are at least as flexible here as their Gentile neighbors are.

It should be added that a similar flexibility is demonstrated in the case of human emergencies, for example, long trips to hospitals, or to other colonies to visit seriously ill relatives. The Brethren simply do not pinch pennies when trips and expenditures are obviously necessary for major human and economic reasons. As one informant commented on decisions of this kind, "We don't get into any kind of trouble with things like that—we couldn't afford to." He meant that the "bosses" would not give him a hard time for making a decision without their full approval, because in the long run such leniency pays off in morale and safety. A similar latitude is shown on small expenditures of between one dollar and fifty dollars. Frequently on a trip to town the manager will buy a needed item out of colony funds entrusted to him for other purposes, and report it to the Householder upon return. This privilege must not be abused, however; the Brethren say that in general it is always better to check with the Householder before making a purchase.

Technical tasks that arise in the course of operations and require a major shift in the labor force can be undertaken at the discretion of the Farm Boss. These decisions do not involve actual expenditures, but they may delay the completion of other remunerative tasks. According to the rules, shifts in task emphasis require discussion and vote; but considerable flexibility is shown in this on a day-to-day basis. In fact, there is much evidence that the Brethren use their formal decision-making apparatus sparingly, lest it be resented. The Jasper colonies differed in this respect, and one colony studied appeared to be unduly cautious. According to an informant, this particular colony was plagued by tension. One common manifestation of colony tension and lack of trust among members is the insistence that every decision be discussed and voted upon.

A number of tasks are relegated to the "routine" category, and hence do not require discussion or special permission: the planting of the garden, once the routine is well established; the planting of most crops; the construction of buildings, once the decision has been made to erect them; the harvesting of garden produce; and the slaughtering and processing of poultry. In the beginning, all such decisions must be planned and discussed; but if by repetition they become routine, the manager or supervisor of the task simply asks the Farm Boss to supply him with the needed workers, or commandeers the female labor force.

In general, the Brethren are relatively rigid when it comes to decisions that involve traditional concepts of diversification or major expenditures, or those that are not urgent. In all other matters they show a sensible flexibility well adapted to their type of operations. There is, however, a *climate* of supervision and control not found on Gentile farms and ranches, where the individual operator is in personal control of his funds, and does not have the problem of allocating a relatively large labor force. Occasionally local people get the impression that the Hutterian managers are "under the thumb" of the bosses, and have to ask for everything they need. However, it is doubtful that they are any less free to make decisions than the managers of the units on a large commercial farm. The fact that they so seldom abuse the privileges given them testifies to the general sense of discipline and commitment, bred by careful socialization, that characterizes Hutterian life.

Styles of Management

While the general procedures of agricultural management are similar in all the colonies, there are individual differences. In the previous chapter we generalized the strategies of economic development and noted that after a period of intensive buildup, the typical colony ceases heavy productive investment, and saves most of its surplus in the form of cash against colony fission. However, it was also noted that some colonies continue to invest more than others, although colonies that do this on a large scale are rare. We attempted to analyze the existing major differences in overall management strategy with reference to productive investment and other features. Although differences were visible in the six Jasper colonies, we needed comparative data in order to be sure of the precise status of these differences. Therefore we visited several colonies in Alberta, including some of the parent colonies of the Jasper groups. This venture gave us an opportunity to examine a larger sample of colonies from the two Leute, Darius and Lehrer, to which the Jasper colonies belong. After our interviews at the Alberta colonies, it became possible for us to define three dominant styles of management, and to consider the extent to which each was associated with the two Leute, and with the various stages of colony economic development. Not all the colonies studied exhibited one of the three styles clearly; it soon became evident that, aside from a few extreme cases, we were dealing with tendencies rather than with clear-cut types.

The three dominant managerial styles we call "relaxed," "balanced," and "pushing." The "relaxed" style is characterized by a tendency to keep investments at relatively modest levels, but to permit the regime to drift toward more profitable enterprises and thus become relatively specialized. Three Darius colonies—two nascent and one mature—exhibited this style, as did one mature colony of the Lehrer Leut. "Relaxed" colonies were not generally inclined to plan carefully, and some had unbalanced equipment and machine inventories. Some "relaxed" colonies were situated in fortunate resource areas, and consequently their specialization was associated with relatively high and assured yields. In two of the Alberta colonies with heavy soils and good rainfall, the emphasis was placed on grain production, and the other possible sources of income were left unexplored. One of these colonies also displayed a pattern of extreme managerial autonomy, in which the various enterprise managers were free to run their sub-enterprises as they pleased, with less direction than is typical. An easygoing Farm Boss was a critical factor here, but this situation also reflected a generally relaxed executive group and the relative permissiveness of most of the members of the colony.

In colonies exhibiting the "balanced" style—one nascent and three mature colonies of the Lehrer Leut—tension was evident in the effort to control the drift toward more profitable production, and to maintain diversification to the fullest possible extent. Controlled expenditure and a very conservative investment policy were also characteristic of this style, and cultural customs were rigorously observed. Strong executive control was evident. Such colonies tended to be critical of the "relaxed" colonies, and to accuse them of poor management. On the other hand, the "relaxed" colonies sometimes criticized the "balanced" ones for being conservative, authoritarian, and bound by tradition. The "balanced" colonies felt their procedures were the most sensible in the light of fluctuating markets and resources; and they viewed uncontrolled drift toward profits as dangerous, since it might result in the neglect of other potentially remunerative enterprises. The executives of these colonies were apprehensive of allowing conditions to develop in which the members might become unemployed through a decline in the market value of the emphasized crop.

The third style of management, which we have called "pushing," is apparently rare; in our sampling, we found it only in one nascent Darius colony and one mature Lehrer group. It is characterized by the deliberate development of many new enterprises, and the expenditure of large sums to establish them, in an effort to maintain the highest possible production in all fields. In general, the "pushing" colonies were more highly diversified, more efficient in agricultural techniques and management, and much less conservative in investments than the "relaxed" colonies. One was quite conservative and controlled in behavior and customs; the other was more lax. The "pushing" colonies were criticized by the others as being "out for the dollar"—that is, for attempting to behave like large commercial organizations—a tendency thought of generally by the Brethren as detrimental to Hutterian cultural and religious integrity. In most cases the critics were supporters of the "balanced" style, who conceived of economic affairs as being indissolubly linked to religion: one does not develop the farm enterprise in order to make money, but rather in order to be able to carry on Hutterian society; therefore commercialization must be checked. The "pushing" colonies had very extensive investments in buildings and equipment, and also were suspected of owning large bank accounts.

The classification of these colonies in terms of "nascent" and "mature" does not reveal a clear pattern, probably because the sample was too small. However, briefer studies of six additional colonies suggested that the "relaxed" and "pushing" styles tended to characterize the younger or "nascent" types. Thus, there is a suggestion that aside from long-term management policies, colonies may manifest more aggressive or profit-oriented techniques in the earlier stages of development, when every effort is being made to accumulate income and pay off debts.

As we have noted, the Darius colonies, both parent and daughter, most often exhibited the "relaxed" style; the Lehrer, the "balanced." The Lehrer were the more conservative, in the sense of conscious adherence to Hutterian traditions of austerity, and sober, efficient "correctness." The Darius were less conservative and more outgoing. They also tended to be less cautious as to new colony establishment, and would permit a colony to start life with less than the necessary financial and human resources. The farming practices and financial management of many Darius colonies tended to be loosely organized, though, of course there were exceptions.

The question of whether or not the Jasper daughter colonies maintained the management style characteristic of their Alberta parent colonies cannot really be answered here, since we could not control the age factor in our sampling. As noted, younger colonies may display certain styles simply because of their level of development. However, in one important case, a Jasper Lehrer colony, the oldest of the six and consequently on or near its affluent plateau, was the leading exponent in the region of the "balanced" style, while its mature parent colony in Alberta was an outstanding example of the "relaxed" style. Significantly, the relationship between these two colonies was not a close one, in spite of the parent-offspring tie. The Jasper group represented a conservative faction that had split away from the parent colony (the normal fission process in this case could be interpreted as a "split," rather than as a simple division). The Jasper colony had much closer relations with another Alberta colony exhibiting similar management practices. The men of these two colonies explained: "We do things the same way."

The fact that one Lehrer colony was thought of by the other colonies in the sampling as particularly "pushing" may be significant. Cultural conservatism and adherence to religious traditions may produce in the colony that practices them a conscious avoidance of over-commercialization; or, conversely, they may lead to extreme efficiency and a single-minded preoccupation with profit. The Lehrer "pushing" colony was not lax in its religious life and in following custom, but the Darius "pushing" colonies were relatively so. Thus commercialization can lead to religious laxity, or a single-minded pecuniary interest, or both. The Hutterites sometimes observe that the greatest dangers to their faith and style of life are prosperity and complete personal freedom; and that in prosperous times they must redouble their efforts to adhere to the traditional customs and beliefs. A little persecution, a little constriction, is safer than ease and plenty.

Farming Practices

In most rural districts with a Hutterian or Mennonite population, it has become a commonplace that the sectarians are excellent farmers—better than most of their neighbors. This particular view was probably not as prevalent in the Jasper region as elsewhere, for the reason that the colonies were younger, and their agricultural techniques exhibited the usual amount of experiment and error. At most, one out of the six colonies—the oldest—had achieved a stable, adapted regime. Although colony managers differ in ability, the need to support a relatively large population on a large, but low per-capita, land area requires a sustained level of relatively high efficiency. It also requires a constant effort to acquire knowledge of improvements in agricultural techniques, which is made somewhat difficult by the limited formal education the Hutterites are permitted. At the same time, it is facilitated by their well-developed mechanisms of intercolony information transfer.

An evaluative analysis of farming practices should take account of several factors. Techniques may be judged on the basis of pure efficiency standards (the extent to which they provide a maximum productive yield at lowest possible cost), or they may be viewed with reference to conservationist standards: that is, granting the need for efficient output, to what extent is this accomplished without harming the available resources? Farming techniques can be analyzed also with reference to the process of innovation, by asking what new techniques and equipment have been adopted, and at what rates. One of the difficulties of existing studies of farming techniques made by agricultural extension agencies is that single standards—adoptions, productivity, management skill, knowledge, and so on—are often applied without reference to reality. A farmer who readily adopts any and all techniques presented to him may do so at the peril of bankruptcy; or a farmer who farms according to the latest extension bulletin may be doing so at the risk of exhausting his soil resources in a decade. A farmer who is an extremely conservative innovator and therefore produces less, may act out of a carefully considered unwillingness to take high risks.

In the Canadian Plains, the decades of drouth and economic depression, coupled with the relative lack of capital, bred extremely conservative attitudes. Most farmers and ranchers of the Jasper region in the early 1960's exemplified this conservative strategic bent. In a study of farming skills and practices for the region as a whole, we determined that the majority of farmers were conservative on innovation, skeptical of untested "gimmicks" and new procedures, cautious in financing, and willing to defer gratification in order to put their enterprises on secure economic foundations. In our study of adaptive selection, we also found that aggressive, innovative, production-minded farmers were very few in number, although they had been more numerous in earlier years. Such people appear to have constituted a very important plurality of all persons migrating out of the region. On the other hand, in recent years better facilities for obtaining loans and building up natural resources have become available, and some of these people have been reappearing in the region. Very inefficient, ignorant, and poverty-stricken farmers, who in the past have found it impossible to remain alive, even at marginal levels, in this extreme environment, have left in droves. Consequently the majority of remaining farmers and ranchers in the region are those in the conservative middle range of skills, who operate their enterprises with great caution and only rarely make risky or expensive investments in additional facilities such as land, machines, and new types of seed.

In considering the nature of Hutterian farming practices,[5] we may first look at the Brethren's position with respect to agronomic and technical innovation. Table 11 summarizes the differences in adoptions between two colonies and the local farmers and ranchers. The data were taken from various manuals and guidebooks, and from information gained in the field with agricultural experts, and were considered indexes of professionally defined excellence in Saskatchewan northern Plains farm culture. Of the two colonies examined here, X and Y, X had the best overall agronomic regime by these standards of any colony in the area, and also was best with respect to financial balance and economic acumen. Y had a lower adoption rate, and a less well-balanced farming program, but on the other hand, Y was a relative newcomer, and X was the oldest colony in the region. While the time difference is partly responsible for the difference in techniques, it is probably not wholly so. The two colonies also exhibited differences in man-

[5] Cf. Riley (1959) for agricultural practices in the South Dakota colonies; Peters (1965, Chap. 7), for the Manitoba colonies.

Table 11—Schedule of adoption of selected items by Colonies X and Y, and by regional farmers

Item	Date adopted by Colony X, or frequency of use[a]	Date adopted by Colony Y, or frequency of use[b]	Date of earliest adoption by farmers or ranchers	Date of general use by farmers or ranchers
Blade cultivators for fallowing	1955	1960	1955, by a few large farmers.	Still not in general use; disc machines more common.
Self-powered grain combines	1950	1958	1950	1956. A few smaller, more conservative farmers still use separators.
Registered seed	1952	Uses occasionally. as early as 1930.	One or two farmers,	Less than half of regional farmers used in 1963.
Registered bulls	1954	1959	1953	Less than half of local ranchers by 1963; majority of farmers used Community Pasture herd, which is registered stock.
Fertilizer	Started use in 1964.[c]	Does not use.	1960, by one or two farmers.	Still very rare: about 10 in region use consistently.
Extension information and services	Uses regularly and systematically.	Uses regularly but not systematically.	Almost never used by ranchers. Used more often by farmers, but not consistently.	
Farm machinery test data	1959. Occasionally used, but farmers prefer own experimentation. Tests often not relevant to use.	Does not use.	Very rarely used by farmers; only 1 in 25 has heard of these reports. Ranchers rarely use; have less need to do so.	

[a] Colony X entered the Jasper area in 1952.
[b] Colony Y entered the Jasper area in 1959.
[c] Another colony, Colony 6, was beginning to fertilize at this time in response to special habitat problems.

agement style attributable in part to the level of literacy and knowledge of their members: as we defined these styles earlier, "X" was a "balanced" colony, "Y" an example of the "relaxed" style.

The following conclusions may be drawn from these data: progressive Colony "X" is well ahead of the Jasper farmers (and especially the ones in the general locality of the colonies—see Chapter 3) with respect to time of adoption and use of a number of key items. It is also ahead of Colony "Y," although "Y" is probably also somewhat more advanced than the average farmer. Allowing for scale differences, some of the best farmers of the region are as advanced as the Hutterites in their modernity, but they are relatively few in number, and their farms tend to be the most richly endowed with natural resources. With respect to particular items like registered seed and bulls, the colonies have an advantage over the individual farmers, since they are able to share supplies and obtain discounts on a volume basis. To some extent, the relatively progressive position of the colonies is not due necessarily to the Brethren's special abilities or disposition toward innovation, but to the scale of colony agriculture, and to the efficient information network between colonies.

We noted above that innovation seems to be correlated with general financial excellence in farming. That is, those who adopt and innovate also do well economically. However, this correlation does not necessarily hold when it comes to conservation of resources. Many of the big, innovative farmers of the region unquestionably abuse their soil or pasture. They may defend these practices in various ways, but there is reason to believe that in time, serious damage will be done. Some of these operators also go deeply into debt, counting on their high productivity to cover them against disaster. The colonies have special problems of their own: Colony "X" is not guilty of abuse of resources (in this case innovativeness goes along with conservation), but "Y" is guilty of irresponsible use of some of its resources. It wastes irrigation water and risks salinization of its irrigated tracts; it overgrazes pastures, and so on. But again these differences between the two colonies with respect to conservation may vanish as "Y" matures.

In any case, conservation of natural resources does not mean the same thing to the colonies as it does to the farmers. On the farms it is combined with extremely conservative, small-scale operation, while in the colonies, it is a phase of large-scale operation. A small farmer conserves because he does not innovate or invest; the colonies conserve *and* innovate and invest. The colonies can afford to conserve because they have enough capital background, due to their scale and their diversification. The big, innovative Jasper farmers often cannot afford to conserve, because they need to keep productivity very high in order to maintain a favorable financial balance.

While colony agriculture is, on the whole, more efficient and more secure financially than the individual farming program, it does not differ substantially in the basic management skills it requires. The Hutterites do not more frequently conduct detailed studies of their management procedures or economic position than the individual enterprisers do. In fact, they do not do so at all, so far as the writer is aware, while some of the Jasper farmers and ranchers *have* submitted to farm management studies in an effort to improve their efficiency. In any case, a large-scale economy has less need for such studies, since deficiencies, or possible improvements, are simply not as apparent. The small farmer or rancher is much more likely to feel that improvements are needed. At best, the Hutterites are limited to simple cost-price computations and projections. Their limited educational level would not permit more sophisticated studies, and the idea of letting outside experts study their management procedures would violate their sense of privacy. The writer was privileged to overcome some of these objections, but to do so required considerable time and patience. Hutterites are basically trial-and-error farmers like most of their neighbors, though they are, on the whole, the very best kind of empirical operators.

The Jasper brethren seem to have been amazed at what they perceived as the backwardness of farming methods in the region. This perception of course was influenced by the situation in the districts in which they chose to settle, since the difficulties of farmers in these districts contributed to the availability of land. However, the Hutterites often show that they feel superior to their Gentile neighbors, whose smaller investments do not permit them the efficiency of large-scale operations. This feeling was apparent in many conversations with the Brethren. They often remarked, "People around here can learn from the Hutterites." In a few specific instances, this comment seemed justified. On the whole, however, it would be neither practical nor possible for the average Jasper farmer to emulate Hutterian agricultural or economic methods.

Another approach to the analysis of Hutterian and Gentile farming practices is to compare them in terms of phases of development with the general North American pattern, especially with the more progressive and richest sectors of Northern Plains agriculture. We may use the term "basic" to refer to a series of standard routines and devices that permit maximum productivity with the use of "extensive" methods of farming; that is, with methods that fall short of intensive development or enhancement of resources.[6] This category

[6] The following describes the farming methods of Colony X, which comprise a "basic" regime with some intensive practices added:

Grain crop rotation was practiced on a one-to-one basis, with half the cropland in summer fallow each year. Tillage of fallow land was carried out with the blade instrument described in the text, which has received the highest recommendation of Northern Plains agronomists. (The hydraulic lifts for the blades permit detailed control of depth of tillage, thus allowing variation in depth in accordance with soil conditions, which is especially important in soils of varying texture. Soils in most of the colonies were alternately very sandy and moderately heavy.) Lighter land was tilled twice during the summer fallow season, and heavier land, four times—another recommended practice. Registered seed was used extensively. Soil was tilled before the seeding operation with the blade instrument and the rod weeder, since the colony discovered that a hoe-drill did not perform the operation efficiently. Hay baling, which is a problem for most livestock operators, had been reduced to a one-man operation by the use of an automatic bale-pickup and stacking machine. Harvesting was carried out by three combines, which operated continuously, and two heavy trucks, which collected the combined grain. The combines were supplied with gasoline in the field. Swathing, a practice that helps to save the grain in large plantings from spoilage by cutting it and laying it on the ground in optimal condition to await harvesting, was routinely done. Spraying for weed and insect control—a practice that has obtained only limited acceptance among local farmers, but is strongly urged by agronomists, was also routinely done. The Brethren's field practices were initially unsuited to the locality; they had been developed on heavier soils in Alberta. Therefore the early years were marked by unnecessary and excessive tillage and other deleterious or mistaken practices. However, within three years the colony, with the help of professional

is comparable to the "conservationist" approach described earlier for the majority of Jasper farmers, who farm carefully on the available natural resources without employing such techniques as fertilization, soil preparation, complex rotational and hybrid plantings, and sprinkler irrigation. (The term "advanced" will be used here to describe specialized and intensive farming techniques and various other labor-saving agricultural devices.) In terms of this distinction, the colonies were ahead of the farmers in some of the basic techniques; that is, as measured by continental or Great Plains development standards, the colonies were performing at a high level of extensive practice. In terms of the advanced standards, the colonies were also ahead of the average Jasper farmer and rancher, but not appreciably so. While such techniques as fertilization, windbreak planting, elaborate fencing, specialized irrigation, the mechanical processing of silage, forage harvesting, machinery for manure disposal, the construction of circular farm buildings, and

---

advice and manuals, had developed appropriate techniques. (For lack of cash, the colony had to begin its farming without sprays, high-priced machinery, and other needed equipment; it acquired suitable equipment only as its financial position improved.) The colony developed water resources in its pasture areas so as to distribute cattle across the pasture in the most economic manner, although water shortages in one case prevented an ideal grazing pattern. Efforts were made to ameliorate this maladjustment by a careful arrangement of fences. Beef cattle were fattened at the colony on a grain ration and suitable supplements. Swine were confined in concrete-floored buildings equipped with power cleaning equipment. Insects around the swine area were kept to a minimum by the use of special preparations. Chickens were supplied with removable wire roosts so that cleaning of the chicken houses could be done with a minimum of effort. All feeding and watering were done by means of automatic devices. The other colonies differed in farm procedures. For example, one colony did not adjust its summer fallow tillage to soil conditions; another used disc implements instead of blades; one did not use feed supplements for its poultry, and did not keep its swine in concrete-floored pens, although its financial position might have permitted the practice. One colony had too much machinery; the rest had too few machines, or had an imbalance, such as too many or too few combines. None of the other colonies used registered seed, but they did buy seed with informal guarantees of quality. While more details could be given, these should be sufficient to indicate the differences. In general, the colony using optimum practices showed more consistency, and a more determined effort to obtain information on the best practices available. This colony was also characterized by an even distribution of skills and knowledge among the agricultural managers; in other colonies, these were uneven. This difference was not simply the result of individual differences, but reflects the general atmosphere of competence: the superior colony made an effort to urge preparation on its managers, and to encourage education and experimentation.

many other things were entering the Jasper region during the period of study, the entire regional population was "going slow" on these things since they involved capital expenditures that were considered doubtful on the basis of past experience. Nevertheless, the colonies were in the vanguard, along with a few (not more than four or five) of the regional farmers and ranchers. As suggested earlier, the colonies are in a better position to introduce these methods since their capital permits less risk; moreover, they usually combine them with sensible consideration of conservationist practices.

Still another measure of farming skill is the level of technical knowledge possessed by an operator. In comparison to most of their neighbors, the Brethren possessed a larger fund of technical knowledge. We noted a respectable number of technical manuals and guidebooks available on colony premises, in the quarters of the executives, in the shops, or in the possession of the agricultural managers. Though acquisition of these sources of information is largely in the hands of the individual Hutterite, some colonies made it a matter of general responsibility to help their members keep up to date.

Farming information is obtained from several sources; particularly from other colonies, and from agricultural extension officials. The Hutterites stated that since the local "ag reps" (as the extension agents are called in Saskatchewan) get their information from the colleges, it is best to go to the original source. Most such contacts were made by letter rather than by visit to the college. Other important sources of information were the large agricultural supply firms. For example, a company in St. Louis, Missouri, that specializes in feeds and feeding regimes for livestock, has special representatives who tour the Hutterian colonies and give demonstrations of feeding routines allegedly "developed especially for the Hutterite colonies." This representative passes out well-written technical manuals that are collected and read avidly by the Brethren.

The Brethren occasionally visit a Federal Government experimental farm about sixty miles from the Jasper area. This establishment has a large staff of highly qualified experts in all fields of agriculture, including gardening and beekeeping, as well as other more highly specialized activities engaged in by the colonies and a few other farmers. Many of the experimental setups at this farm are geared to the special needs of large-scale operators like the Brethren.

The Hutterites complained to us that much of the agricultural extension literature circulated by official agencies is either too general for their specialized purposes, or is geared to small-scale operations. This was especially true, in their view, of the official *Guide to Farm Practice in Saskatchewan,* a standard publication issued by the College of Agriculture and given very wide circulation throughout the Province. They were more appreciative of the specialized manuals on livestock, forage crops, and so on issued by this agency. They criticized the services of the local "ag rep" on similar grounds: while they respected the man and his knowledge, they felt his recommendations were relevant mainly to the needs of the smaller individual farmer, not to those of large commercial enterprisers like themselves.

The move into Saskatchewan brought the Hutterites into the driest and most variable part of the northern Plains, where they have been required to make changes in the farming methods developed by the parent colonies in Alberta. Since we knew the date of entry of each of the Jasper colonies, it was possible to study the rate at which they acquired new devices and procedures. We found that the colonies required an average of four years after date of entry to adapt methodologically to the special conditions of the Jasper region. Some colonies did it in three, and some in six. All appear to have realized what changes were necessary almost immediately after entry, except the first colony to come, which had to experiment. The extensive information network between colonies permitted a rapid dissemination of pertinent adaptation information; but differences in finances, literacy level, and general ability to utilize information were sufficiently great between colonies that some were able to put information to good use much sooner and more efficiently than others.

Agricultural development at the enterprise level is more than a

simple problem of learning or adoption. It also involves investment opportunities, capital, exposure to various media, and local
resources. An important distinction should be made between techniques that simply require definite knowledge, and those which
are possible only if labor and finances permit. In the case of the
Jasper colonies, our study had to begin with the fact that knowledge
of suitable farming techniques is extremely widespread among the
Hutterites, and is readily available to the Brethren through inter-
colony communication and exchange. Consequently, though there
are marginal differences from colony to colony, the overall picture
is one of relative uniformity. Interchange of farm information takes
place even between colonies that have had acrimonious disputes,
since the farm enterprise managers are free to visit and discuss
matters of common concern among themselves even though their
respective Elders are in disagreement.

In one such case involving the two Jasper colonies most seriously
at odds, the swine bosses regularly exchanged ideas on how to
construct concrete swine barns and manure carriers; and the farm
bosses did likewise with regard to new cultivating implements.
A particular method of barn construction developed by one colony
was copied by three other colonies during the 1960's.

The fact that the colonies were not identical in their agronomic
approaches is attributable in part to their geographical location and
resources, but also to the differences in skills and ability among the
various enterprise managers and executives. As already noted, other
differences in farming methods among the colonies can be attributed to age and financial ability. With one exception—the high-
altitude colony, Colony 6—the colonies that had been in the Jasper
region the longest had the best farming techniques: they had
sufficient time to adapt to the conditions of the region, to conduct
experiments on their resources, learn from other colonies, and above
all, to accumulate the capital needed for investments. Often a colony was forced to delay its changeover to new techniques simply
because of a lack of money: this was particularly true when the
purchase of labor-saving machinery, proper implements suited to
the soils of the region, and the construction of expensive structures

like feed-mills and granaries, feed lots, hog barns, and the like were involved. One case in point is that of summer fallow tillage. In this region of uneven topography and light soils, a horizontal-blade implement with a hydraulically controlled lift to vary penetration is far better than a vertical-disc implement, which disturbs the soil and encourages erosion and blowing. An incoming colony learns this routinely, but a horizontal-blade implement, and a proper tractor to pull it, is very expensive: it costs at least $6,000 for a suitable outfit. Until the colony can find the money or the credit to buy one, it will make do with its cheaper disc cultivators, possibly brought with it from the parent colony. Time may also be lacking to train machine operators in the techniques of handling the big blade outfits. This is a case where the adoption of suitable farming techniques is almost entirely dependent on the purchase of the correct machinery.

To an increasing extent, commercial farming in the Plains is subject to the control of technique by investment possibility. But this is not always the case. The use of a blade implement must be coupled with a knowledge of both the blowing proclivities of the light soils and the exact amount of penetration needed to kill the weeds without unduly disturbing the soil. These techniques can be communicated by language, or an operator can ride on a neighboring colony's machine to learn by observation, but in the long run, actual ownership of equipment and constant experimentation is the best teacher. It took two of the Jasper colonies four years to refine their summer fallowing, after they had acquired the correct machinery. In any case, a colony in its early stages, before machines are available, or before the skills associated with them have been developed, may give an impression of lack of knowledge —which is deceiving, since in nearly all cases colonies eventually adopt the appropriate devices and techniques.

However, colonies do differ in their receptivity to new devices and procedures, as well as in the time it takes them to develop new methods. Other things being equal, colonies that emphasize literacy will be ahead of the others in innovation and management, since they make a point of acquiring and reading technical literature.

Some colonies, particularly the "balanced" type, will engage in conscious experimentation more consistently than those whose management skills are not sufficiently developed. Many colonies that lack technical skills and knowledge nevertheless acquire sophisticated techniques relatively rapidly, simply by copying from their more progressive brothers. Thus, Hutterian agriculture develops as a unit, not singly, by colony; and this is facilitated by the fission process, which leads to a flow between colonies of pertinent agricultural information.

NINE

Hutterian Enterprise
and Individual Enterprise

We will conclude our presentation of Hutterian agricultural economy by comparing the production, yields, and expenditures of a typical colony with those of Jasper individual farm enterprises. This is not a professional economic analysis, for neither the time nor the skills adequate to such a task were available during field work; but rather it is an attempt to illustrate the impressive economic and adaptive advantages of colony agriculture. We will also present data concerning consumption habits—a vital issue in the comparison of Hutterian and Jasper Gentile culture.

In these comparisons we shall consider the colony as a single enterprise, or at least as a federation of enterprises. In Saskatchewan, the accepted legal status of the Hutterian colony is that of an incorporated cooperative enterprise. This status defines the colony for taxation purposes, and allows it to take advantage of certain tax benefits reserved for cooperative organizations.

While considering the colony as an enterprise comparable to the individually owned farm, we should remember that the colony's communal property system does not permit the distribution of returns to the component nuclear families or to individuals on a cash-share basis. All money goes into a common bank account, and the needs of the individual families are met by collective decision. This control over proceeds is the practical basis of consumption austerity, and the source of the Hutterian colony's financial strength.

The colony selected for this comparative study was one of the oldest in the region. Most of its debts had been retired, and it was about to enter what we have designated as the third, or "plateau" stage of development, where it could begin to save toward its eventual fission. It had a "balanced" economy and an efficient, though perhaps overly conservative, system of management (over-conservative at least from the point of view of some of its young managers). The Gentile enterprises selected for comparison include one of the oldest, largest, and most productive mixed farms in the region, which was about to enter its third generation of management at the time of our study. (We will refer to this enterprise as "Farm X.") The farm was diversified mainly on a grain-livestock basis; grain was its major source of income, and cattle and swine were next in importance. Two other enterprises—a large cattle ranch and the component farms of a large kin group considered as a unit—were subject to less intensive comparative analysis.

Table 12 presents production and yield data for selected commodities raised by the colony and by Farm X. Though the farm shows a somewhat higher yield for wheat, the two are about equal in rye production. It is doubtful that the slight advantage shown by the farm is very meaningful in light of the great yearly variation

Table 12—Comparison of the production and yield of selected commodities in a Hutterian colony and in Farm X (two-year average)

	Colony[b]			Farm[c]		
Item[a]	*Production*	*Proceeds*	*Yield*[d]	*Production*	*Proceeds*	*Yield*[d]
Wheat[e]	25,000[f]	$32,400	9.8	8,000[g]	$12,800	10
Rye[e]	3,000[h]	$ 3,000	30	2,500[i]	$ 2,500	29
Calves[j]	80	$ 8,000	$100[k]	. . .	. . .	. . .
Yearlings[j] . . .	75	$ 9,550	$127.33[k]	36	$ 5,500	$152.77[k]
Hogs[j]	600	$24,000	$ 40[k]	115	$ 5,000	$ 43.47[k]

[a] Figures on poultry, sheep, wool, and forage are omitted, since Farm X sells none of these items.
[b] Holdings: 15,000 acres.
[c] Holdings: 1,920 acres.
[d] Per cultivated acre.
[e] In bushels.
[f] On 2,527 acres.
[g] On 800 acres.
[h] On 100 acres.
[i] On 85 acres.
[j] Figures given in head.
[k] Price per animal.

in yields typical of the region, and it seems fair to conclude that both enterprises are producing crops at relatively high and nearly equal levels of efficiency. During the years selected for the analysis, there was relatively abundant moisture; in dryer years, wheat yields would have been smaller.

In the production of yearling beef and swine, the farm shows a better per-animal average than the colony. While Farm X has had difficulty maintaining steady livestock production, it apparently has been able to maintain a satisfactory regime during the periods when it could do so—especially in cattle "finishing." Colony livestock practices were more like those of a ranch than those of a farm, for the colony's herd was large, and while animals were finished in the colony feed lot, there was somewhat less intensive feeding, and for a shorter period, than in many smaller farm feeding regimes. Moreover, the colony's feeding operations were somewhat crude; the Jasper colonies had not yet refined their livestock practices, since in Alberta grain production had been given greater emphasis. The farm used better methods and consequently produced heavier finished stock.

Table 13 demonstrates the savings made possible by colony consumption austerity. The totals and per capita figures for such items as fuel for passenger vehicles, clothing, publications, and recreation are evidence of the financial advantages of consumption restraint. The advantages of cooperative sharing of business expenses are clear in the per capita figures for farm machine fuel and annual machinery payments. It should be added, of course, that these per capita advantages do not mean that the colony's larger number of people were poorly nourished or lived in poverty. The members of this colony lived well by Hutterian standards; that is, they enjoyed an abundance of simple food, lived in sparsely but attractively furnished quarters, and owned first-class farm equipment. Some of the colonies in the region that had not reached a plateau of affluence exhibited similar per capita advantages, but their annual balance sheet showed a much smaller surplus, or even a deficit—just as the colony used in this comparison would have done in its earlier years. Farm X, on the other hand, showed a deficit every

Table 13—Selected annual expenditures[a] for a Hutterian colony and a large mixed farm

Item	Colony[b] Total expenditure	Colony[b] Per capita expenditure	Farm[c] Total expenditure	Farm[c] Per capita expenditure
Automotive fuel for trucks, tractors	$5,700	77.02	$2,815	703.75
Automotive fuel for passenger vehicles	500	6.76	1,000	250
Heating fuel[d]	1,835	24.79	600	150
Average annual machinery payment	2,000	27.03	1,500	375
Clothing[e]	3,500	47.30	700	175
Household maintenance	1,920[f]	25.94	250	62.50
Publications	50	.68	200	50
Recreation,[g] entertainment	2,500	33.78	1,500	375
Municipal taxes	5,609	75.80	740	185

[a] Certain items differ from those on 1963–64 balance sheets on Tables 14 and 15, owing to the fact that the figures here were averaged over a five-year period.

[b] 74 persons.

[c] 4 persons.

[d] Includes fuel for heating stock pen water, barns, etc.

[e] Mostly unfinished materials for colony; ready-mades for farm.

[f] Includes expense of furnishing one apartment for newly married couple; about one marriage per year.

[g] "Recreation" for colony consists of refreshments, treats, and gifts provided locally at weddings and at Christmas. For farm family, it might mean parties, dinners, short trips, a vacation home in Hills, an annual major vacation to Florida, etc.

five years or so—although this deficit was always made up by bank loans or bumper crop yields.

Tables 14 and 15 present data on production returns for both the colony and the large mixed farm. It is apparent that the colony kept a closer balance between its various income-producing activities. While wheat was a major source of income for both colony and farm, the colony obtained a substantial amount of its income from various other commodities; and the total income from all these other activities was considerably larger than the wheat income alone. This was not true of the farm, which relied heavily on its wheat crop. As a result, Farm X's annual income fluctuated by as much as $10,000. An item like eggs, which brought in little more than petty cash to the farm, was a major income source for the colony; while custom labor, which was a minor source of income

Table 14—Balance sheet for Hutterian colony, 1963–64[a]

INCOME		OPERATING EXPENSES (cont'd.)	
Wheat[b]	$ 45,000	Electricity	$ 1,000
Hogs	24,000	Veterinary services and supplies	860
Eggs	17,344	Welding supplies	502
Yearlings	9,550	Goslings	438
Calves	8,000	Seeds	319
Lambs	6,750	Breeding sires	300
Wool	3,600	Interest on loan	250
Rye	3,000	Telephone	150
Cows	1,650	Cattle trucking	100
Bulls	1,500	Bees[g]	62
Chickens	850	Wool sacks	27
Dairy cattle	630	Total	$ 49,927
Geese	324	OTHER EXPENSES	
Sheep	200	Family cash allotments	6,300
Produce consumed[c]	10,000	Loan to other colony[h]	5,000
Total	$132,398	All clothing materials[i]	3,500
OPERATING EXPENSES		Gifts, refreshments[j]	2,500
Annual machinery payment		Food essentials	2,500
(avg. over 10 yrs.)[d]	10,000	Household furnishings[k]	1,200
Automotive fuel	6,200	Drugs	811
Municipal taxes	5,609	Household expenses other	
New building	5,000	than heat	720
Sprinkler irrigation equipment	5,000	Dental[l]	396
Consumable supplies[e]	3,675	Medical expenses[m]	282
Income tax[f]	3,000	Miscellaneous items	200
Heating fuel	1,835	Newspapers, etc.	50
Repairs and maintenance	1,700	Total	$ 23,459
Fencing supplies	1,500	Grand total	$ 73,386
Animal and plant sprays	1,400	Grand total including land	
Grain treatment	1,000	purchase of $27,000	$100,386
		Net income	$ 32,012

[a] A "good" year, owing to good crops and sales of stored wheat. No unusual expenses. Maximum savings possible.

[b] This is somewhat greater than average. The total includes some wheat stored from previous bumper crop year. Also note that all forage crops were fed to livestock; in other years, some were sold.

[c] Retail market value of garden produce, meat, etc. consumed.

[d] This will drop by half shortly—the figure represents accumulation stage.

[e] Hardware, lumber, electrical wiring, paints.

[f] An average figure; higher or lower in some years.

[g] Bought annually; production of honey rising, will be higher in future. None sold as yet.

[h] Interest-free; indefinite repayment time. At least one such loan put on books each year.

[i] Somewhat higher than most years, owing to special bulk purchase of cloth. All materials bought unfinished.

[j] Mostly for holidays and wedding celebrations.

[k] Cost of outfitting one new married couple. Colony has about one marriage per year.

[l] Government medical care does not cover dental fees.

[m] Figure low because of Provincial medical plan; these fees paid to private clinics for special services.

for the colony, was a major one for the farm, where it equaled the annual machinery payments. The value of food produced by the colony was ten times that produced by the farm; but the per capita value of the farm's home food production was substantial, and the total equaled its average annual machinery payment. (This is some-

Table 15—Balance sheet for Farm X, 1963–64[a]

INCOME		OPERATING EXPENSES (cont'd.)	
Wheat	$ 12,100	Sprays	$ 304
Yearlings	4,967	PFRA pasture fees[g]	233
Rye	2,315	Fire insurance	226
Custom labor	1,000	Interest on loan	200
Hogs	636	Veterinary fees and supplies[h]	165
Eggs	218	Welding supplies	152
Home-produced food		Grain treatment	120
consumed[b]	1,000	Purchase of purebred boar	60
Total	$ 22,236	Cattle trucking	50
		Total	$ 14,370
OPERATING EXPENSES[c]			
Automotive fuel[d]	3,815	OTHER EXPENSES	
Purchase of feeder cattle	3,229	Recreation, vacations	1,500
Annual machinery payments[e]	1,000	Groceries	1,200
Municipal taxes	740	Clothing	250
Heating fuel	600	Household maintenance	250
Labor wages	600	Publications	200
Hail insurance	544	Medical expenses	50
Misc. consumable supplies	500	Drugs	50
Electricity	500	Total	$ 3,500
Feed and supplements[f]	500	Grand total	$ 17,870
Seed	500	Net income including retail value of home-produced food consumed	$ 4,366
Repairs and maintenance	332		

[a] A relatively "low" year, owing to reduced feeder cattle operation resulting from growing ground water shortages in the vicinity. A "high" year would yield a gross income of about $35,000.

[b] Retail value of home-produced food consumed.

[c] This family had no telephone, because no local line was available. No income tax was paid in 1963–64.

[d] For trucks, tractors, and passenger vehicles.

[e] Average for five-year period.

[f] The remainder of the cattle forage was supplied by home-produced grain, and by hay cut on local road allotments or on shares for local ranchers or the Community pastures.

[g] As on all farms in the neighborhood, the feeder cattle were pastured throughout the warm months in the local Community Pasture, and were then fed through the winter at the farm.

[h] Includes breeding fees.

what unusual, for home food production on farms is usually less significant.)

Tables 16, 17, and 18 detail and summarize per capita and per acre returns for farm and colony. A comparison of these ratios points up the difference between colony and farm with respect to operating efficiency. Because it has no labor expenditure, and possesses a large amount of pasture land, the colony has much lower operating expenses per acre than Farm X does. It also has a lower machinery investment per cultivated acre than the farm, owing to its labor efficiency and large scale of operations.

Current studies of farm business in the Northern Plains reveal that the larger the acreage of a grain-livestock farm in any of the lighter (poorer) soil zones, the lower the operating and labor costs will be.[1] Machinery costs are low up to 1,200 acres; above that point, they are higher in proportion to the amount of total acreage involved. Figures on machinery investment at Farm X seem to illustrate this, although in this instance the rise may have been partially the result of a special interest in machinery on the part of the farm's operator. On the other hand, the colony's machinery investment was lower than would be predicted on the basis of these management studies, and reflected the fact that the colony's relatively large labor force used its machines with great efficiency.[2]

In every per capita income category but one, the farm was ahead of the colony. With regard to gross income per working man, the colony surpassed the farm by more than $2,000.[3] This reflects the operating efficiency made possible by a large, well-equipped labor

[1] For figures on Saskatchewan, see H. D. McCrorie and others (1963), especially p. 27, and Tables 3a–3g.

[2] It should be pointed out that the colony had other equipment that the farm did not need: refrigeration equipment, automatic feeding devices for chickens and hogs, bakery and meat-cutting machines, elaborate feed grinders, and similar items. In the early phases of colony economic development, purchase of these items is a heavy drain. The colony studied here had already paid for all these special devices. If the comparison had been made earlier in the life of the colony, the competitive position of the colony on machinery items would have been sizable. Nevertheless, the various sources of savings in colony operation make possible a rapid and efficient debt retirement not possible within the farm economy.

[3] We defined the male labor force as being made up of all men between the ages of 15 and 35. This includes all the apprentices, field hands, and managers, but does not include the Elders.

Table 16—Investment value of Hutterian colony, 1964

Land		
Actual price paid for land (1951–63)	$260,000	
Value at current prices in district	285,000	
Value determined by multiplying tax assessment by 2	128,700	
Probable value in "walkaway" sale[a]	200,000	
Estimated value used for this computation		$200,000
Farm products on hand[b]		
Livestock	111,200	
Feed and forage	22,450	
All other products	3,000	
Total		136,650
Machinery and tools[c]		
Farm machines and vehicles	30,050	
Tools, shop equipment, refrigeration and feeding devices, etc. . .	11,104	
Total		41,154
Household and kitchen[d]		
Household equipment and furnishings	3,500	
Food preparation equipment	3,000	
Total		6,500
Other items[e]		
Buildings	53,889	
Electric lines	378	
Fencing	7,700	
Dugouts	2,426	
Wells	604	
Total		$ 64,997
Grand total		$249,301
Grand total including estimated land worth		449,301
Actual "walkaway" sale price		400,000
Bank net worth computation[f]		250,000

[a] A "walkaway" sale is one in which the entire establishment, with most properties, is sold as a unit. Values for the colony were estimated by four local farm operators and businessmen. All figures were within $5,000. The estimators all used much higher figures for land than the bank did. The "walkaway" sale price rather accurately reflects the values current for the period, although because of the large size of the colony holdings, and the specialized building layout, it is highly improbable that a private operator would ever buy it as a unit.

[b] At 1964 market prices.

[c] Cost depreciated on declining balance. All capital items were depreciated according to standard procedures established by farm management researchers of the University of Saskatchewan College of Agriculture.

[d] Cost depreciated on declining balance.

[e] Depreciation figured with various standard techniques.

[f] As computed by bank for figuring collateral value. These bank net worth statements are always conservative, and the assessors use lower valuations for land than are current.

force. Farm X is capable of achieving comparable returns in a good year, but must be prepared to accept much lower per-man returns in bad years, when its relative lack of diversification results in lowered income. Barring extensive drouths and other unavoid-

Table 17—Investment value of Farm X, 1964

Land		
Actual price paid for land (1927–29)	$ 7,000	
Value at current prices in district[a]	112,500	
Value determined by multiplying tax assessment by 2	17,800	
Probable value in "walkaway" sale	50,000	
Estimated value used for this computation		$ 50,000
Farm products[b]		
Livestock on hand	5,600	
Feed and forage on hand	2,000	
Stored wheat	2,000	
Total		9,600
Machinery and tools[c]		
Farm machines and vehicles	23,958	
Tools and shop equipment	6,537	
Total		30,495
Household and kitchen[c]		
Household furnishings	400	
Kitchen equipment	200	
Total		600
Other items[d]		
Buildings	12,658	
Electric lines	370	
Dugouts[e]	500	
Fencing	800	
Total		14,328
Grand total		$ 55,023
Grand total including land		105,023
Actual "walkaway" sale price[f]		150,000
Bank net worth computation		75,000

[a] The difference between current price and tax-assessment computation here is greater than in the case of the colony, since grain cropland sells for much higher prices than pasture, and all of the farm's land was used for grain for sale and feed, whereas only 3,000 acres of the colony land was used for crops.

[b] At 1964 market prices.

[c] Cost depreciated on declining balance.

[d] Depreciation figured with various standard techniques.

[e] New: cost value.

[f] Enhanced value for land was used by estimators.

Table 18—Per capita and per acre returns and investment values for Hutterian colony and for Farm X[a]

	Colony[b]	Farm[c]
Per capita gross cash income	$122,398, 74 persons = $1,654.03	$21,236, 4 persons = $5,309.00
Per capita net income[d]	$22,012, 74 persons = $297.46	$3,366, 4 persons = $841.50
Gross cash income per working man	$122,398, 15 men = $8,159.86	$21,236, 3.5 men[e] = $6,067.42
Gross cash income per gross acreage	$122,398, 15,000 acres = $8.15	$21,236, 1920 acres incl. rented land = $11.06
Per capita investment value	$449,301, 74 persons = $6,071.63	$100,023, 4 persons = $25,005.75
Investment value per gross acreage	$449,301, 15,000 acres = $29.95	$100,023, 1920 acres = $52.09
Per capita net worth[f]	$250,000, 74 persons = $3,378.37	$75,000, 4 persons = $18,750.00
Net worth per gross acreage	$250,000, 15,000 acres = $16.66	$75,000, 1920 acres = $39.06
Operating expenses per gross acreage	$49,927, 15,000 acres = $3.32	$14,370, 1920 acres = $7.48
Net income ratio[g]	$22,012 ÷ $122,398 = .18	$3,366 ÷ $21,236 = .16
Machinery investment per cultivated acre	$30,050 ÷ 3,000 = $10.01	$23,958 ÷ 1,920 = $13.40

a It should be understood that the figures we are using here are those for a particular crop year, 1963–64, and are not averages. We were unable to compile sufficiently detailed figures on all production units on a multiple-year basis to obtain an average, but feel that the objectives of our analysis are served by those of a particular year: spot-checks with other farms and colonies for other years indicated that these ratios appear to express the principal economic differences in the two forms of enterprise quite adequately.

b A good year; colony near peak of development; expenses stabilized.

c A "low" farm year.

d For colony, per capita net income is really a kind of "undistributed surplus."

e Number includes hired help; one full-time man and one half-time man. The labor force and population of this farm is normal for the region. Occasionally additional men are hired, but the local average is 3.5 men per farm.

f Bank computation.

g The net income ratio for a "high" year might be $10,000 ÷ $35,000, or .29.

able disasters, a colony, once established, can easily maintain a favorable ratio.

The colony's operating expenses per acre were less than those of the farm—another indication of high efficiency. As expected, the net worth estimations of the farm were high. The colony's net income ratio was generally more favorable than that of the farm, but in a good year the farm ratio nearly equaled the colony ratio. It is evident, therefore, that the farm can manifest as high efficiency as the colony when conditions are favorable.

A "walkaway" sale is one in which an entire establishment, including most properties, is sold as a unit. The difference between the bank net worth computations and the "walkaway" sale prices of the colony and the farm (shown on Tables 16 and 17) highlights an important aspect of agricultural economy in North America, and an important difference between colony and individual enterprise. The fact that bank valuations were made at about half the potential market value of the enterprises demonstrates the fact that because of its speculative value, agricultural property can command almost any price. In recent years, this has meant that many farm and ranch enterprises have drifted into a position characterized by what economists call "negative profits." In other words, regardless of actual returns, the cost of raising livestock and crops is lower than the price obtained *only* if all interest on investment is excluded from the analysis.[4]

So far as the writer knows, the colonies never calculate interest on investments. The colony "intellectuals" are aware that the property would bring high prices if it could be sold, but this is of no interest to them, since when a colony buys land it buys it forever. The Hutterites invest not in money values but in social values: in

---

[4] As many farmers and ranchers realize the implications of their position, they sell out and use the proceeds to invest in businesses likely to yield higher returns. Those who decide to remain in agriculture are highly committed people who like the occupation and simply ignore the fact that in terms of current standards, their returns are not commensurate with the value of the property. Ranchers know they could sell their places to urban hobbyists looking for tax shelters at almost any price; if they refuse, it means they like ranching. Farmers who decide to stay seek to enlarge their holdings, which helps to increase productivity and avoid "negative profits," but here, too, strong commitment to the country and agricultural society is evident.

the continuity and stability of the colony. The proprietor of Farm X was well aware of his position, and discussed it at great length—the inducements for him to sell out were very powerful. Such an issue would probably never be raised in the colony, but if it were, it would be definite evidence of disorder and breakdown within the colony system.

The fact that many ranchers and farmers stay on in spite of the unstable nature of their financial position suggests that they resemble the Brethren in at least one respect: they are committed to a particular way of life, and they view their property as tangible evidence of their commitment. However, in the case of the colony, commitment is built in, so to speak; it is a consequence of the whole system; whereas for the individual operator, it is a matter of personal or family decision.

In these computations of colony and farm operations, we have not included labor as a cost or as an income gain. This is because its inclusion would have required a longer and more detailed study of colony operations than we were prepared to make (as already noted, colonies do not keep records of labor productivity). However, some general observations are possible. As a colony enters its mature stage, work becomes lighter, and the labor force can adhere to a more relaxed schedule than it followed in its early years. This increased leisure is an expression of increased income, which manifests itself this way rather than through increased consumption benefits. In other words, this means that the fall in per capita "income" represented by increasing colony population is compensated for to some extent by increased leisure. This effect of profit is not felt by the average farmer, who must work assiduously until forced to retire, if he is to support a family and build up an enterprise to pass on to his son.

If a mature colony is being run by a group of "pushing" executives and managers, it may decide to continue to increase its productivity by establishing new enterprises or expanding existing ones. However, the colony must consider that an increased scale of operations also means increased costs that may threaten savings put aside for fission; moreover, new enterprises are time-consuming. Consequently the Hutterites, especially those in the "balanced" colonies, favor marginal gains and a reduced work schedule. The colony managers realize that prosperity can be almost as troublesome as economic difficulty. As a Gentile remarked of the Brethren: "They know how to do it, all right, but these big outfits have their problems, too. When they get rich, they don't know what to do with the young men . . . and if they keep getting bigger, they get their money all tied up."

Other Comparisons

On Table 19, the amounts of acreage, local land taxes, income, and population supported during an average year by one colony are compared to like figures for the largest cattle ranch in the region. Large ranches are the only individually operated enterprises in the area that come close to the colonies in acreage and in income. (However, while the colony owned its land, the ranch in question leased most of its 16,000 acres from the Provincial government.) Colony cattle holdings are generally smaller than those of the larger ranches—there are about 1,000 head to a large ranch, as compared to 250 head to an average colony cattle operation.

Table 19—Economic comparison of a Hutterian colony and a large cattle ranch in the 1960's

Item	Colony	Cattle ranch
Taxed acreage	13,009	16,726
Tax assessment	$41,900	$40,100
Tax paid	$ 2,514	$ 2,236
Gross income	$90,000	$75,000
Net income	$20,000	$22,000
Population	98	4

The ranch had a much higher per capita income than the colony did, although since the ranch was operated as a company, the income was shared among a larger number of recipients than is indicated on the table. The ranch was usually in debt to various types of creditors: stockholders, bankers, private lenders, cattle dealers, and so on. Still, the family of four who owned the ranch and were fully supported by it enjoyed a very comfortable income and had a consumption level much higher than that of any Hutterian nuclear family unit in the colony. This was the only family unit and the only individuals fully supported by the ranch income.

The colony gross income was $25,000 higher than that of the ranch. Since its acreage was larger, this is not surprising; however, there are additional reasons for its prosperity. Much of the colony crop land was submarginal for crop production, and hence was not as continuously productive as the excellent and efficiently used grazing lands of the ranch. The difference in income was created mainly by the fact that the colony developed diversified enterprises, and did so efficiently. The ranch net income was slightly higher than the colony's, which might be explained by the low overhead associated with extensive livestock production. In terms of income per acre alone, the colony was more productive than the ranch ($6.91 per acre for the colony, as against $4.48 for the ranch); however, in terms of per capita income, the ranch had the advantage.

A comparison of another kind can be made by studying a group of farm families related in the male line who farm near each other

Table 20—Economic comparison of a Hutterian colony and a non-Hutterian kin group for the period 1953–64

Item	Colony	Non-Hutterian kin group
Taxed acreage	17,726[a]	12,228
Tax assessments	$ 64,350[a]	$46,317
Taxes paid	$ 4,110	$ 2,770
Population, 1953	66	35
Population, 1964	73	29
Per capita tax, 1953	$ 62	$ 70
Per capita tax, 1954	$ 57	$ 94
Gross income, 1964[b]	$100,000	$60,000
Per capita gross income, 1964[b] . . .	$ 1,500	$ 2,070
Net income, 1964[b]	$ 30,000	$15,000
Per capita net income, 1964[b,c]	$ 424	$ 517

[a] For district land only.
[b] Data for 1953 not available.
[c] "Undistributed surplus."

in the same district (see Table 20). Economically, such an arrangement resembles a Hutterian colony spread out, with individual related nuclear families all bearing the same surname, but each owning and operating its own land. As it happens, several of these family groups inhabited the district now occupied by the western Jasper colonies, and one or two remain, although reduced in population and number of farms. It will be recalled that kin groups of this type developed from a classic European pattern whereby fathers established their sons on tracts of land near the paternal farm— a pattern poorly adapted to the Jasper habitat and economy.

Most of the farms in the kin group studied produced both grain and cattle, with grain providing most of the income. Hence their economy is not strictly comparable to that of the colony, with its extensive diversification. Nor were their inter-family ties as strong as those among the Brethren; they did not practice much more cooperation than one might find among any neighboring non-related farmers in the region.

Note that the population of the colony grew, while that of the kin group dwindled, which means that the per capita tax load of the colony decreased while that of the kin group grew heavier. The per capita income figures show that the individual farmer had an advantage throughout. However, the colony net income was twice that of the kin group, though it owned barely half again as much land. This difference was the result of the Brethren's diversification, and their use of a pooled labor force and other measures of efficiency. It is possible that if the kin group families had been able to cooperate and diversify as effectively as the Hutterites, they might have been in a sounder economic position. The declining population of the kin group reflects the out-migration of many family members, who found that the increasing costs of small-scale farming in this habitat were not compensated for by the prevailing market prices. In some cases the kin group's failing farms were bought up by the colonies—a dramatic illustration of the superior competitive position of colony agriculture in the Jasper region.

TEN

Social Differentiation and Social Control

While this study has dealt with only six of the more than 160 Hutterian colonies now in existence, the chartered uniformity of Hutterian social life makes some generalization possible. We approach this task with the usual scientific diffidence, and with the anticipation that the conclusions in these two final chapters will be the object of criticism and revision. If they have originality, it derives from the fact that we studied the Brethren primarily as entrepreneurs and administrators, rather than as religious sectarians.

Our approach led us first to examine the relationship between the Brethren's egalitarian social system and their functional role differentiation. The utopian communalists of the American frontier and those of the Israeli kibbutzim have had difficulties maintaining a balance in this relationship: with the former, the stresses resulting from the practical need to assign tasks of differing responsibility and skill in an officially egalitarian society led to dissolution of some of the communities. There have been difficulties in Hutterian colonies with this problem, but on the whole they have had considerable success in controlling divisive tendencies. They have managed to maintain productive incentive while avoiding the prestige differentiation that so often arises when incentive is fostered.

A second theoretical consideration is the relationship between cultural patterns and technological and commercial change. For almost five hundred years, with one or two lapses, the Brethren have maintained their traditional way of life in spite of exile, forced migration, persecution, wars, and natural disasters. Moreover, they have adapted technologically and economically without sacrificing their social identity. In Chapter 11 we shall inquire into the basis of the Hutterian ability to accept technical change without serious alteration of the culture.

Social Differentiation

The present chapter is concerned with the sources of social differentiation and strain in the Hutterian social system. The problem has a special cogency in the Hutterian case, because while the overt values of Hutterian religious sociology reject individuation and differentiation, it is apparent that no human society can exist without some degree of these. Social and economic tasks, and the abilities required to perform these tasks, necessarily differ; and a human society is no more a homogeneous mass than an insect society is. Clearly, absolute equality is an ideal that in practice is always modified.

Summarizing the materials and discussions presented in earlier chapters, we can distinguish three important sources of differentiation in Hutterian society: (1) the practical need for assigning people to different tasks and responsibilities in the conduct of a diversified agricultural enterprise; (2) the influence of the institutional frames of the external world and the visible way of life of Gentile neighbors, from which the Hutterites learn that individuals do strive for personal success and are accorded recognition for their accomplishments; and (3) biological tendencies. The natural endowment of individuals is not uniform, and differences lead individuals into the performance of tasks of differing degrees of complexity and social significance, or they seek these tasks.

The first two sources of differentiation seem clear enough. Hutterites are required to assign people different roles in their organizational structure. They recognize that the "outside" is seductive and corrupting, and hence must constantly fight against "temptation"; i.e., self-seeking and social cleavage. However, the third source presents a theoretical problem. In occasionally holding to it, we are assuming that biological differences automatically and universally produce individuation. However, in fact we cannot prove this. Emile Durkheim acknowledged biological differences, but felt that men had to be taught to be individuals. If he is correct, then there is no biological cause of differentiation in Hutterian society. Rather, we would have to argue that differentiation is caused by the same processes as in other societies: by men learning to want to be different from each other. This argument would hold even if we grant the processes of technical and administrative role differentiation. There is no reason to assume that these processes automatically impart desires for individual difference and success, since men could, presumably, simply learn them as roles. During the Moravian period, the Hutterites maintained a much larger number of trades, occupations, and professions among their members than they do now, without any apparent serious tendency toward individual aspirations that posed a threat to communal solidarity.

On the other hand, we have pointed to the existence in Hutterian writings of statements that appear to assume that men are inherently individualistic and consequently prone to quarrel and compete with each other. Some of these statements go back to the sixteenth century, but there is reason to believe that the fear of the tendency, or the emphasis upon its converse—egalitarian brotherhood—may be stronger today. Our historical evidence is not sufficient to be certain of this, however, and the issue cannot be pursued. We can only argue that modern Hutterites possess *both* the overt doctrine of egalitarian brotherhood and a set of covert attitudes concerning its opposites—which implies that they believe men are not really egalitarian by nature, and Christianity must teach them to be so.

Whether Hutterian differentiation is due to a universal biosocial process or whether it is a wholly cultural process cannot be determined. However, the empirical situation seems clear enough: Hutterites take enormous pains to train their children and themselves in egalitarian patterns, and in the repression of self-seeking and other individuating tendencies. Likewise, they seek to repress all destructive forms of social cleavage. We must conclude, then, that in addition to learning something about social uniformity and communalism, the Hutterite also learns something about its opposites. Some of the latter comes from the Hutterian experience itself and some from the outside, but it is hard to measure the quantities with precision.

Social Stability

A number of factors are responsible for the stable quality of the Hutterian social order:

Preadaptation, that is, the early choice of a model with high survival value, such as the late medieval noble estate with its efficient management and economic rationality; primary group solidarity, the acceptance of the *colony frame of existence,* with its relatively small population and primary-group mechanisms of social control; *gratification and security,* supplying responsible jobs for a majority of men by colony fission, and guaranteeing their retirement; *isolation* and "boundary maintenance," that is, the choice of a rural locus far from the disintegrating influences of urban life and economy; *austerity,* or the rejection of consumption aspirations and their individuating effects; *social control,* or the institutionalization of mechanisms that penalize interpersonal conflict and competition, or keep them within bounds; and finally *socialization,* the indoctrination of the children with a system of religious or sacred values that define the entire scope and meaning of Hutterian existence.[1]

[1] This list includes the general conditions regarded by most contemporary anthropologists as necessary for a stable and unchanging social system and culture (see Voget, esp. pp. 266–67). However, while the social system is unquestionably stable and the religious idology unchanging, Hutterian technical and economic culture is subject to extensive and continual change; hence the conditions that define "stability" here obviously do not enforce conservatism throughout the entire culture. The point is that often the "change" theorized about by anthropologists is not *planned* or rationally controlled change, but unforeseen changes occurring as "drift" or as automatic consequences of cultural borrowing or communication. The Hutterian case concerns planned change, and therefore many of the generalizations do not apply. (Foster, pp. 145–62, lists various factors that constitute "motivations"

These factors all reinforce and define the communal framework; and it is this framework that shields the Brethren from the world. Hutterites do not read sociology textbooks, but they have a profound understanding of the nature of social integration, and how it may be achieved with minimal compulsion. Outsiders, misunderstanding these techniques, sometimes mistakenly assume that the Brethren mistreat and imprison their dissenters. It is difficult for those outside the colonies to comprehend the nature of a social system that effectively controls individual impulses in a benevolent way.[2]

Since the essence of Hutterian life is communalism—a managed democratic order in which every male member is accorded equal treatment and given an equal share of wealth—one basis of colony stability is the relative absence of socially differentiating tendencies. However, we have also explained how the instrumental organization requires functional differentiation. We note therefore that the colony system contains a series of paradoxes. First, it is ideally without status, but actually status does exist there; second, it is ideally free of individual competition, yet a kind of functional competition is an important feature of the economic order; third, while communal life is ideally its own reward, in reality the economy and demography are constantly being adjusted to provide individuals with rewarding jobs and thus keep them satisfied with colony life.

Among the Hutterites, status and competition take covert or suppressed forms, and rarely threaten the harmony of the communality. The latency of these phenomena is not the result of some diffuse process, but is in part the consequence of training during early childhood, both in the German school and in the family circle.

---

stimulating change: prestige, economic gain, competition, friendship, play, religion, dignity, and pride. Nearly every one of these factors is ruled out as a legitimate force in social life by Hutterian communal ideals, and accordingly, the social organization does not change. But the technology and economy do—and in the absence of Foster's criteria. This is so because of the planned character of Hutterian change.)

[2] P. A. Sorokin (1954) has called Hutterian culture a truly altruistic one. This is quite correct; but the price paid for the Brethren's achievement can be viewed as much too high for the majority of humans. The Hutterites are a small and special people; their goals do not include proselytizing, and they are content simply to serve as models of Christian living.

The Hutterites consider the child a sinful being, but unlike the Puritans, they do not hold him responsible for his state. Rather, responsibility rests with the adults, who must teach the child the Christian way, not censure him and burden him with guilt feelings. Thus, the Hutterites largely substitute moral training and bureaucratically supervised conformity for dependence on the individual conscience.

The German School is the chief agent of this training, and consequently its curriculum involves the entire culture and social order of Hutterian life. The child is taught to respect his elders because of their constant labors and care for his welfare. He is trained to avoid attachment to personal possessions, ambition, and the exercise of interpersonal aggression. His textbooks are nineteenth-century German-language readers filled with moral tales and rhymes; Hutterian religious books; and, of course, the Luther version of the Bible. He is not exposed to contemporary culture, nor given any knowledge of worldly affairs and institutions, although children are given such exposure in the public school sessions held at the colony. The teachers in the German School and in the pre-school kindergarten are kindly shepherds and stern parental figures by turn: they not only teach, but also punish, counsel, and supervise, and also attend to all of the children's physical needs during the time they are at school. Intensive help is given the slow learners, with the general objective of keeping all pupils at the same level. The particularly intelligent child is often encouraged to read at home, in technical fields or in Hutterian religious and historical literature, but not to "show off" in class. Teaching methods are traditional: the endless copying of lessons into notebooks alternates with individual and group recitation and the rote learning of Biblical and catechistic texts. At Sunday School, religion is stressed, but the methods of learning are the same; in addition to copying and memorizing, the children hear a sermon by the teacher, who in some colonies is also the Second Minister. These techniques are carried over into the adult church services, where the sermons are mechanically delivered, the responses and chorales are stereotyped and automatic. By the time the child is old enough to attend the adult church services (12 years), he has learned all the responses and hymns and most of the Biblical texts and sermons by heart. At the German School, lazy or disobedient pupils are punished by being made to stay after school and repeat lessons, or are given a quick strapping by the teacher. Though corporal punishment is not resorted to where warnings will suffice, children and those in their teens who commit serious wrongs are punished, usually by both the teacher and parent, who take turns with the strap and the word. Hutterites sum it all up with the aphorism: *Erziehe den Baum wenn er klein ist; gross ist desto härter, oder sogar unmöglich* ("Train the tree when it is little; when the tree is large, the job is just so much harder, or even impossible").

These thoroughgoing methods produce the Hutterian consensus, an element of conformity in the Hutterian personality that shows up in psychological tests. In the study by Kaplan and Plaut,[3] the "normal" Hutterian personality revealed by projective tests was remarkably homogeneous and had content duplicating the major features of Hutterian culture as viewed from the outside. There was remarkably little difference between individual protocols; and there were "no status differentiations," and little "overt competitiveness." The descriptions of the Hutterian personality revealed by these protocols contain no surprises for one who has read accounts of Hutterian culture.

However, there is something one-sided in this description. In the first place, the content of socialization is really dual: the overt and much-emphasized side is that of communalism and the repression of individualism, but on the other hand, the very presentation of this side means that its opposites are also communicated in a latent fashion. The very fact that the child as well as the adult is constantly enjoined to avoid self-seeking and acquisitive behavior means that he is aware of the things that he must avoid and suppress. Hutterites talk about the temptations of "the World," and of the corrupt nature of man, which is their nature too—they are not

---

[3] Kaplan and Plaut (1956); see esp. pp. 17 and 91. See also Eaton and Weil (1955).

ignorant of them. In this negative and latent sense, Hutterites also learn that men are individualistic, that society is stratified, and that they themselves must fight temptation. It would seem that there is another side to the Hutterian personality, which Kaplan and Plaut did not pick up in their tests.

The emphasis on consensus in the Kaplan-Plaut protocols obscures the fact that when one gets to know them well, one sees that Hutterites are far from uniform, and that their responses are highly varied. There is variation in precisely the things mentioned above: in the desire, and perhaps its secret satisfaction, of acquiring possessions; in degrees of subtle manipulation in order to advance one's own interests; in styles of factional maneuvering. There also exists variation in outward behavior: men range from withdrawn, thoughtful, somber persons to outgoing, humorous "characters." Women tend to conceal spontaneity from outsiders, but when friendships are made, there is considerable difference in responsiveness and intellectual interests. Kaplan and Plaut, of course, were not concerned with overt character manifestations, but with what they believed to be underlying character structure; however, the social significance of the latter may not be as great as the former. Certainly overt behavior is of vital significance in assigning functional roles: the most serious and stable-appearing individuals get the managerial jobs; and the seemingly frivolous remain as field hands, only moving upward into the higher echelons of responsibility as they develop sobriety. Homogeneous behavior is especially apparent on formal and ritual occasions: at church, in the dining hall, on visits to town, or in front of outsiders. Homogeneity may be seen as that aspect of behavior under the control of the cultural demands for interpersonal harmony: the emotional flatness of Hutterian behavior as seen from an external point of view is part of this configuration. However, when the Hutterites interact with friends, or engage in purely recreational activities, they often exhibit emotion and even deviance freely. At the same time, it seems evident that there is a constant suppression of individuality at work, especially in potentially tense interpersonal situations.

The Brethren's recognition of marginal or latent individuality is expressed in the fact that they take considerable pains to see that deserving individuals obtain responsible positions as rewards for their abilities. This recognition is covert, and is expressed through the electoral system, which is theoretically the will of God in action. The practical reason for this recognition is that it preserves colony harmony through the avoidance of resentment and frustration. At the same time, the individual *must* suppress overt signs of ambition or frustration. Man-hour productivity differences are not recorded, lest individuals feel discriminated against; pains are taken to equalize hours of work; and managers and Elders strive to give everyone a sense of involvement in colony affairs. Nevertheless, individuals differ in their ability to do certain things and to commit themselves to the general round of activities, and this, Hutterites believe, must be reckoned with, and also constructively exploited in the interest of colony stability and continuity.

The complex rules and regulations governing the Brethren's behavior are administered humanely, and persuasion is used more often than punishment or threats. Young people are expected to be a bit "wild"; everyone is allowed to violate a rule or be a bit ambitious occasionally; this is excused if it does not become a habit. The constant example of people doing their job in a small, face-to-face society functions effectively as a source of motivation.

The Hutterites also hold many rules to be effective only in a *pro forma* sense; that is, they often do not enforce them with sanctions implying a profound moral breach. For example, the writer once presented exhibitions of color slides in the colony dining hall at the request of the Elders. After the second or third show, the writer was asked by one of the Elders not to do this any more, since one of the other colonies might hear about it, and "make a fuss." That very evening the Elder was in the writer's cottage on the colony premises viewing a special selection of slides of other colonies, arranged by the writer at the Elder's request! Many rules are of this nature: the public appearance is the important thing, not the behavior itself.

Consensus, egalitarianism, and conformity to rules and regulations cannot entirely conceal the existence of certain differences in privilege and the presence of de facto competition. Agricultural managers are often excused from heavy field work, and they may drive to town without permission or preparation (usually they make a point of taking one or more of the field hands with them). The colony "intellectuals," who tend to associate with one another rather than with the less well read and less articulate members of the colony, are usually the ones assigned to accompany visitors on tours and on special visits to town. There are slight differences, too, from member to member, in quantity of personal possessions, because of differences in opportunity.

The practical question is whether the terms individualism, aspiration, privilege, prestige, and competition accurately describe these various manifestations. Such terms are clearly the products of the study of an individualistic society in which these phenomena are identifiable and are, in fact, formal, overt, sanctioned aspects of many spheres of institutional life. It is true that to some extent the individualistic, egalitarian pattern of North American social structure resembles the Hutterian in its normative denial of status; but on the other hand, it recognizes competition and even glories in it; and certainly some areas of the society overtly acknowledge status differentiation as well. It is suggested here that in Hutterian society we are dealing with a case where there coexist: (1) a normative denial of differentiation and competition; (2) a latent belief that individualism will out, because of imperfect human nature; (3) instrumental needs for differentiation; and (4) effective mechanisms for eliminating or mitigating the effects of these needs. Hence, ideal and real coincide to a remarkable degree, though not perfectly.[4] Hutterites are simply North American human beings,

---

[4] This would imply that the Hutterian social system comes very close to a homeostatic system or a mechanical model of equilibrium. This model, though still to some extent a basic point of departure for theories of culture change, has been more or less rejected by most anthropologists concerned with change (e.g., Voget, p. 231, and Theodore Schwartz, pp. 360ff). Schwartz stresses social interaction and the weaving of unique individual perspectives into the social fabric as the factors responsible for continuing imbalance or change in culture. However this may be, change is a relative thing, and so is homeostatic balance. In comparison to many other societies, large and small, the Hutterites closely approach a balanced functional homeostasis; and this means that the "steady state" model applies more cogently in their case. The important issue in the Hutterian case, however, is not

with values that the rigorous social system cannot entirely suppress or change, and which are partly generated by the system. Hutterian institutions are, in many ways, "outside" institutions that have been adapted to colony use; and as such, they have certain requirements that must be accommodated.

During the writer's intensive work with one colony, he was sponsored by a family in which nearly all the men were in managerial or executive positions. The members of this family had educated themselves to a greater degree than many others, and therefore they could speak with greater authority and objectivity about Hutterian life. The writer noted that his visits to families outside this group of intellectuals were taken as a compliment by those he visited—as though his presence conferred a higher "status" upon his hosts, and signified that they were "as good as" the "elite" (all the writer's own terminology). Individual members of such families would seek to create incidents in order to lure the writer into their apartments.

The problem presented by the Kaplan-Plaut protocols, then, is simply that the psychological absence of what they called "status differentiations" does not quite match the reality of Hutterian life, but that, at the same time, it *does* reflect the existence of institutional mechanisms that control such differentiation. One cannot say that aspiration, status, and competition do not exist, or that the psychological and structural foundations are absent, but only that they are brought under extensive control by institutionalized means. It is quite possible that when Hutterites do behave in ways describable by qualified terms of differentiation they are simply not aware they are doing so; and that when they are asked questions on attitudes or are given psychological tests dealing with these phenomena, they respond in a negative fashion.

---

the presence or absence of homeostasis, but rather the way in which the Brethren *control* Schwartz's mechanisms of interaction and integration of unique perspectives in order to obtain both stability and change. Thus the Hutterites achieve a level of rationality higher than that of most societies; Hutterian society and its changes are controlled not only by indirect ecological pressures, political factors, and individual responses, but also by the society's collective will. The forces leading inevitably to change in other social systems are used by the Brethren to control and limit change in their own.

The training received by the Hutterites in childhood is reinforced by a series of positive social devices that incorporate the
adult individual in the decision-making apparatus and give him a
sense of identity; by a set of sanctions against interpersonal conflict that hold the individual accountable before the entire group
for his behavior; and by the toleration of pragmatic exceptions to
the rules.[5] This ingenious system of social control, itself entirely
sanctioned by religious beliefs and commands, is remarkably resistant to external influences; and, when it functions optimally, it
keeps the social order of the colony on an even keel. From the Hutterian point of view, the atmosphere it creates is one of constructive
conformity, in which the individual is so thoroughly socialized
that even though he may be beset by anti-social desires or aspirations, he will be able to control them for the good of the group.

This system is not, however, foolproof, and behavioral deviance
continually crops up. In many colonies one finds a few young men
conducting private lives of their own: smoking behind the barn,
stealing from the colony's stock of wine, taking clandestine trips
to town, even carrying on love affairs with girls from the neighboring ranches or farms. John Hostetler has found that nearly all the
male defectors from colonies are men who have not held managerial or executive positions, and who are beginning to doubt that
they ever will. Most of these men leave the colony for jobs on the
outside, sow their wild oats for a year or two, then discover that
their training and education are too limited to command the satisfactions and advantages of the upward mobility that one can find
in the colony life; and that their socialization in the Hutterian
system has not provided them with the highly competitive and outgoing personality needed to get along outside. (Girls leave more
rarely, and when they do, it is usually permanently, for marriage
with a Gentile.) The high rate of return of the men speaks for the

[5] These means have been described in other chapters. It is important to note,
however, that control is exercised not only by specific procedures like public
apology, but also by the value system itself. It should be recalled that prestige is
suppressed because Hutterites believe that to be accorded prestige is blameworthy;
that is, if an individual receives marks of prestige from his brothers, it is his "fault,"
and he should be censured accordingly.

relative effectiveness of the contemporary colony system in providing rewards for its population; but it is also one more proof that personal aspiration, and pleasure at receiving recognition, exist in a latent form in Hutterian society, even though negatively sanctioned, a fact that the Brethren themselves, in the light of their doctrine of human fallibility, are the first to admit.

Still another way of analyzing the situation is to consider it in the light of the opposition between the individual and the communal spheres of participation—what is "my" world, and what is the colony world. The Hutterites seek to maximize the latter, and minimize the former; in fact, it can be said that their belief system makes no allowance for the personal sphere whatsoever—although there is the latent feeling among members that it exists. The Israeli kibbutz offers a sharp contrast: here the development of the personal world is encouraged to a large extent. The individual is expected to have his own hobbies and intellectual interests, and he is permitted to participate in the larger society and culture to a considerable extent. Consequently the kibbutz experiences considerable difficulty with loss of ideological and social commitment, and its regular loss of members and whole families results in a static or declining overall population. The kibbutz also seeks to reward its disaffected members with creature comforts and other inducements to remain—a measure that is also practiced in the colonies, but not to any great extent, since the colony socialization system is most effective in impressing communal ideals and austerity. In the Hutterian colony, the individual is expected to find his satisfactions in colony life, and effective socialization prepares him for this search. In this sense, the "repressive" social system of the colony is a means of both protection and gratification. In the kibbutz, these functions appear to be out of balance.

Social Tensions and Leadership

There are certain conditions under which colony stability and integration are likely to give way. To study the breakdown of any formally organized group, and the means of its regeneration, it is necessary to begin the analysis with an understanding of the group's formal organization and mechanisms for carrying out specific tasks (this structure was described in Chapter 6). It will be recalled that this system of "managed democracy" depends heavily upon leadership by the executives and Elders. These men steer the colony in appropriate directions, control the allocation of labor and funds, keep the books, disseminate information, adjudicate disagreements, and censure the disobedient. Their authority in such matters is supported by the colony's religious beliefs and held in check by the assembly's democratic decision-making process. The bosses therefore have considerable responsibility, but they must also submit to considerable control.

The basic problem confronting every Hutterian executive (and by the managers, though in different degree) is simply that while he is given a distinct role with responsibility and authority, he is not entirely free to exercise that authority, and, even more important, he is not given any public credit or prestige for exercising it effectively. If he behaves as if he were entitled to prestige, he is guilty of the sin of pride; indeed, if some of his fellow brethren confer such prestige upon him, the situation is considered to be evidence of a social sickness in the colony that requires correction. Even more, any sign that a Hutterite is willing to accept public approbation is counted as evidence of a defect of character on his part, and is considered even more reprehensible than the behavior of the brethren who show him deference.

While these difficulties accompany the role of leader and administrator, other problems of integration exist as well. Colonies may experience the evils of factionalism, arising from disagreements over policies of expansion or development or out of quarrels between the nuclear family units. Deviant behavior on the part of individuals may get out of hand, owing to weak or indecisive leadership, but the reassertion of strong authority may also be carried to excess and cause dissension. If defection becomes habitual, or if a colony begins to be characterized by creeping carelessness and slipshod performance, it is considered by other colonies to be on the verge of breakdown and dissolution.

In the course of the field work, we acquired considerable information on these symptoms and processes of tension, and the control devices used to restore order. In most instances, all the difficulties mentioned above were present. We concluded that a "trouble case," if reasonably severe, always involves the elements of leadership, authority, cleavage, factionalism, and individual deviance and dissent. Hutterites themselves are inclined to single out leadership as the primary cause, as well as the cure, of these social ills. A healthy colony is a colony with executives and managers who are able to control factionalism and deviant behavior, and also to provide the marginal or covert rewards that keep Hutterites contented and committed to the system.

One characteristic pattern of difficulty appears to emerge when the Minister, or other executive with responsibility, is unable to control quarreling and cleavage, or behaves in such a way as to encourage it. One common pattern is found in the colony that has enjoyed a long period of harmony and development under the benevolent guidance of a patriarch, and then after acquiring a new Minister or Householder, begins to exhibit signs of trouble. In such a case there is evidence that the leadership of the previous patriarch was sufficient to hold in check, but not to eliminate, potential sources of difficulty among the Brethren. Once his resolute and "charismatic" authority is relinquished to a man less skilled or less trusted, covert difficulties come to the surface. This situation gives us further reason to believe that latent prestige and aspiration are indeed important factors in Hutterian society.

Trouble also can arise when a Minister does not correctly carry out his duties to censure individuals for infractions of the rules. Hutterian regulations are quite specific: a person who has committed a breach of the rules must be requested by the Minister to stand up in the public assembly meeting and apologize for his action. This apology ends the matter. Ministers have been known to make accusations unfairly, after insufficient examination of the facts, or to require more than one apology. When such incidents occur, resentment can become acute. Such resentment opens hidden flaws in the social fabric, and cleavage results. Executives have also been known to exhibit favoritism in the kinship sense: to ignore the misdemeanors of their own nuclear family members, but to make certain that the infractions of the members of other families were given full censure. This sort of thing can intensify the inherent tendency toward nuclear kin-group cleavage that exists to some degree in every colony, but which under normal circumstances is manifested simply by a mild clannishness. In extreme cases, family solidarity can affect the voting process, for example, when the sons of executive-fathers vote consistently along lines they know their fathers favor, and against the sons of another executive.

Another source of trouble is over-dogmatic assertion of authority by Ministers and Householders. The most important day-to-day issues in Hutterian life concern the management of the farm enterprises and the overall development of the colony economy. We have shown elsewhere that this is a peculiarly delicate matter since it includes elements of both progress and conservatism. A colony must develop, but only to a point; it must avoid dedication to acquisitiveness and yet establish solvency and a regular rate of profitable return. Whether an executive encourages the more energetic managers unduly, or unduly inhibits them, the effect is to accentuate the everpresent differences over the "progress" issue. In every colony there are men who understand the need for growth and investment, and who may therefore push things too fast or hard; likewise there are men with conservative cultural or financial policies, who fear progress and investment. An executive must keep these factions in balance, or risk an open confrontation.

Similar problems emerge when the lines of authority become blurred. According to Hutterian procedures, the Minister is in charge of spiritual and behavioral matters; the Householder, the instrumental. However, Hutterites also hold that the Minister is entitled to intervene in practical affairs when the occasion warrants it. The patriarchal charisma of the Minister is considered to override all other mandates of authority, but only when circumstances are extreme. If a Minister asserts his authority where others feel it is not needed, thus compromising the role of the Householder, nuclear kin will form ranks on both sides of the controversy, and cleavage will develop. These problems can become acute when a colony lacks a suitable man for the Householder role, and the incumbent is a kind of figurehead, controlled and manipulated by the Minister, an executive, or a manager.

When trouble develops, the net balance of stability and tension will determine whether or not the fabric can be reunited. A "healthy" colony is not necessarily one that is free from tension—for all colonies have some ongoing tension—but is, rather, a colony which routinely finds ways to overcome these tensions. The most common solution (aside from appealing to the Leut Council of Ministers—always a last resort) is for the managers and executives to carefully manipulate things so as to blunt the effects of the behavior of the executive, or the factions and their leaders. Because of the nature of Hutterian values, an open break must be avoided at all costs, and the existing institutions of Hutterian decision-making must be used to regain control and integration. An executive can be replaced by the normal voting procedure; his decisions can be voided in various ways; he can be reasoned with in private, and possibly talked into conforming with those who seek the social health of the colony; he may be persuaded to "lay off" individuals he is persecuting. In the great majority of trouble cases, one or more of these methods work, and a breakdown is avoided.[6]

One of the Jasper colonies, Colony 6, which experienced severe difficulties during the early years of its founding, originally branched off from an Alberta group that lacked substantial resources, and could provide Colony 6 with only minimal funds and equipment. The new colony's executives soon realized that environmental conditions on the plateau required extensive agricultural adaptation and therefore considerable cash outlay. The Householder arranged for loans, but crop failures and other difficulties caused by resource problems prevented repayment. Lacking capital for the construction of adequate buildings and heating, the col-

---

[6] The importance of the fission process and the small size of the colonies in reducing tension must also be emphasized. Quarrels between leaders are often resolved by dividing the colony and thus separating the contenders. Hostetler (1964, pp. 185–98) has noted that in Amish society, too, divisiveness is controlled by migration.

ony members suffered from exposure, and began to develop signs of frustration and despair at their inability to establish a viable agricultural regime. The First Minister was an old, rather feeble and gentle man, who became discouraged by the colony's hardships and lacked the strength to exert influence over the members. The Householder, an unstable and not particularly competent man, had quarreled with the other Brethren, run up debts in town for his own and colony expenses, and had lately become obsessed with the idea that the other colony members were plotting against him. By its third year, the colony, foundering under its uncertain leadership, was destitute. Its social structure was disintegrating, and its young people had begun to leave to seek a better life on the "outside." At this point, some of the colony members took their problems to the Leut council, which decided to act. The colony's entire population was taken back into the parent group; the Householder was demoted to field hand, and the aged Minister was retired. A new group of vigorous young colonists was sent to the daughter colony location, where they undertook with the encouragement of the Leut a program of bold innovation that finally succeeded in raising the colony to economic viability. By 1965, the colony was well on its way to becoming another monument to Hutterian adaptability and industry.

The case of Colony 6 illustrates how in extreme circumstances wavering and destructive leadership must be controlled by external intervention. The Brethren of Colony 6 were incapable of action, or perhaps the usual manipulative techniques proved inadequate. In this case, the colony's situation was also aggravated by the discomforts and anxiety caused by the bad climate and by the failure of the farming program.

The Psychopathology of Leadership

There is no question but that the emphasis given to leadership by the Hutterites is an accurate reflection of their attitude toward the structure of their social system. The tendencies of the colony members toward factionalism and individuation, which are generated in part by the need for functional differentiation, are subject to control by wise and paternal executives who know how to exercise authority without abusing it. Among the forty-odd colonies in the southeastern part of Alberta and the southwestern region of Saskatchewan, at least four had experienced significant tensions during the 15 years preceding the field research for this study; and an additional two colonies were slowly breaking apart. Details are lacking on most of these cases, and it is impossible to be certain of causes, but leadership problems appear to have been involved in all instances of disturbance. Of the four colonies worst beset, one no longer exists: most of its members joined other Hutterian groups, and the remainder divided the colony land among themselves.

The number of cases of severe difficulty within this group of forty colonies has not been sufficiently large to establish a trend, but it is great enough to require vigilance, and the colonies therefore watch each other carefully. Each minister is responsible not only for the social health of his own colony, but in a general way for the welfare of all others as well, especially those within the same Leut, and most particularly those in the same intermarrying group. The abuse of authority and the collapse of leadership can have far-reaching results. Nepotism may become the rule on the managerial level; the rate of defection may increase, as men excluded from decisions decide to leave colony life; the young people, sensing the lack of authority, may begin to run wild, and it may become difficult to obtain wives for the colony men, since no woman wants to join a troubled colony. Colony members may increase their associations with Gentiles, and in extreme cases may become employees in Gentile businesses. Individual colony families may begin to appropriate the proceeds of separate enterprises. Very quickly, the fabric of communal life disintegrates.

Our task is to attempt to account for the behavior of the leaders. The Hutterites themselves sometimes generalize bad leadership behavior by referring to it as "spiritual illness"; that is, they perceive the leader as suffering from a disturbance of his relationship with God—in secular terms, he is suffering from a mental illness or neurosis. This brings us to a consideration of the "mental health" and personality of the Hutterites. Eaton and Weil (1955, p. 102) cite the relatively high incidence of manic-depressive behavior among colony leaders and their wives, and refer to the distinctive Hutterian "psychosis" analyzed in Kaplan and Plaut and called by the Brethren themselves *Anfechtung* (literally, "temptation," or "attack").[7] Anfechtung is described as involving guilt feelings, doubt, fear, and withdrawal from colony society. These symptoms manifest themselves in varying degrees, depending upon situations and extremity. The writers also approvingly note the high rate of cures effected by the restorative powers of colony society itself. (Our own observations indicate a high frequency of use by the Brethren of professional psychiatric services provided by the Province, but this particular issue is not our concern here.)

The theoretical question is whether Anfechtung is the correct term for the pattern of deviant behavior among Ministers and Householders described earlier. The general outline is similar, but the writer's data indicates a broader range of response and differing implications for the colony social situation than in other cases of deviant behavior. Some kind of stress is clearly evident, and an etiology of Hutterian anti-social behavior must include an analysis of the nature of this stress.

We noted previously that the Minister and the Householder have a great deal of power, but that this power is subject to careful control. The division of responsibility is reasonably clear, but the duty of the Minister to prevail in particular cases also introduces a note of potential strain. Both executives are also under great pressure to maintain the colony image, for the Brethren are particularly concerned with warding off criticism and persecution. The House-

---

[7] *Anfechtung* has been discussed by Eaton and Weil (1955) and Kaplan and Plaut (1956). The Eaton-Weil study is essentially a statistical survey that reports the incidence of various symptoms in the populations of a number of colonies. The frequency of *Anfechtung* reported in this survey was misleadingly high, according to Kaplan and Plaut, who argue that the disease is vaguely defined, and that individuals diagnosed as having it display a high rate of recovery. Actually both publications report that psychosis, whatever its incidence in the colonies, does not appear to injure the social fabric—that is, the "mental health" of the Brethren is good, and they have a "good adjustment" to their cultural pattern (Kaplan and Plaut, p. 8).

holder is in an especially vulnerable position. Though he has considerable authority, he is only *primus inter pares,* and cannot make unilateral decisions, no matter how much pressure is brought to bear on him by the agricultural managers. Consequently he must often deny their requests. The Householder role thus resembles that of the president of a large corporation, whose powers are subject to the many checks and balances exerted by the board of directors and the vice presidents. This analogy holds true in the financial sense as well, for many colonies are in the $100,000 gross income class, and the funds over which the Householder has control are quite substantial.

Thus, while the Householder has enormous responsibilities, his powers are limited. However, if anything goes wrong with the colony or its relations with the outside, he, "the boss," will be held responsible. Often these internal and external forces are in very delicate balance, and only a very wise and skilled leader can maintain order. Householders sometimes resign; the writer became acquainted with one who retired because he found his duties too heavy. He did not break down emotionally, but asked to resign because he felt that he was not equal to the task, and found it difficult to decide among the many competing demands. His own difficulties, however, were slight in comparison to those that can arise in the midst of work in a new colony, especially when the colony is poor or badly situated.

The emphasis placed on the Householder role accords with the actual importance of the role to the colony's welfare. This importance accounts for the Brethren's insistence on the need to "watch carefully" over the actions of the Householder, and to make certain that his grip is firm and his mind clear. The duty of watchfulness falls to every man, but especially to the Minister, and this situation, however necessary it may be, is also a source of potential friction and anxiety.

The Minister is in a position similar to that of the Householder, since while he is responsible for the mental and social health of every member of the colony, he must at the same time avoid doing anything to disturb the balance. He is also expected to set a perfect example of conduct in his own behavior, and not to favor any one person or kin group. In a colony with serious latent cleavage and hostilities, this balancing act can be extremely difficult to maintain. Consequently the Minister can easily begin to suspect colony members of resisting or deliberately provoking him—just as they in turn might construe his actions as unfair. If mutual suspicion develops between the Minister and the Householder, the situation is made worse.

There is a suggestion here that Hutterites may be especially vulnerable to feelings of lack of acceptance by their fellows. Any indication that the colony is not in complete accord with the executive may be taken by him as an attack, or at least as evidence of distrust. Likewise, any disciplinary action he might take could become the source of fear that he had "rejected" someone, or upset the communal equilibrium. Kaplan and Plaut (pp. 99–100) discuss what they call "uncertainty of acceptance" as a general pattern among Hutterites; they refer to content in their Thematic Apperception Test protocols that were interpreted as showing strong needs for "affiliation and comradeship" and "even greater" fears of lack of support by other human beings and rejection of the individual by the group. If these social and emotional patterns are basic to Hutterian personality, the especially vulnerable roles of the Minister and Householder would be likely to generate considerable stress.

Interestingly enough, Kaplan and Plaut regard their findings as "surprising," owing to the fact that Hutterian life is lived out in the midst of close kin and in terms of an ideology of communal sharing and group welfare. The present writer is inclined to reverse the equation: communal life breeds a sense of alienation and fear of rejection. That close family life can have this effect is well known to psychiatrists, novelists, and psychocultural anthropologists.

In Chapter 5 we described the avoidance techniques and the tendencies toward "awayness" that characterize Hutterian social life. The demands of the nuclear family, the extended kin group, and the colony community frequently conflict, and the Hutterite finds

himself in an ambivalent position. Withdrawal to avoid this conflicting situation may generate fear and guilt, which are expressed
as Anfechtung. The Householder and the Minister are especially
vulnerable in this regard. They must make decisions and bear responsibilities that can alienate them from others; but if they "withdraw," they endanger the life of the whole community. The situation can reach a point where especially sensitive individuals begin
to suspect hostility on every side—and in this super-Christian culture, hostility is a sin. Kaplan and Plaut state on page 75: "Hutterian
men give the impression of strength and stability principally, we
believe, because of their close adherence to Hutterian dogma, which
provides a comprehensive guide and support for them. When the
relationship to the dogma is changed and it is no longer paternal
and supportive, but instead becomes threatening, the individual is
overwhelmed by his own weakness and becomes depressed and
anxious. This ... is the soil from which Anfechtung develops."
This particular mechanism may work for the majority, but our
findings suggest that for the Minister and the Householder, an alternative pathway of reaction is available: they can respond to their
feelings that the "dogma" (really, the colony system as a whole) is
hostile, by accusing it—that is, the other Brethren— of conspiring
to injure them and prevent them from doing their jobs properly.
The comment by several informants that paranoid-like reactions
often "run in families" is interesting, since it suggests that some
predisposition may exist that renders certain individuals especially
sensitive to pressures.

It would seem that all is not roses in the Hutterian earthly para-
dise. The Brethren themselves have always recognized this; their
literature contains statements to the effect that they do not find
their way of life easy, but that since it is "Christ's way," they have
no choice but to persevere. Informal discussions with Hutterites
yielded confirmation of this: when you live in close proximity, they
would say, year after year, with the same people, under the taboo
against interpersonal conflict, you learn how to avoid them; at
times even to retreat into your own nuclear family group in order
to drain off hostilities and avoid irritations, and thus preserve your

sanity, and your ability to cooperate—the essential virtue demanded by large-scale collective agriculture. Visiting patterns in the colony showed surprising variety—some members rarely saw anyone other than work companions, spouse, and children; others were more gregarious, and had one or two intimate companions, usually siblings. The isolates were usually borderline cases of Anfechtung, and there were at least two in every colony studied.

Lest this discussion give an impression of an emotionally vulnerable and precariously balanced people, we should recall again that the number of colonies that actually go under because of leadership breakdown are very few. Moreover, the Hutterian system in North America has been up to now economically and demographically healthy, and shows no signs of general decay. Our major point here is simply that a certain emotional price must be paid for being a Hutterite, and that a few weak spots exist in this remarkable system of "managed democracy."

ELEVEN

Cultural Conservatism
and Technological Change

The ability of the Brethren to adapt to a variety of environments, both natural and social, has been a major theme of this book. We have described their strategies of adaptation to the Jasper milieu, pointing out how their efficiency and determination, and the scale of their economy, permits them to buy tools, avail themselves of resources, and experiment with agricultural techniques. We have noted that this adaptability is not a recent thing, but appears to go back to the Moravian period, when the Brethren were stewards on the estates of nobles. As a result of these traditions of adaptability, efficiency, and rationality, the Hutterites are able to accept modern technology and business methods without feeling compromised. It also can be argued that whatever the historical basis, the Brethren have been forced to accept these things in order to support their rapidly growing population in a period of rising costs of production.

If the historical argument is correct, then the adoption of modern technology and commercial methods was a matter of conscious decision, and hence there is simply no "problem" of change comparable to that found in tribal and peasant societies that have had technology thrust upon them. To a large extent, that is our position. However, it begs the question of effect. We are still required to show why changes as drastic and far-reaching as mechanization and commercialization have not had greater consequences for Hutterian culture and identity. After all, the Brethren are taught to reject luxuries, rejoice in hardship, distrust affluence, and avoid forming a material orientation. On the face of it, modern mechanization and commercialization do appear to threaten at least indirectly certain key values in Hutterian culture.

These problems have been the major topics of a variety of works on the Hutterites that have appeared since the 1930's.[1] In these writings, the various authors have noted that, while adoption of modern technology and some aspects of consumer economy have resulted in substantial change and breakdown in many tribal and peasant cultures, the Brethren appear to have taken similar changes in their stride. On the other hand, research on modernization since World War II has indicated that the prognostication of breakdown, or of its opposite, accommodated change, is a difficult one, because of the independent effects of the many variables involved.[2] The nature of the traditional culture and social system, the way changes are introduced, and the relationship of the tribe or community to the national society contain many variant possibilities. The Brethren's success in accommodating change is thus not as much of a surprise as it might have been a generation ago.

We may begin the discussion by referring to a well-known paper

---

[1] Eaton (1952); Serl (n.d.); Eaton, Weil, and Kaplan (1951); Deets (1931).

[2] Manning Nash found that Maya Indians employed in factories did not suffer extensive social and cultural change, because they could control its effect by residential and other ecological factors, and because Maya culture contained built-in mechanisms (possibly analogous to Hutterian traditional economic rationality) accommodating wage labor and other aspects of industrial life. J. M. Halpern found that while the peasant must give up his pastoralism for factory work, he retains his village ethnic identity. In these and other cases the common factor appears to be residential stability—the ability to remain living in a traditional enclave. This finds an analog in the Hutterian case of colony isolation. Spicer, in his monumental study of the Southwestern Indian's retention of his old culture in the face of Spanish and American domination, points to another key factor: the ability of the Indians to retain their traditional economic base, since none of the conquerors was especially interested in changing it. The Hutterian case is analogous, since the patterns of North American agrarian economy permit them to retain their own enterprise system. Norman E. Whitten, Jr. found that among the Ecuadorians in his study, "the social structure has moved toward increasing rationalization while at the same time expanding traditional ways of getting things done" (p. 198). This is so because the rationalization of the social structure permits the local people to obtain what they want from the larger national society. The Hutterites are not in quite the same situation, since they do not rationalize or change their social structure—however, their basic agrarian social structure contains built-in rational economic devices, which serve the same "broker" function as such devices do in the Ecuadorian case. At the same time, the Hutterites resemble Whitten's group in the sense of retaining their traditional internal system.

by Joseph Eaton (1952), in which he viewed the phenomenon of change as a case of "controlled acculturation"—the result of the persistent efforts of the Hutterites to control the rate of social change by defining the areas in which change is to be approved. When the pressure for change becomes too strong and the rules are violated widely enough to threaten respect for law and order, the Hutterian leaders "push for formal change of the written law before it makes too many lawbreakers" (p. 338). Eaton illustrates this process by citing changes in the *Ordnungen,* or written rules of the Schmieden Leut over a period of years, and by one quotation from an "outstanding leader" of the Hutterites who expresses a cool view of the need for careful, cautious adjustment to change, and maximal conservation of basic values. Eaton does not, however, show how actual decisions for change were made in the context of Hutterian life; the examples are all from the Ordnungen.

There is, of course, no doubt that certain aspects of Hutterian culture have begun to alter, and that there is possibly some tendency to accept more of the culture of the "outside." For example, though passenger vehicles were still taboo in many colonies in the early '50's, they are now found in every colony. In the '40's the only animal feeds purchased were protein supplements; today a variety of special feeds for poultry and livestock are routinely used. Items of personal or household convenience such as electric razors were rare in the '40's; today they are relatively common. However, in the area of personal adornment the traditional austerity prevails.

On the basis of our research findings, we feel that distinction should be made between the adoption of technological changes and the adoption of consumer and luxury goods. The former changes concern the colony as a whole, but the latter, the individual members only; the former relate to efficiency in production, and the latter to personal desires, and hence to basic values like humility and selflessness. To equate the two levels of change is to confuse the issue and vitiate the significance of particular conclusions.

Most of the Schmieden Leut rules cited by Eaton concern consumption. This is understandable, since it is personal acquisition that most seriously threatens the Community of Goods. The psy-

chological structure of the situation as described by Eaton is undoubtedly correct, and conforms to the writer's own observations:
the individual Hutterite experiences a "silent struggle within the
heart" (Eaton 1952, p. 338) between the traditional austerity and
the temptations of the rich culture of the outside. Sometimes leaders
have met this struggle by making judicious concessions at key
points. Each Leut has its Council of Ministers, which decides on
the areas of tolerance—areas defined by changes in the individual
colonies. Each colony has the right to make changes in the rules
governing consumption, though they must not depart too radically
from the general limits established by the Ordnungen of the Leut,
and any change must be sanctioned by the Leut council. Consequently there is a complex interplay of colony changes and sanctioned Leut changes; and sometimes the Leut simply acknowledges
existing changes by elevating them to the level of formal rules. (On
occasion, the Leut council turns the clock back by checking "undesirable" changes that have emerged.) It would seem, therefore,
that Eaton's presentation is mainly correct, but not complete
enough to give a true picture of the circumstances under which
changes occur.

With respect to the adoption of modern technology, the situation
today differs from that described by Eaton. As noted, the Leut controls are exerted principally over consumption. John Hostetler, who
has studied the Ordnungen of all three Leute, states that the majority of all rules concern clothing—the visible symbol of conformity. On the other hand, technological changes are almost entirely a matter of colony decision, and the Leut has relatively little
authority or interest here. Technology serves the goal of healthy
maintenance of the colony, and so long as it does not introduce
personal differentiation in property, it can be accepted. It is based
entirely on communal ownership. Moreover, Hutterian technology
is not industrial, but agrarian—the Brethren are not required to
work in factories.

Thus, the Hutterites adopt only those economic and technical
devices they perceive as having a clear and useful function in maintaining and strengthening the colony. Our Hutterian informants

consistently gave pragmatic explanations of such changes: "We began to go in for heavy machinery about fifteen years ago, because we had to increase production." "You can't survive out here without good machines." "With as much light soil as we have, the only way we could keep it from blowing was to invest in that Noble Blade outfit and tractor—the whole thing cost $6,500, but it kept the soil from blowing." "We probably shouldn't buy another combine this year, because it is such a big expense, but we get caught short by bad weather nearly every fall." "We had to put in that new feeding system for the chickens because we got more eggs, and we needed that money to pay off debts a few years ago." The writer found no reason to disbelieve these explanations, or to seek for some subtler motivation. In every case, the conversion to modern methods of production and accounting were instituted because they strengthened the economic health of the colony. It should be noted also that the Hutterites often have more and better machines than their Gentile neighbors, and that they regard their mechanization as a symbol of their superior farming techniques. Their economic superiority arises out of community, and the Brethren realize it. Thus the acquisition of better machines functions to conserve rather than to destroy Hutterian values.

In one sector of technology the Brethren do seem to exert a conscious policy of restriction or cautious progress: that is, in the use of machines by the women. Some colonies permit women to drive the little garden tractors that are now used extensively for hauling wagons and people around the colony premises. But so far as the writer knows, no colony allows its women to drive regular farm tractors, trucks, or passenger vehicles. The reason the Brethren show caution here is obvious: the culture of the women remains the most conservative sector of Hutterian life, and care must be exercised in adopting anything that might result in unemployment or aspirations for equal rights among them.

The dynamics of the resolution of issues concerning machinery purchases would appear, in most cases, to follow the pattern described in Chapter 8, that of the debates over the hog-manure disposal project. Large, expensive projects often divide the colony into conservative and progressive factions. When the conservatives find that their practical objections have been dissolved by effective counter-arguments, they fall back on moral objections, which center on the theme that Hutterites should work hard and not let the colony fall prey to elaborate technological schemes. Throughout the history of the Brethren in North America, the conservative element has generally lost out to the modernists and practical men, who have been able to show that continued economic and social health demands judicious spending for the sake of efficiency.

At the same time, these "modernists," if they are to be effective, must be highly conservative in their adherence and commitment to Hutterian beliefs and social practices. The quickest route to innovation in a healthy colony is to work within the existing frame of cautious and sanctioned change—not to resist it. In most colonies, the most effective innovators are the young managers who are also the best Hutterian scholars, and who are demonstrating their competence not only by efficiently managing their enterprises, and cautiously suggesting improvements, but also by preparing themselves for governing roles in later life.[3] Thus so long as Hutterian values remain influential, the system will persist as a means of achieving innovation and change, as well as of controlling or resisting them.[4]

[3] This phenomenon of the "conservative innovator" is well known in ordered societies undergoing change. The writer has observed it in the case of Japan: in the early history of Japan's modern era the bulk of the modernizing changes were instituted by the cultural conservatives (see Bennett and McKnight, pp. 101–13). Among the Japanese educated in the United States and returned to Japan, those who were most effective in communicating their new knowledge and producing innovations were those who adhered to routine Japanese social and cultural patterns (see Bennett, "The Innovative Potential," pp. 246–51).

[4] This raises the question of the role of values in cultural change. The Hutterian case would seem to be clear enough: values are part of an explicit theological charter, and are comprehensive enough to order decisions on almost all spheres of life. At the same time, the values are flexible enough to permit change in adaptive directions. This situation does not differ greatly from that observed by other investigators; e.g., those who worked on the Harvard Five Cultures Project, which was concerned with the value systems and adaptations of various groups in the "Rimrock" area of New Mexico. In their summary of the role of values, Vogt and Albert, Chapter 1, note that the cultural changes among the five groups did not involve drastic changes in existing values, but rather that most changes were encompassed within the existing cultural framework. Subsequently, however, new

Verne Serl (n.d.) is concerned with another facet of Eaton's concept of "controlled acculturation": the relationship of the acculturation process to the face-to-face interaction of colony life. Eaton believes that the strength of primary group mechanisms is such as to permit the efficient communication needed in a program of planned change. This is an echo of similar ideas appearing in the earlier studies by Deets in the late 1920's and early 1930's, and implicit in Horsch (1931) and others. These writers stress that the fact that Hutterian life is always lived out in the context of single, relatively small, face-to-face groups has been the major reason for the system's stability and resistance to change.

Serl (p. 5) points to this fact, but in addition observes that the primary group context of Hutterian life leads to "common background and experience of colony members," which in turn results in "a common interpretation of the situation at hand." Change takes place, but it is not recognized, "and therefore does not give rise to the anxiety and frustration characteristic of social situations in which alternative views compete for acceptance." In Serl's view, controlled acculturation is an overly mechanistic term for orderly accommodation and change; he wants to substitute the hypothesis that Hutterian culture changes without stress because the Hutterites lack any awareness that change is taking place. Since all changes take place in the context of the microcosm—in which, despite some restlessness, there is general agreement on goals and dogma, hence little chance for disputes and factionalism—the ethos of Hutterian culture always has maximum opportunity to assert itself, regardless of how strongly it is challenged.

---

values appropriate to the respective "niches" occupied by the five cultures slowly emerged. Hammell, pp. 199–215, had related findings to the effect that a value system could remain intact and homogeneous even though actual behavior became heterogeneous, with the values functioning as rationalizing and reassuring mechanisms. The basic question therefore is how flexible a given value system may be in permitting adaptive decision-making. The second key question concerns the general milieu; that is, do there exist factors which permit maximal retention of a given value system, or adherence to its requirements, by permitting only minimal departures from it? Hutterites adapt well not only because their values have appropriate flexibility, but also because the milieu of Great Plains agriculture permits relative ecological isolation and autonomy, thereby permitting minimal or selective adaptation to the larger culture.

The relatively small number of people involved, and the face-to-face quality of daily life undoubtedly play some part in stability and change. But do they merely encourage the growth of a common frame of reference? The colony is a rationally controlled environment, with elaborate mechanisms for ensuring conformity and for involving nearly everyone in decision-making; therefore, the effect of the primary-group atmosphere is felt not merely as some vague, Durkheimian solidarity, but through explicit measures of administrative social control. Moreover, the primary-group spirit itself contains certain dangers, if it takes the form of family solidarity at the expense of colony unity. As noted in a footnote to Chapter 10, the Hutterites take over the typical human process of perspectival novelty arising in social interaction (Schwartz 1962) and use it rationally for the purpose of controlling change—in the spirit of Eaton's theory but in not quite so simple a manner. The rationality of the system consists of erecting a complex formal organization that allows for individual perspective and motive while at the same time controlling or, upon occasion, suppressing them. In everyday language, one might say that the Hutterites are very strict with each other but in a very humane way.

In any event, changes and adoptions must always be considered from the viewpoint of the Hutterites themselves. It would be wrong to assume that the adoption by the Brethren of, say, an air-conditioned combine or some such spectacular gadget, would have greater cultural consequences than the adoption of the practice of occasional smoking. The Hutterian view would be that the combine facilitates colony continuity and strength, and that cigarettes threaten them; hence a colony can adopt the use of air-conditioned combines without changing culturally, but cannot adopt smoking or the possession of transistor radios without drastically altering its views on personal austerity.

One might argue that the issue is not this simple, since the use of air-conditioned combines might conceivably lead the users to wish for a more comfortable environment, which in turn might lead them to demand more comfortable living quarters, and so on. Of course, this possibility cannot be entirely disallowed; technological adoptions do have halo effects. However, the answer is simply that, for the present, Hutterian norms are sufficiently strong to make the kind of careful discrimination we have just described possible, and a carryover to domestic existence highly unlikely.

The Eaton hypothesis is mechanistic, sociologistic, and oversimplified. Serl's is culturological, and also oversimplified. Neither is wrong; both have gotten at part of the truth. However, to seek for answers to the always complex process of change in human society in the form of single factors is to misrepresent this process. We have noted that Eaton's hypothesis probably works best with reference to items of personal consumption that present a clear challenge to the Community of Goods. Serl's hypothesis would appear to apply to the technological aspect of change in which colony, rather than personal, interests are involved. Serl points out that the managerial personnel of the colony have extensive contact with outside agencies and persons, and yet such contact does not result in defections or in seductions by consumer culture. There is no mention in his paper either of consumer goods or of personal adornment and conveniences.

Several writers (e.g., Serl, p. 5) cite the Brethren's view of a "fixed and unchanging universe" as another factor in their permitting change to take place with a minimum of conflict. The mechanism operates as follows: various textual references in the Bible and in the basic writings of men like Peter Rideman serve to define the communal basis of Hutterian life. So long as these general principles are observed, it is the business of the Elders and the colony Leut to define the nature of contemporary issues, and to find their solutions, and these solutions become part of the body of Hutterian tradition. In contrast to many other fundamentalist sects, the Hutterites do not use Biblical references to cover *all* daily affairs, thereby limiting the possibilities of choice. Within certain parameters, whatever the Hutterites do is traditional, i.e., is in line with the teachings of their fathers.

There is much to be said for Serl's interpretation. In the course of our study we noted comments by Hutterites that would seem to confirm this theory of change and ideological autonomy. "Cars don't interfere with our life, since we own them in common," and such statements as, "It doesn't matter what color we paint our buildings; there isn't anything in the book that says we have to have them white, or gray, or anything," were common. The instrumental basis of Hutterian life—the cooperative and communal farm—has its own momentum, and requires flexibility at many points as a sheer matter of economic survival. One colony decided to cover its buildings with asbestos siding instead of painting them because this covering, though unattractive, would be cheaper than frequent repainting. The decision was made quite rationally on the basis of the money involved. The point is that the Hutterites are free to make such decisions on the basis of the ideological mechanism described by Serl, and the immediate circumstances of the decision may be entirely practical, or even impractical: for example, many colonies, especially the Lehrer, insist on paint instead of asbestos siding, although they know it is expensive—because they like it, and because they feel they need to present a good appearance to their non-Hutterian neighbors.

Data from the Jasper Gentile community provided us with comparative information on the rate of adoption of agricultural innovations among the various groups in the study region. On this score, the Hutterites ranked high: they have accepted more innovations than most of their neighbors, and are often more progressive in outlook; but they have to be shown that the particular innovation is worth the money, and they are often as hard to convince as their conservative Scottish neighbors. Therefore what puts the Hutterites ahead in the long run is not their favorable attitude toward innovation, but the sheer scale of their operations. The net worth of a colony near the peak of its development is at least $275,000, which means that its credit is virtually unlimited; and once the Brethren are convinced of the need for an adoption, they are financially free to make it. Many of their Gentile neighbors will never have the requisite cash or credit to innovate successfully.

However, not only do individual colonies differ on their rate of acceptance and expenditures, but the Leute differ also. One of the key points of difference is the access to printed technical information, and the desire to accumulate and read this. Some colonies forbid any "useless" expenditure on books and publications; others permit or even encourage the practice. Some colonies are not inclined to encourage the young "intellectuals" in the managerial group, in their intense cultivation of literacy as a compensation for the lack of a high school education. These differences can be critical, since the existence of one or two "intellectuals" in a colony can mean the difference between abundant knowledge of new technology and management procedures, and complete ignorance of them. In general, we found that the Brethren have more respect for learning than their neighbors in typical "backward" Great Plains districts do, and that this contributes to their rate of innovation. The Hutterites are proud of the fact that they can do so much with so little formal public education.

Conclusion

We have noted that the current North American phase is the second Golden Age in Hutterian history. The three groups who migrated from Russia in the 1870's were remnants of many colonies who had recently abandoned the practice of communal living; this divergence from dogma had occurred at least once before. In our opinion, the exceptional stability of the American colonies may rest mainly on the adaptive success the colonies have enjoyed in the United States and Canada. In spite of attempts by non-Hutterites in the Dakotas and in Alberta to restrict them, the colonies on this continent have, on the whole, prospered and expanded without serious hindrance or persecution, thus achieving maximum satisfaction and rewards.

These considerations suggest that the conventional view of Hutterian society as an anachronistic system that somehow resists the effects of modern change is a limited one. Hutterian society is what it is: a Christian body practicing communal living. To do this successfully within the agricultural mode, it is necessary to farm efficiently and without serious interference. Wherever the Hutterites have found favorable conditions, they have done well, and have adopted whatever means were necessary to further their ends. Their austerity is dictated by dogma, but austerity is necessary if they are to accumulate the savings they need to finance colony fission and care of the aged. The Brethren have one basic instrumental problem of change—they must continually curb individual expenditures in order to maintain adequate savings—but this problem is probably no more acute now than it has been in the past. Cooperative farming is as difficult today as it ever was, and just as successful.

Though Hutterian life is stable by any standard of comparison, its stability is a dynamic phenomenon, in which change is accommodated when it is necessary for the continuity of the colony system. The Hutterites teach us that the preservation of the integrity of a traditional culture is possible, given good management, an enormously strong social system, and a clear sense of cultural identity. Moreover, the Hutterian experience teaches us that the dangers are constant: the Brethren are threatened by both extreme privation and extreme prosperity; the "World System" in every period has offered temptations and hostility. These must somehow be fought while at the same time meeting the world on its own terms.

There will be more changes.[5] If land purchases are increasingly restricted, the colonies will be forced to find some routine way of losing population, since they will be unable to divide and therefore will be unable to provide their population with the satisfying activities that help the members maintain identity and motivation.

---

[5] The position on culture change taken by the writer is simply that change is best studied as a continuous process and not as a movement from one end-state or stable point to another. The latter, or stop-and-start theory of change is associated with the older tradition of acculturation theory in anthropology, and it is characterized by concern for a typology of end-states. For example, see Dozier who distinguishes six: rejection, assimilation, compartmentalization, fusion, reactive adaptation, and stabilized pluralism. All these reactions have characterized Hutterian responses to the "outside" at one period or another or in one colony or another. The problem is not the typological nature of the reaction, but the process of adaptation represented by the choice of one or another strategy.

Gadgetry probably will continue to find its way slowly into colony culture, and the young people will probably develop a greater sense of independence, an attachment to modernity. Secondary education will eventually arrive—it is already starting in the Manitoba colonies. There will be more defectors and restlessness; and perhaps many of the colonies will dissolve, leaving behind a hard core of committed Brethren who will foster the Community of Goods in some other, more isolated region. Perhaps some will take a middle way. Here the remark of one of our Hutterian friends may be prophetic: "If they [the Elders] ever decide to let in radios, I am going to see to it that we make them ourselves. That's the Hutterian way."

BIBLIOGRAPHY

Bibliography

Arndt, Karl. "The Harmonists and the Hutterites," *American German Review*, X (1944), 24–26.

Arnold, Eberhard. Children in Community: a Survey of the Educational Work of the Bruderhof Communities. London, 1939.

———. The Hutterian Brothers: Four Centuries of Common Life and Work. London, 1940.

Arnold, Emmy. Torches Together: The Beginning and Early Years of the Bruderhof Communities. Rifton, New York, 1964.

———. Eberhard Arnold. Rifton, New York, 1964.

Barnard, Chester I. The Functions of the Executive. Harvard, 1950.

Bennett, John W. "The Innovative Potential of American-Educated Japanese," *Human Organization*, Vol. 21 (1962–63), pp. 246–51.

———. "Communal Brethren of the Great Plains," *Trans-Action*, Winter 1966.

———, and Robert McKnight. "Approaches of the Japanese Innovator to Cultural and Technical Change," *Annals of the American Academy of Political and Social Sciences*, Vol. 306 (1965), pp. 101–13.

———, and Iwao Ishino. Paternalism in the Japanese Economy. University of Minnesota, 1963.

Bestor, Arthur E. Backwoods Utopias: The Sectarian and Owenite Phases of Communitarian Socialism in America. University of Pennsylvania, 1950.

Birdsell, J. B. "Some Environmental and Cultural Factors Influencing the Structuring of Australian Aboriginal Populations." *American Naturalist*, no. 87 (1953), pp. 171–207.

————. "On Population in Generalized Hunting and Gathering Populations." *Evolution,* no. 12 (1958), pp. 189–205.

Boyd, Hugh. New Breaking: An Outline of Cooperation among the Farmers of Western Canada. Toronto, 1938.

Bozeman Conference. *Risk and Uncertainty in Agriculture.* Proceedings of Research Conference on Risk and Uncertainty held at Bozeman, Montana, 1953.

Canadian Mental Health Association. The Hutterites and Saskatchewan: a Study of Inter-group Relations. Unpublished. Regina, Saskatchewan, 1953.

Clark, Bertha W. "The Hutterian Communities," *Journal of Political Economy,* Vol. 32 (1924), nos. 3 and 4, pp. 357–374, 468–486.

Clements, F. E. "Climatic Cycles and Human Populations in the Great Plains," *Scientific Monthly,* September 1938.

————, and R. W. Chaney. Environment and Life in the Great Plains. Carnegie Institute of Washington, Suppl. Public No. 24, 1936.

Cohen, Eric. Bibliography of the Kibbutz. Jerusalem, 1964.

————. "Progress and Communality: Value Dilemmas in the Collective Movement," *Informational Review of Community Development,* nos. 15, 16 (1966).

Cohn, Norman. The Pursuit of the Millennium. New York, 1947.

Conkin, Paul K. Two Paths to Utopia: The Hutterites and the Llano Colony. University of Nebraska, 1964.

Cook, Robert C. "The North American Hutterites: A Study in Human Multiplication." *Population Bulletin,* no. 10 (1954), pp. 47–107.

Cooperstock, Henry. "Cooperative Farming as a Variant Social Pattern," reprinted in Blishen *et al.,* Canadian Society. Glencoe, Ontario, 1961.

Cummings, Elaine, and David M. Schneider. "Sibling Solidarity," *American Anthropologist,* Vol. 63 (1961), pp. 498–507.

Darin-Drabkin, H. The Other Society. London, 1962.

————. Patterns of Cooperative Agriculture in Israel. Tel Aviv, 1962.

Dawson, C. A. "Group Settlement: Ethnic Communities in Western Canada." Vol. VII of Canadian Frontiers of Settlement, W. A. Mackintosh, ed. Toronto, 1936.

Deets, L. E. The Hutterites: A Study in Social Cohesion. Gettysburg, 1939.

————. "The Origin of Conflict in the Hutterische Communities," in *Publications of the American Sociological Society,* no. 25 (1931), pp. 125–135.

Dozier, Edward. "Differing Reactions to Religious Contacts among North American Indian Tribes," *Akten des 34. Internationalisten Amerikanistenkongresses.* Vienna, 1962.

Eaton, Joseph, Robert J. Weil, and B. Kaplan. "The Hutterite Mental Health Study," in *Mennonite Quarterly Review,* January 1951.

Eaton, Joseph W. "Controlled Acculturation: A Survival Technique of the Hutterites," *American Sociological Review*, no. 17 (1952), pp. 331–340.

———, and Albert Meyer. Man's Capacity to Reproduce: The Demography of a Unique Population. Glencoe, Ontario, 1954.

———, and Robert J. Weil. Culture and Mental Disorders. Glencoe, Ontario, 1955.

Elton, G. R. Reformation Europe: 1517–1559. London, 1963.

Fenwick, Robert W. "Hutterites Destroy Value of Land, Montanans Say." *Denver Post*, July 14, 1948.

Firey, W. Man, Mind, and Land. Glencoe, Ill., 1959.

Fischer, Hans. Jakob Huter: Leben, Froemmigkeit, Briefe. Newton, Kansas, 1956.

Fletcher, E. A. Constitution of Hutterian Brethren Church and Rules as to Community of Property. Winnipeg, Manitoba, n.d.

Foster, George M. Traditional Cultures and the Impact of Technological Change. New York, 1962.

Francis, E. K. "The Adjustment of a Peasant Group to a Capitalistic Economy: The Manitoba Mennonites," *Rural Sociology*, Vol. 17, p. 335.

Freilich, Morris. "The Natural Experiment, Ecology and Culture," *Southwestern Journal of Anthropology*, no. 19 (1963), pp. 21–39.

Fretz, J. Winfield. "An Evaluation of the Hutterian Way of Life from the Sociological Point of View," in *Proceedings of the Conference on Mennonite Cultural Problems*, no. 5 (1946), pp. 89–93.

Fried, Morton H. "Land Tenure, Geography, and Ecology in the Contact of Cultures," *American Journal of Economics and Sociology*, 11 (1952), 391–412.

Friedmann, Robert. Hutterite Studies. Goshen, Indiana, 1961.

———. "An Epistle Concerning Communal Life: A Hutterite Manifesto of 1650," in *Mennonite Quarterly Review*, III (1960), 249–274.

Gee, Wilson. The Social Economics of Agriculture. New York, 1954.

Geertz, Clifford. Agricultural Involution: The Process of Ecological Change in Indonesia. University of California, 1963.

Gross, Paul S. The Hutterite Way. Saskatoon, Saskatchewan, 1965.

Halpern, J. M. "Yugoslav Peasant Society in Transition: Stability in Change," *Anthropology Quarterly*, Vol. 36 (1963), pp. 156–82.

Hammell, E. A. "Social Rank and Evolutionary Position in a Coastal Peruvian Village," *Southwestern Journal of Anthropology*, Vol. 18 (1963), pp. 199–215.

Heady, E. O. "Extent and Conditions of Agricultural Mechanization in the U.S.," in J. L. Meij, ed., Mechanization in Agriculture. Chicago, 1960.

Hedges, James B. Building the Canadian West: The Land and Colonization Policies of the Canadian Pacific Railway. New York, 1939.

Hofer, Peter. The Hutterian Brethren and their Beliefs. Starbuck, Manitoba, 1955.

Horsch, John. The Hutterite Brethren, 1528–1931. Goshen, Indiana, 1931.

———. "The Hutterian Brethren, 1528–1929: A Story of Martyrdom and Loyalty," in *Mennonite Quarterly Review* (1929), 11, 97–102.

Hoselitz, Bert. "Tradition and Economic Growth," in Braibanti and Spengler, eds., Tradition, Values, and Socio-Economic Development. Duke University, 1961.

Hostetler, John. Amish Society. Johns Hopkins Press, 1963.

———. "The Communal Property Act of Alberta," *University of Toronto Law Journal,* Vol. 14 (1961), pp. 125–29.

———. The Hutterites in North America. New York, 1967.

———. "Persistence and Change in Amish Society," *Ethnology,* Vol. 3 (1964), pp. 185–98.

———, and Calvin Redekop. "Education and Assimilation in Three Ethnic Groups," *Alberta Journal of Educational Research,* VIII (1962), 189–203.

Hutterian Brethren of Manitoba. "The Hutterian Brethren and Their Beliefs." Pamphlet, n.d.

"Hutterian Brethren of Montana." Augusta, Montana, 1963.

Infield, Henrik F. Cooperative Communities at Work. New York, 1945.

———. Cooperative Living in Palestine. London, 1946.

———. "Sociometric Structure of a Veterans' Cooperative Land Settlement," in *Sociometery,* 10 (1947), no. 1.

———. Utopia and Experiment: Essays in the Sociology of Cooperation. New York, 1955.

———, and J. B. Maier, eds. Cooperative Group Living: An International Symposium. New York, 1950.

———, and K. Freier. People in Ejidos. New York, 1954.

Kaplan, Bert, and Thomas F. Plaut. Personality in a Communal Society. University of Kansas, 1956.

Klassen, Peter. The Economics of Anabaptism. Unpublished dissertation, University of Southern California, 1962.

Knill, William Douglas. Hutterian Education: A Descriptive Study Based on the Hutterian Colonies within Warner County No. 5, Alberta, Canada. Unpublished thesis, Montana State University, 1958.

Kraenzel, C. F. The Great Plains in Transition. University of Oklahoma, 1955.

Labes, Emanuel. Handbook of the Moshav. Jerusalem World Zionist Organization. Jerusalem, 1962.

Lévi-Strauss, Claude. Structural Anthropology. New York, 1963.

Lincoln, James F. Incentive Management: A New Approach to Human Relations in Industry and Business. Cleveland, 1951.

Lipset, S. M. Agrarian Socialism. University of California, 1950.

Littell, Franklin. The Anabaptist View of the Church. Boston, 1958.

Lockwood, George B. The New Harmony Movement. New York, 1905.

Loserth, Johann. "The Decline and Revival of the Hutterites," *Mennonite Quarterly Review*, IV (April 1930), 93.

———. "Crafts of the Hutterian Brethren," in Mennonite Encyclopedia, I, 728–30.

MacEwan, Grant. Between the Red and the Rockies. University of Toronto, 1952.

Mackintosh, W. A. Prairie Settlement: the Geographic Background. Vol. 1, Canadian Frontiers of Settlement. Toronto, 1934.

Mange, Arthur. The Population Structure of a Human Isolate. Unpublished dissertation. University of Wisconsin, 1963.

McClelland, David C. The Achieving Society. New York, 1961.

McHale, Thomas R. "Econocological Analysis and Differential Economic Growth Rate," in *Human Organization,* Vol. 21, no. 1 (1962).

McHenry, Dean E. The Third Force in Canada: The CCF, 1932–1948. University of California, 1950.

Meij, J. L. Mechanization in Agriculture. Chicago, 1960.

Moorhouse, H. J. Deep Furrows. Toronto, 1918.

Morton, Arthur S. "History of Prairie Settlement." Vol. 11 of Canadian Frontiers of Settlement. W. A. Mackintosh, ed. Toronto, 1938.

Murphy, R. F., and J. H. Steward. "Trappers and Trappers: Parallel Process in Acculturation." *Economic Development and Cultural Change,* IV (1954), 335–55.

Nash, Manning. Machine Age Maya. American Anthropological Association Memoir, No. 87. 1958.

Nelson, L. The Mormon Village. University of Utah, 1952.

Nesbitt, Leonard D. Tides in the West: A Wheat Pool Story. Saskatoon, Saskatchewan, 1962.

Nordhoff, Charles. The Communistic Societies of the United States (first published in 1875). New York, 1961.

Odum, E. P. Fundamentals of Ecology. Philadelphia, 1953.

Park, R. E. "Succession: An Ecological Concept," in *American Sociological Review,* no. 1 (1936), pp. 171–79.

Park, Thomas. "Beetles, Competition, and Populations," in *Science,* Vol. 138, no. 3548.

Pascal, R. Communism in the Middle Ages and the Reformation: Waldenses and Anabaptists," in John Lewis, ed., Christianity and the Social Revolution. New York, 1936.

Patton, Harald S. Grain Growers' Cooperation in Western Canada. Harvard University, 1928.

Peter, Karl. "The Hutterites: Values, Status, and Organizational Systems," in *Journal of the Sociology Club of the University of Alberta*, Vol. 2 (1963), pp. 55–59.

Peters, Victor. All Things Common: The Hutterian Way of Life. University of Minnesota, 1965.

———. A History of the Hutterian Brethren, 1528–1958. Dissertation, Georg August University at Göttingen, 1960. Published by the University of Minnesota Press, 1965.

Plath, David. "The Fate of Utopia: Adaptive Tactics in Four Japanese Groups," in *American Anthropologist,* no. 68 (1966), pp. 1152–62.

Priestly, David. A Study of Selected Factors Related to Attitudes toward the Hutterites of South Dakota. Unpublished dissertation. South Dakota State College, 1959.

Rideman, Peter. Account of Our Religion, Doctrine, and Faith (1565). translated by K. Hasenberg. London, 1950.

Riley, Marvin P. "Agriculture on South Dakota's Communal Farms," in *South Dakota Farm and Home Research*, Vol. 10, no. 2 (1959).

———. The Hutterite Brethren: An Annotated Bibliography. Agricultural Experiment Station, South Dakota State University, 1965.

———, and J. R. Stewart. The Hutterites: South Dakota's Communal Farmers. South Dakota State University, 1966.

Robinson, Will. "Communism," in *The Wi-Yohi,* IV, 1–6. South Dakota State Historical Society publication, 1950.

Sakakibara, Gan. "Study of the Hutterite Brethren: A Strophe of the Sociology of Religion," in *Aoyama Keizai Ronshu* (1962), Tokyo.

———. Junkyō to Bōmei Hataraito no Yon-hyaku-go-jū-Nen (Four Hundred and Fifty Years of Hutterite Martyrdom and Exile). Tokyo, 1967.

Sauer, Carl. Land and Life. University of California, 1963.

Schilling, Arnold J. The Music of the Hutterites of Tchetter Colony. Unpublished dissertation. University of South Dakota, 1965.

Schneider, David H., and George C. Homans. "Kinship Terminology and the American Kinship System," *American Anthropologist,* no. 57 (1955), pp. 1194–1208.

Schonfield, Hugh J. The Passover Plot. New York, 1965.

Schwartz, Charles. The Search for Stability. Contemporary Saskatchewan Series, 1. Toronto, 1959.

Schwartz, Theodore. The Paliau Movement in the Admiralty Islands. American Museum of Natural History Anthropological Papers, Vol. 49, No. 2, 1962.

Serl, Vernon C. Stability and Change in Hutterite Society. Unpublished dissertation. University of Oregon, 1964.

———. "Stability and Change among the Hutterites," in Herbert C. Taylor, ed. *Research in Progress.* Western Washington College of Education, n.d.

Sharp, Paul F. The Agrarian Revolt in Western Canada. University of Minnesota, 1948.

———. Whoop-up Country: A Study of the Canadian-American West. University of Minnesota, 1955.

Shelly, Paul R., and others. "Implications of the Hutterian Way of Life for other Mennonite Groups," in *Proceedings of the Conference on Mennonite Cultural Problems*, 5 (1946).

Smith, C. H. The Story of the Mennonites. Newton, Kansas, 1950.

Sommer, Donald. "Peter Rideman and Menno Simons on Economics," in *Mennonite Quarterly Review*, XXVIII (1954), 205–23.

Sorokin, P. A. "Techniques of Contemporary Free Brotherhoods: the Hutterites of the U.S.," in The Ways of Power and Love. Boston, 1954.

Spicer, Edward. Cycles of Conquest. University of Arizona, 1962.

Spiro, M. E. Kibbutz: Adventure in Utopia. Harvard University, 1956.

Stamp, L. Dudley, ed. A History of Land Use in Arid Regions. Columbia University, 1961.

Steward, J. H. "The Concept and Method of Cultural Ecology," in Theory of Culture Change. University of Illinois, 1955.

Strange, H. G. I. A Short History of Prairie Agriculture. Winnipeg, 1954.

Talmon, Yonina. "Pursuit of the Millennium: The Relation between Religious and Social Change." *Archives Européenes de Sociologie,* III (1962), 125–48.

———. "The Family in a Revolutionary Movement: The Case of the Kibbutz," in Nimkoff, ed. Comparative Family Systems. New York, 1965.

Thomas, Norman. "Hutterite Brethren," *South Dakota Historical Collections,* Vol. 25 (1951).

Thomas, William L., Jr., ed. Man's Role in Changing the Face of the Earth. University of Chicago, 1956.

Thornthwaite, C. W. "Climate and Settlement in the Great Plains," *USDA Yearbook,* 1941.

Tyre, Robert. Douglas in Saskatchewan: The Story of a Socialist Experiment. Vancouver, B.C., 1962.

Voget, Fred. "Cultural Change," in B. J. Siegel, ed., *Biennial Review of Anthropology,* pp. 232–33. Stanford University, 1963.

Vogt, E. Z., and Ethel Albert. People of Rimrock. Harvard University, 1966.

Waldner, Marie. "The Present Day Social Customs and Cultural Patterns of the Hutterites in North America," *Proceedings, Fifth Annual Conference on Mennonite Cultural Problems* (1946), Berne, Ind.

Walpot, Peter. "True Surrender and Christian Community of Goods," from the Great Article Book, 1577. Translated by K. Hasenberg and published as an article in *The Mennonite Quarterly,* January 1957.

Webb, Walter. The Great Plains. New York, 1931.

Weber, Max. The Protestant Ethic, and the Spirit of Capitalism. Translated by Talcott Parsons. New York, 1904.

Whitten, Norman E., Jr. Class, Kinship, and Power in an Ecuadorian Town. Stanford University, 1965.

Williams, George H. The Radical Reformation. Philadelphia, 1962.

Wolkan, Rudolf. Die Hutterer. Vienna, 1918.

————. Geschichtbuch der Hutterischen Brüder. Vienna, 1923.

Wright, Jim. Prairie Progress: Consumer Cooperation in Saskatchewan. Saskatoon, Saskatchewan, 1956.

Yates, S. W. Saskatchewan Wheat Pool. Saskatoon, Saskatchewan, 1947.

Zakuta, Leo. A Protest Movement Becalmed: A Study of Change in the CCF. University of Toronto, 1964.

Zieglschmid, A. J. F. Die Alteste Chronik der Hutterischen Brüder. Ithaca, New York, 1943.

————. Das Klein Geschichtbuch der Hutterischen Brüder. Philadelphia, 1947.

INDEX

Index